JAC

THE Expanded & Updated
WHISTLER
BOOK

AN ALL-SEASON OUTDOOR GUIDE

GREYSTONE BOOKS

D&M PUBLISHERS INC.

Vancouver/Toronto/Berkeley

For Louise
For Derrick and Dixon Thompson
For Randy Stoltmann and John Clarke (Xwexwselken)

Copyright © 2009 by Jack Christie

09 10 11 12 13   5 4 3 2 1

Greystone Books
A division of D&M Publishers Inc.
2323 Quebec Street, Suite 201·
Vancouver BC Canada V5T 4S7
www.greystonebooks.com

Library and Archives Canada Cataloguing in Publication
Christie, Jack, 1946–
The Whistler book : an all-season outdoor guide / Jack Christie.
—Rev. and updated ed.
Includes index.
ISBN 978-1-55365-447-6

1. Whistler Mountain Region (B.C.)—Guidebooks. 2. Outdoor recreation—British Columbia—Whistler Mountain Region—Guidebooks. I. Title.

FC3845.W49C56 2009   917.11′31045   C2009-903763-7

Editing by Naomi Pauls and Derek Fairbridge
Cover and text design by Peter Cocking and Naomi MacDougall
Cover photograph by Graham Osborne, www.grahamosborne.com
Photos by Louise Christie
Maps by David A. Lewis
Printed and bound in Canada by Friesens
Printed on acid-free paper or Printed on acid-free paper that is forest friendly (100% post-consumer recycled paper) and has been processed chlorine free or Printed on paper that comes from sustainable forests managed under the Forest Stewardship Council
Distributed in the U.S. by Publishers Group West

We gratefully acknowledge the financial support of the Canada Council for the Arts, the British Columbia Arts Council, the Province of British Columbia through the Book Publishing Tax Credit, and the Government of Canada through the Book Publishing Industry Development Program (BPIDP) for our publishing activities.

Contents

. . . . .

Preface

. . . . .

I F YOU can't enjoy yourself in Whistler, you're dead and you don't know it. For Whistler, like Mecca, is one of those fabled places, and one to which adventurers flock year-round to indulge in the invigorating powers of the great outdoors. In fact, on the sky-blue morning of July 2, 2003, Whistler's Village Square was *the* place to be. That's when the International Olympic Committee announced that Vancouver-Whistler would host the 2010 Winter Games. Thousands of people jammed the square to cheer the news with the same over-the-top enthusiasm accorded local hero Rob Boyd following his historic World Cup downhill ski victory on Whistler Mountain in 1989, and snowboarder Ross Rebagliati when he returned home after his gold-medal-winning run at the 1998 Nagano Winter Olympics.

Village Square will undoubtedly be the scene of more such gatherings in the years leading up to 2010—and beyond. For just as the square anchors the heart of British Columbia's stellar resort municipality, Whistler's world-class reputation as a four-season outdoor recreation hub energizes the entire Sea to Sky corridor, from Squamish to Lillooet.

As tourism replaces logging and mining as the key employer in the Sea to Sky corridor, the average age of those living in the region is continually dropping. Kids around the world dream of making a career here—and not just on the slopes of Whistler Blackcomb in winter but as river guides and mountain bike instructors in summer. Therein lies the major shift that has occurred here in the past decade: Whistler's metamorphosis from a winter resort to an internationally renowned year-round destination.

Many of the young professionals fueling this all-season boom first experienced Whistler as kids while vacationing with their families, whether they drove up from the Lower Mainland or flew in from halfway around the world to catch the buzz. Over the years, they've personally witnessed the amazing growth in both winter and summer activities in Whistler, as snowboarding, mountain biking, and kayaking have become as popular today as hunting, fishing, and skiing here were with their grandparents.

The Whistler Book is written with this new breed of outdoor adventurer in mind. Every chapter details the activities best suited to each locale within the Sea to Sky corridor, but the focus is squarely on those outings most likely to bring family and friends together regardless of individual ability. After all, it's not just how skilled you are, it's how much fun you're having that's important.

I hope this book will lead readers to places of tranquility and reflection, places where the rewards far exceed the effort spent in reaching them.

Enjoy.

Creating *The Whistler Book* required encouragement and patient assistance from many, especially my wife, Louise, whose photographs are a constant reminder of our good times in the Sea to Sky region. Special thanks to Rob Sanders of Greystone Books for keeping the faith. Anne Rose, Naomi Pauls, and Derek Fairbridge provided staunch editorial wisdom while Susan Rana managed this edition with a steady hand. David A. Lewis mastered the maps.

Over the past three decades I've been grateful for the encouragement from local pioneers, such as the late Rose Tatlow, editor emerita of the *Squamish Times*, and Florence Petersen, founder of the Whistler Museum. Nora Gamboli shared memories of her mother, Joan Matthews. In Pemberton, Molly Ronayne and Margaret Fougberg answered many questions.

Timely advice came from Charlie Hou on the Gold Rush Trail; Perry Beckham of the Squamish Rockclimbers Association; B.C. provincial toponymist Janet Mason; Vicki Haberl at BC Parks; and forester Don MacLaurin.

Many thanks to Whistler Blackcomb, including Christina Moore, Tabetha Boot, Michelle Leroux, Amber Tourau, Ryan Proctor, Arthur DeJong, Rob McSkimming, Brian Finestone, and Stuart Osborne; Jan Jansen and Randy Simmons at the Resort Municipality of Whistler; Cindy Burr, Janice Greenwood-Fraser, Carla Mont, and Mika Ryan at Tourism British Columbia.

A tip of the hat to Mike Duggan, Paul Morrison, Jacquie and Juergen Rauh, Doug Perry, Irene Wolf, Brigit and Bill Sirota, Fred and Lori Xavier, Jane McRae and Gordon White, Larry Emrick, Ruth Tubbesing, Brian Jones, Dave Sarkany, Charles Campbell, Bob Purdy, Brian Murfitt, Monica Hayes, and Kirsten Hodge.

On-going thanks to Dan McLeod and Yolanda Stepien, Charlie Smith, Martin Dunphy, and staff at the *Georgia Straight*; Bob Barnett at *Pique* Newsmagazine; Mark Forsythe at CBC Vancouver.

The works by the following have all been helpful resources: Frances Decker, Margaret Fougberg and Mary Ronayne at Pioneer Pemberton Women Publishing; Grant Lamont and Charlie Doyle; Dawn Hanna; Jim McDonald; Kevin McLane; Anne McMahon; Maggie Paquet; Betty Pratt-Johnson; Randy Stoltmann; William Mathews; Wayne Suttles; Gordon White; Michel Beudry; Cheryl Coull; Richard and Sydney Cannings; Stephen Vogler; Brian Finestone, and Kevin Hodder.

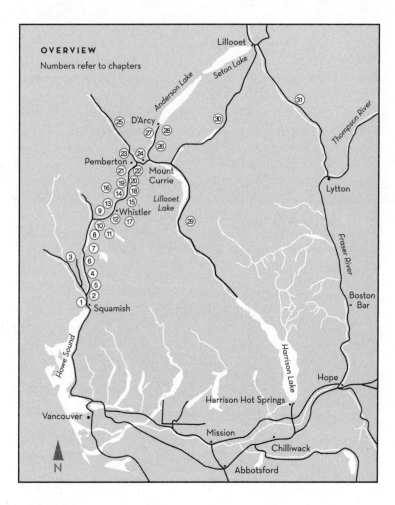

OVERVIEW
Numbers refer to chapters

Lillooet

Anderson Lake

Seton Lake

31

30

Thompson River

25 · D'Arcy

27 28

26

23 24

Pemberton ·

21 22 · Mount Currie

19 20

16 14 18

13 15

9 12 · Whistler

17

Lillooet Lake

10 8

11

7

29

Lytton

3

6

4

5

2

1 · Squamish

Howe Sound

Fraser River

Boston Bar

Harrison Lake

Hope

Harrison Hot Springs

Vancouver ·

Mission

Chilliwack

Abbotsford

N

LEGEND

——	Road	🌲	Campground with picnic facilities
-------	Trail	ⓘ	Information
——	Railroad	Ⓥ	View
-··-··-	Park boundary	Ⓟ	Parking
•——•	Chairlift/Gondola	㊇	Highway
•—••	Gate		

⊼	Picnic site
∧	Mountain peak
�	Dike/Dam
⩊	Marsh
⋈	Bridge

Introduction

. . . . .

THE THIN veneer of civilization around the Sea to Sky corridor suggests a coziness that can be deceptive. Even here in the southwestern corner of the province, where half of B.C.'s population resides, those who do not respect the wilderness often face uncompromising consequences. Venture much beyond sidewalk's end and you come face-to-face with a landscape shaped by thick pans of glacial ice that until quite recently covered the entire landmass. So strong was the force exerted by this ice that, as it retreated, it cast a ragged impression in the bedrock.

Travelers can get an inside look at these fantastic features without being extreme adventurers. Although you will experience the churning natural forces still at work in the aftermath of the most recent ice age, with proper preparation and a confident spirit you can negotiate this landscape safely. Guaranteed you will emerge with vivid memories of your encounter with the wild side of life.

Weather: Current weather information for the Sea to Sky region is available from Environment Canada. For recorded weather forecasts for Howe Sound–Whistler Village, call 604-664-9021. On-line weather information is available from Environment Canada's website: www.weatheroffice.ec.gc.ca. Generally speaking, November and February are the two wettest months in coastal British Columbia, while May and September—when the weather is at its best and there are fewer travelers—are two of the most enjoyable months for exploration.

Campground Reservations: Travelers can reserve campsites in three provincial campgrounds in the Sea to Sky region up to three months in advance of a visit and can stay as long as fourteen days. The BC Parks reservation line—1-800-689-9025 throughout Canada and the United States, or 604-689-9025 in Greater Vancouver—operates daily between March 1 and September 15; for detailed information, call between 7 AM and 7 PM Pacific time Monday to Friday, and between 9 AM and 5 PM Pacific time on Saturdays and Sundays. If you are reserving on one of the three long weekends in summer, there is a minimum three-day charge. Long weekends during reservation season occur on Victoria Day (the Monday nearest May 24), B.C. Day (the first Monday in August), and Labor Day (the first Monday in September). At present, a surcharge of $7 per night is added to the regular camping fee of about $20 per night, with a maximum surcharge of three nights even if you are reserving for a longer stay.

No-Trace Camping: According to ancient Chinese philosophy, a good walker leaves no tracks. The same could be said about camping. A good camper leaves no trace. There are six basic principles of limited-impact camping:
> Plan ahead and prepare
> Camp and travel on durable surfaces
> Pack it in, pack it out
> Properly dispose of what you can't pack out
> Leave the landscape undisturbed
> Don't light a campfire unless you have to

This may seem like a lot to remember—and something of a bother. After all, camping is supposedly an escape from the regimentation of daily life. Who needs a lot of rules? Well, Nature does. One easy remedy is to use recyclable containers. Try mixing up a drink with fruit crystals in your thermos before you set out. That way there are no pesky cans or bottles to lug around in your pack or dispose of once emptied. Try to take as much precooked food as possible. If you have to heat food, use a lightweight camp stove. These days, too many campgrounds have no underbrush. Years of campfires have left their mark.

So have the footsteps of campers who venture beyond their tent pads. Limited impact also means being wary of where you walk. Don't go off the beaten path: trails, boardwalks, bridges, portages, even game routes. If you know it's going to be wet and muddy, wear gaiters and sturdy boots. This will make it easier to stay on the trail in even the most extreme conditions. Take responsibility for your actions. As they preach in golf, replace your divots. It takes decades for a rutted landscape to repair itself.

Bear Advisory: Consult a guide such as *Backcountry Bear Basics* by David Smith. Subtitled *The Definitive Guide to Avoiding Unpleasant Encounters,* Smith's book is an easy read that anyone preparing for a backcountry journey should refer to before setting out. The information contained in it is well researched and helps separate factual evidence from half-baked research and uninformed opinion. For example, the speed with which bears move means that even track stars should never flee from a bear or attempt to scale a tree. That's one race you'll never win.

If a bear spots you in the backcountry, stand your ground. Even better, if you spot a bear first, quietly slip away. Only when a bear enters your campground should you make as much noise as possible in an attempt to drive it away. The rarity of bear predation on humans is a sign that we don't often fit their prey image like marmots, mice, and salmon do. Still, most knowledgeable wildlife biologists, such as David Smith, are unwilling to dismiss predation as an unnatural act or the desperate deed of a starving or slightly crazed bear.

Food-conditioned bears pose the most dangerous threat to humans. Once a bear has tasted food prepared by humans, all else in its diet pales in comparison. Remember: A fed bear is a dead bear. Hundreds of black bears and grizzlies, so-called "nuisance bears," are shot each year in B.C. For their well-being and your own, only use trash barrels that are bear-proofed. Most refuse containers in Squamish and Whistler as well as in provincial parks are sturdily designed.

Mountain Biking: The difference between cycling and mountain biking is often subjective. For some, mountain biking means riding on a road that isn't paved. For others, mountain biking is just not a challenge if the path doesn't go straight down a mountain and involve hopping the bike over rocks, boulders, fallen trees, and hand-built ramps and bridges. For the purposes of this book, mountain bike trails usually involve at least the possibility of single track, a trail that's only wide enough to accommodate one bike at a time.

Snow Trekking: Backcountry winter adventuring is a league apart from skiing on patrolled runs. Before you head out, prepare yourself for any eventuality. Learn to handle demanding winter camping conditions and discover how to anticipate and avoid avalanche hazards. The Canada West Mountain School (47 West Broadway, Vancouver; 604-878-7007 or 1-888-892-2266; www.themountainschool.com) has been offering mountain safety instruction since 1982. It has expanded considerably in the past several years to include introductory backcountry courses for snowboarders and ice climbers as well as skiers. Weekend ski treks for novices begin in early January and continue through March. As well, avalanche safety programs for skiers and snowboarders begin in early December and continue through March.

Once you're comfortable with backcountry winter conditions, consider making an extended foray in March and April. Spring snow conditions are generally the most favorable of the year, which is why many skiers and snowboarders plan backcountry expeditions as the sun strengthens and provides longer daylight hours.

The Alpine Club of Canada's Vancouver section posts information about trip schedules plus a variety of other useful listings and links, including weather reports, avalanche advisories, and road conditions, at their website: www.accvancouver.ca.

Hiking: When planning a hike, consider carefully what to take in your pack. Conditions can change quickly in this mountainous region, and it pays to be prepared for any eventuality. Here's a list of the most critical items to bring with you:

> Minimum of 1 liter (roughly 1 quart) of water
> Plenty of high-energy foods such as nuts and raisins
> Sunscreen (minimum SPF 15)
> Sunglasses and a hat
> Extra-warm clothing (not cotton)
> Emergency equipment including a whistle, knife, headlamp, lighter, candle, and large plastic bag or space blanket
> Maps or a guidebook
> Emergency first-aid kit
> Insect repellent

Finally, file a trip plan with someone who loves you as to your exact destination, the time you plan to return, and the license plate number of your vehicle. An informative, pack-sized guide to have handy is *Outdoor Safety and Survival*, by Judi Lees.

Freshwater Fishing: a good source to consult before you set out is the BC *Fishing Directory and Atlas.* Few anglers can resist supplying advice and information to anyone asking for helpful tips. It's a given that local store operators will know about the lakes and streams in their areas and will be able to recommend what flies or lures to try according to the season. Catch-and-release with a single barbless hook has become the byword for anglers fishing ocean-bound streams and rivers in the Sea to Sky region of B.C. Once you've hooked a fish, do not overly tire your catch or grab at it when landing it, which can cause abrasions that in turn lead to disease. Simply grasp the shank of the hook and lift the hook bend upwards for the most effective release. Attitude means a lot in fishing. Remember that the essence of sport angling is to try to hook a fish on the most sporting terms you can handle. Use light tackle with artificial lures, barbless hooks, and delicate leaders, adhering to the philosophy that a trout is much more valuable as a living challenge to your skill than as part of a meal.

SQUAMISH

SQUAMISH AREA

. . . . .

> LOCATION: East end of Howe Sound, 60 km (37 mi) north of Vancouver, 58 km (36 mi) south of Whistler, 95 km (59 mi) south of Pemberton

> ACTIVITIES: Camping, cycling, fishing, hiking, kiteboarding, nature observation, picnicking, mountain biking, rock climbing, viewpoints, walking, whitewater rafting, windsurfing

> HIGHLIGHTS: Waterfalls, climbing walls, estuary trails— all within sight of each other

WELCOME TO the self-proclaimed outdoor recreation capital of Canada. That may seem like a grandiose claim, but a quick scan of the recreational opportunities in Squamish—or "Squish," as it's affectionately known—offers quick verification. Despite the town's veneer of newness, however, this diversity is not a recent phenomenon. For more than a century, day-trippers have been exploring the mountains, rivers and lakes that surround this tight-knit community of 16,000 at the head of Howe Sound. Members of the Vancouver Natural History Society, for example, regularly journeyed here by boat in the early 1900s on their way to the alpine meadows of nearby Mount Garibaldi. The society, bolstered by the local government, successfully lobbied in the 1920s for the creation of 1947-square-km (752-square-mi) Garibaldi Provincial Park. By the 1930s, hundreds of hikers were trekking and skiing in the provincial park's Diamond Head region, which affords panoramic views of the Squamish area.

New road and rail connections—including the Squamish Highway (Highway 99), which first connected Whistler and Vancouver

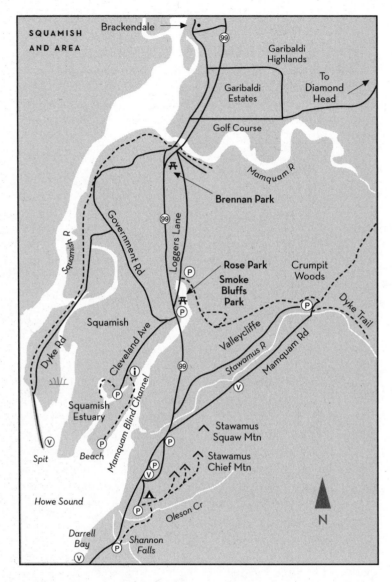

in the 1960s—conveniently coincided with a flood of interest in the area's natural charms. Rock climbing on the Stawamus Chief, a freestanding granite monolith that rises beside the highway at the town's southern entrance, caught national attention in 1961 when

Jim Baldwin and Ed Cooper made the first successful ascent while crowds of more than 10,000 looked on.

Climbers put Squamish on the map—and more than a few magazine covers—as the town began to quietly cement its reputation in outdoor recreation circles. And success bred success. In the 1970s, when the upstart sport of windsurfing took off, a new kind of tourist blew into town. There may not be much surf where the Squamish River meets Howe Sound along the town's western perimeter, but this confluence is one of the most challenging and easily accessible stretches of water for windsurfers on the West Coast. Predictable winds fan the shoreline. Thanks to these strong blasts, kiteboarding is the latest extreme sport to hit Squamish.

Another technologically innovative piece of sports equipment, the mountain bike, arrived on the scene in the 1980s. The trail-building efforts of volunteer groups such as the Squamish Off-Road Cycling Association (www.sorca.com) and the Squamish Trails Society (www.squamishtrails.ca) ensure that new routes appear each year. At last count there were 122.

Roll all these activities together, and you can see why past decades have seen scores of fresh-air enthusiasts leave their footprints—and fingerprints—in and around Squamish. It's one of my favorite year-round destinations, with a sea-level location that guarantees its low-elevation trails remain snow-free most of the year. The Test of Metal (www.testofmetal.com) endurance mountain bike race in June, softball tournaments in July, and Squamish Days Loggers' Sports (www.squamishdays.org) on the first weekend in August draw crowds throughout the warm-weather months. Just as numerous are the birdwatchers who gather in January for the annual eagle count or to stroll the estuary dike trails with binoculars in hand looking for trumpeter swans.

It's important to note that Highway 99 isn't the town's main street. That honor more properly belongs to Cleveland Avenue. Not that you'd know it. Any sense of the historic downtown core is all but shuttered from view, thanks to a strip of fast-food franchises that line the west side of Highway 99, which the late Squamish pioneer Rose Tatlow labeled "Hamburger Row." Tatlow, who was named honorary senator by the municipal council in recognition of her lifelong service to the community, lived on the shore of the Mamquam Blind Channel directly across from Cleveland's intersection with Highway 99. Little evidence of her modest residence remains other than several fragrant honeysuckle vines. Instead, leafy Rose Park (see page 20) offers a tranquil resting place from which to contemplate the placid surroundings. While Tatlow, who died in 1998, might have condemned town planners for allowing the likes of Taco Bell to dominate the landscape, I'm certain she would have been tickled to have the architecturally pleasing Squamish Adventure Centre as her neighbor.

With the opening of the *Whistler Olympic/Paralympic Park*, Squamish has also begun to position itself as a snowshoeing and Nordic skiing destination. Aside from the well-known trails at Diamond Head in Garibaldi Park (see chapter 2), local businesses are promoting the 2010 Olympic cross-country skiing facilities in the Callaghan Valley (see chapter 9), which are just a 30-minute drive north. Squamish presents another choice besides Whistler for people looking for affordability, right in the middle of the action.

> **SHANNON FALLS PROVINCIAL PARK** &

Access: Entrance to the park is well marked, at the traffic lights on the east side of Highway 99, south of the Stawamus Chief roadside pullout.

There is a fine viewpoint at the Squamish lower town limits, 1.6 km (1 mi) south of Shannon Falls on the west side of Highway 99. This is just above the spot where British naval captain George Vancouver and his crew camped while surveying Howe Sound in 1792. The Garibaldi viewpoint marks the approach to a remarkable series of geographical formations, including the eye-catching granite Stawamus Chief Mountain and B.C.'s third-highest waterfall—Shannon Falls, linked to the Chief by a 2.5-km-long (1.5-mi) trail. The white veil of water drops 335 m (1099 ft) from an easily spotted ridge above Highway 99 to a creekbed below that empties into nearby Howe Sound. In the late 1800s, the falls drove a wooden waterwheel to provide energy to a nearby sawmill. In the 1970s, their pure water was used to brew beer. These days the falls deliver mental refreshment to those seeking a soothing getaway from life's hectic pace.

Shannon Falls is a tourist magnet during summer months, with a parking lot that's usually full by noon on weekends May through September. A fee of $3 per vehicle per day is charged year-round, or $1 per hour if you're just stopping by for a quick look. Two large picnic areas accommodate families and groups who like room to stretch out and play while barbecuing. The falls maintain a constant roar while the nearby Chief's south face looms on high; many visitors understandably take advantage of this striking backdrop for photographs.

It takes only a few minutes to walk up to the falls from the parking lot. A well-built system of smooth trails, wooden staircases, and bridges leads to two viewing platforms near the base of the falls. On a hot day, the combination of mist from the falls and shade from some impressive large trees provides the perfect tonic, especially if you climb the stairs leading off to the left just before the main viewing spot to a higher vantage point at the base of the falls where fewer visitors venture. A breeze stirred by tons of falling water whips the mist into billowing clouds, making this an ideal place to get a natural facial. I particularly enjoy visiting here in fall when leaves on broadleaf and vine maple trees display vibrant colors.

To combine a visit to the falls with a walk to the Stawamus Chief, take the well-marked trail that leads 2.5 km (1.5 mi) north from the parking lot along the base of Goat Ridge. It crosses a small bridge at Oleson Creek that links with the Chief's primary hiking route.

> **STAWAMUS CHIEF MOUNTAIN**

Access: The main entrance to Stawamus Chief Provincial Park, along with nearby climbers' access parking lot, lies on the east side of Highway 99 south of the Mamquam Forest Service Road intersection.
Ability Level: Strenuous

The Stawamus Chief is the sentinel of the Squamish Valley. As you journey north on the Sea to Sky Highway from Vancouver, the sight of this 702-m (2303-ft) granite monolith comes as a relief, the signal that the highway's sinuous twists and turns lie behind now. To appreciate its majesty, pull over for a good look from the provincial park's roadside viewpoint on Highway 99.

To the trained eye, the mountain's smooth-faced apron of blue-gray rock reveals dozens of vertical routes to ledges from which to take in the bigger picture. The action in the parking lot below, where climbers spread out their ropes and pitons, carabiners and camming tools, daisies and aiders, belay and rappel devices, harnesses and chalk bags and all-important gear slings, is evidence of the amount of equipment and serious preparation required to make even a basic climb of the Chief's west face. (Information on climbing routes on the Chief and other climbs in the Squamish region can be gleaned from Kevin McLane's *The Climbers Guide to Squamish.*)

From the Base: One of the easiest routes at the base of the Chief begins at the well-marked climbers' access parking lot beside Highway 99 just north of the Chief's more prominent viewing zone. Follow the welcoming Apron Trail that leads a short distance uphill through the forest and connects with the Grand Wall area. An easy stint of free climbing deposits you on a ledge from which most climbers begin to rope up. Even if you go no higher, you can now claim to have climbed on the Chief. Enjoy an unobstructed view of the town spread below. Unlike the monolith, which took an estimated 60 million years to assume its present shape, the transformation of Squamish's formerly industrial waterfront seems to be occurring in the blink of an eye.

Hiking Up: If you're more inclined to slip on a pair of lightweight hiking shoes and throw some snacks and water into a backpack, consider two alternatives to storming the walls. These routes may make you feel like you're climbing a clandestine staircase to gain access to the turrets of a castle—especially if you begin early, before everyone else who knows the way shows up too.

There are two approaches to the Chief's trailhead. One leads from nearby Shannon Falls Park (see above); the other begins a short distance above the Highway 99 roadside viewpoint. From Shannon

Squamish Spit

Falls, signs point the way. Travel time to the Chief is 30 minutes on this well-maintained trail, the first half of which leads over level ground through an alder forest. Once it reaches the base of the mountain, the trail begins to climb beside the smooth granite rock face, which is covered in places by green lichen. A small bridge over Olesen Creek, gurgling through a cleft in the mountainside, provides a good glimpse of Howe Sound below. The Chief Peaks Trail begins across the creek.

The trailhead in Stawamus Chief Park lies beside the 63-site campground (16 vehicle and 47 walk-in sites; see www.env.gov. bc.ca/bcparks for details). This is where out-of-town climbers are typically ensconced. Park here. Once on foot, you'll pass a spacious cooking shelter with picnic tables, stainless steel counters, and food lockers to help deter bears.

Pay particular attention to the cautionary signs posted at the foot of the first of a series of steep staircases. As BC Parks takes pains to point out, "This is *not* a 'walk in the park.'" Also listed are recommendations to dress properly and avoid injury. Equally telling are the older markers affixed to the trees by the Federation of Mountain Clubs of B.C., which maintained the trail before the establishment of the provincial park here in 1997. They say: "To all peaks carry water." There is little shade on much of the trail, so pack plenty of fluids.

Stawamus Chief Mountain has three summits, each one progressively higher and separated by deep clefts. At the outset, a common trail leads upwards towards all three. It then divides into two separate routes. Along the trail the handrails are smooth and well oiled from constant use. The bridge to the Shannon Falls Trail soon appears over Olesen Creek where a bench provides good views over Howe Sound and the ripples where the outflow of the Squamish River meets the tidal action. Several distinct shades of green delineate the zones of dissolution as fresh and salt water blend. This is a good place to assess how much higher you want to climb. It helps if you are as psyched as the climbers on the Chief's smooth face.

Wood and stone stairs lead upwards beside Olesen Creek. Potholes in the creek brim with clear water. The cool sounds of the rushing water help your frame of mind on a hot day. At the junction 40 minutes beyond the bridge, the majority of hikers head for the South (or First) Summit, a 7-km (4.3-mi) round trip. There's no loss of face in joining the relatively easier conga line to the South Summit (elevation 600 m/1969 ft), particularly if you are hiking with young children or dogs. That said, I recommend the numerous rewards—such as some modest rock climbing and a great view of a notch on the Chief's north face—if you choose the slightly more challenging route to the modestly higher Centre (Second) and North (Third) Summits, an 11-km (6.8-mi) round trip. In fact, one of the most pleasant options, particularly if you have an extra hour's time, is to follow the loop that links both.

No matter which summit you choose, be prepared for an unrelenting regime of up, up, and up (and the resultant knee-knackering corollary of down, down, down). Pace yourself by monitoring your breathing. Never climb so fast that you can't breathe through your nose—the most effective way to feed your oxygen-starved muscles. This also ensures you take the time to enjoy your surroundings. Unlike the stark openness of the Chief's apron, its hiking trails lead beneath tall stands of ramrod-straight Douglas fir. These provide shade as welcome as the steady breeze that funnels round the mountain off Howe Sound. The constant owl-like hooting of one or more male blue grouse accompanies you.

> SOUTH SUMMIT

During the entire climb, you will find yourself walking up, around, next to, and under the solid granite of the Chief. The trail is smooth and wide in most places. And the higher you climb, the more exhilarating it becomes, until, finally, near the top and above the treeline, you reach a broad and open windswept spot. The most difficult part is now behind you; relax and contemplate the lunch menu on this final section. From here you can see Shannon Falls in profile to the south, with the ribbon of Highway 99 curving beyond until it goes out of sight past the Garibaldi viewpoint. To the north, the Squamish River cuts through the valley between Brackendale and Howe Sound. Across the water to the west are the glaciated peaks of the Tantalus Range.

Your imagination may begin to work overtime as you approach the edge of the cliffs. Thinking about the sheer walls below is dizzying. My legs always tremble involuntarily up on the Chief, as if the Earth were moving—strange, considering that underfoot is one enormous piece of rock. It's a bit of a test of will to get close to the edge as the wind blows over the top. If you're feeling particularly intrepid, have someone hold onto your ankles while you lean over for a look. It's not as dangerous as it feels, but obviously it's best to be cautious.

> CENTRE AND NORTH SUMMITS

If you take inspiration from rock-climbing tales yet are not prone to tackle the Chief's sheer front face, you can still thrill to visceral contact with the rough granite walls via the Chief's back route—just below the Centre Summit, where bolted lengths of chain and a metal ladder have been placed to assist hikers. Once on top, views quickly open up as the forest gives way to low-lying scrub pine, evidence of the summit's dry and windswept environment. Note: Keep careful track of the orange markers designating the route. Owing to the scarcity of trees, the markers thin out at both the Centre and North summits, where dabs of orange paint on rock indicate the way. As you look across to the South Summit, the geography of the Squamish Valley is suddenly revealed.

Several rewards await you for carrying on as far as the North Summit (elevation 650 m/2133 ft). For one, as you make your way up the cleft between the two, you pass a dramatic viewpoint at the top of the North Gulch, where the walls are fortress-steep. Even better, once on the summit, the sound of an unnamed waterfall cascading down the slopes of an adjacent ridge drowns out the buzz of traffic, the drone of airplanes, and the nattering of hiking groups rising from far below. Find yourself a picnic spot sheltered from the constant breeze (which does help keep the bugs at bay in summer) and spread out.

To the north, Mamquam Glacier's white face shares the horizon with the Diamond Head formation (see chapter 2); to the south, the peak of Sky Pilot Mountain dominates Goat Ridge, where the headwaters of Shannon Creek gather above the falls. As you make your way down off the North Summit and descend through a narrow, boulder-filled canyon, pay careful attention to the route markers. Your spirits will be buoyed by the satisfaction of having made the climb and a sense of relief at getting safely down after all the drama up top, but your toes will be shoved into the front of your hiking shoes for the next 90 minutes, so choose socks and footwear accordingly. This hike is an adventure and an accomplishment. You'll never pass the Chief again without remembering that wonderful shaky feeling you had at the summit.

> **SMOKE BLUFFS PARK**

Access: Turn east off Highway 99 onto Loggers Lane at the Cleveland Avenue intersection. Head north past Rose Park for 1 km (0.6 mi) to a gravel driveway and a paved parking lot opposite the Squamish Adventure Centre where a sign depicts a climber. Outhouses and a notice board flank the trail.
Ability Level: Moderate

Rock climbing around Squamish is not limited to the Chief. Just as popular are the Smoke Bluffs, a ridge that rises above the Mamquam Blind Channel to the north, on the east side of Highway 99. These small cliffs are laced with cracks that appeal to climbers of all abilities. And unlike many of the routes on the Chief, those on the Smoke Bluffs (or simply the Bluffs) are shorter—though no less intimidating in places—and much easier to reach. Thanks to their southern exposure, the granite walls also dry quickly in the morning sun. In fact, it's the moisture evaporating from the walls that gave the bluffs their name. Climbers groom the rock faces with wire brushes to obtain an ideal smoothness.

After years of lobbying by the Federation of Mountain Clubs of B.C. and the Climbers Access Society of B.C., in 2006 a public climbing park was created at the Bluffs, not just for rope hangers but for everyone to enjoy. An aerial map posted in the climbers' parking lot details various trails and several viewpoints—the best lie above Pixie Corner and beside Penny Lane, as well as beside Burgers & Fries, the most frequently climbed cliff in Canada. Wood and rock staircases lead up to one section called the Octopus's Garden. Farther west, the loop trail narrows as it curves between two smooth granite walls where small groups of climbers regularly practice. They won't mind you watching if you are quiet; safe climbing requires complete concentration.

> **SQUAMISH ESTUARY TRAILS**
Access: Turn south from Highway 99 onto Cleveland Avenue (the town's main drag) to Vancouver Street; then head three blocks west to the trailhead and the Squamish estuary.
Ability Level: Easy

The interpretive loop trail that leads through the town's oceanfront estuary makes a fine wildlife-viewing walk. A wooden sign posted at the Vancouver Street trailhead bears a detailed map of the estuary and the grassy dike trail that rambles west past a massive new housing development and log-sort yard beside channeled waterways to Cattermole Slough, home to two hundred bird species, such as meadowlarks and sandpipers as well as overwintering waterfowl such as goldeneye, bufflehead, mergansers, and trumpeter swans.

Meadow Trail leads out on the estuary proper where uncluttered views really open up, with the smooth granite walls of the Stawamus Chief displayed to great effect. Equally arresting, if the skies are clear, is the dagger point of Atwell Peak and its broad-shouldered companion, Dalton Dome. Together they dominate the skyline of Garibaldi Provincial Park to the north. The trail follows the Central Channel atop the Heritage Dykes, the oldest human-made structures in Squamish. In the 1890s, Chinese laborers built these ramparts to reclaim the marshland for hayfields. Herons, Canada geese, and a host of ducks and seabirds work the channel. Strategically placed benches provide good viewing perches. Allow 45 minutes to complete the loop.

The narrow dike path is bordered by brick-red rosehips, and drifts of sedges pattern the surface of the slough. The white stalks of pearly everlasting rival Shannon Falls' snowy tresses, which can be seen cascading down the slopes to the south of the Chief. Spires of solitary, stunted Sitka spruce anchor the estuary's perimeter. Bright yellow cedar waxwings flit among the snags, seemingly oblivious to the strong winds, which power kiteboarders aloft in the distance. Wild roses scent the air. Breezes riffle the tall grass. From midsummer through fall, a palette of colors is on display, from blond cattails backed by an evergreen forest to silver poplar leaves framed against a robin's-egg-blue sky.

Farther inland, two additional estuary trails—*Forest Loop* and *Swan Walk*—lead through wooded areas to the west of the BC Rail spur line. The easiest way to reach both trails is to follow Bailey Street, an industrial gravel road that curves around the north end of Chieftain Centre off Cleveland Avenue near Highway 99. Several approaches to the estuary trails are clearly marked here. Take *Swan Walk* for the best chance of spotting the trumpeter swans. These majestic honkers sport the largest wingspan of all West Coast birds.

> ### SQUAMISH HARBOUR DOCK
Access: At the intersection of Vancouver Street and Loggers Lane in downtown Squamish.

Until rail and road connections were opened in the 1950s, visitors from Vancouver arrived via boats, which often docked in the

Mamquam Blind Channel. Prior to a disastrous flood in 1921, the Mamquam River flowed into Howe Sound along this channel. These days, the quiet backwater that extends to Rose Park (see below) almost drains dry at low tide. A paddle in this tranquil spot provides an excellent way to appreciate many of Squamish's natural features, such as the Malamute—the "mini-Chief"—that rises sharply from the water directly across the Mamquam Blind Channel from the harbor dock adjacent the Squamish Yacht Club. A ramp here provides easy access to the channel for both hand-carried vessels and boat trailers. Best times to put in are early in the day before breezes begin to freshen on Howe Sound. One of my favorite sights out on the water is an oceangoing canoe paddled by a dozen or more members of the Squamish First Nations.

> **SQUAMISH MUNICIPAL PARKS** &

Access: Adjacent to the district Forest Service office on the east side of Highway 99, on the south side of the Mamquam River Bridge.

At *Brennan Park*, a large community leisure center with an indoor swimming pool anchors the playing fields. There are tennis courts beside the Mamquam River and picnic tables dotting the recreation trail. You can explore the Mamquam via this dike path to its mouth at the Squamish River. In summer, when water levels are low, there are also good sandbars to fish from.

Loggers Lane leads south beside the park and its campground for visitors, many of whom come to compete in tournaments or the annual Squamish Days Loggers' Sports on the first weekend in August. It then meanders past the Smoke Bluffs trailhead to *Rose Park*, named in honor of Squamish pioneer Rose Tatlow, whose home once stood beside the Mamquam Blind Channel. The recently minted park is dedicated to the memory of Squamish's pioneer families, such as the Carsons and the Wrays, and their sections of the park are formally planted with flowers, cherry trees, and trellised Interlaken seedless grapes that will soon bear fruit. Rose Tatlow, whose homesite, along with an adjacent property to the north, is more sheltered from the sounds of highway traffic, would have approved of the new picnic table on a small deck by Lily's Garden, with its views of the slough and the climbing bluffs.

Access: From Highway 99, follow Cleveland Avenue, the town's main street, to its south end. Cross the train tracks, then turn right onto an access road which leads to the beach.

Piles of driftwood lie jackstrawed along the shoreline of Nexen Beach. At first glance, Nexen's hard-packed, dark surface appears more like a mudflat where it stretches out into the shallow reaches of Howe Sound, the southernmost fiord on the North American coastline.

Bounded by an abandoned wharf to the south and an active cargo dock on the north, Nexen Beach is the centerpiece of an ambitious waterfront redevelopment plan set to unfold over the next decade. A passenger-ferry terminal, hotel, conference center, arts center, and more are envisioned to rise on the 28-ha (69-acre) site. Dozens of wave riders gather at Nexen Beach in July for the North American Windsurfing Championships. An onshore wind blows here with the same sustained intensity that draws windsurfers and kiteboarders to the Squamish Spit, north of Nexen at the mouth of the Squamish River. Nexen Beach is envisaged as a wind-sport training area. Design modifications in windsurfing boards make Nexen Beach the logical place to launch. These newer boards are fatter, a tad shorter, and more rectilinear than previous models. Their most radical design feature is a meter-long (yard-long) center fin that provides greater stability and allows these boards to carry

> ## WHAT'S IN A NAME?

. . . .

ALTHOUGH THERE have been attempts to translate "Squamish" as a First Nations expression meaning "mother of the wind," there is no linguistic root for the name. The original European explorers rarely recorded the names of the native people they encountered; according to noted Northwest Coast anthropologist and linguist Dr. Wayne Suttles, none can be identified with names used later. The name appeared in a 1907 study as "Squawmish," referring to the aboriginals who still inhabit two dozen settlements along the Squamish River.

a much larger sail. Launching one is best done in shallower water than is found at the Spit, which makes Nexen Beach an ideal place to practice.

An extensive paved area behind the beach also offers a place for novice kiteboarders to practice their kite-handling skills. If you find Nexen Beach somewhat underwhelming, for instant relief just raise your eyes to the twin sights of Stawamus Chief Mountain's Grand Wall and nearby Shannon Falls' white scarf of cascading water. The view is reason enough to pay the beach a visit. One of the beach's most novel features is a curved straw bale-and-adobe "fort" above the high-tide line, a legacy of the popular Squamish Equinox Music Festival (SERF) held in June. "Fort Nexen" provides a much-needed windbreak behind which bathers can warm up while at the same time offering unobstructed views of ocean action.

> **SQUAMISH SPIT**

Access: Windsurfer signs indicate the Squamish Spit turnoff, west from Highway 99 at the traffic lights onto Industrial Way, then guide travelers past the West Coast Railway Heritage Park to the unpaved dike access road.

The Squamish Spit is a 4-km (2.5-mi) finger of dike at the mouth of the Squamish River where it flows into Howe Sound. This narrow piece of land helps keep the harbor free of silt so that large freighters can tie up nearby. But as windsurfers have long known, there's also no finer place to catch an ocean breeze. As predictable as the sunrise, each day around noon a strong wind carries across Howe Sound. And woe betide those caught out on the turquoise-toned waters unprepared to ride this zephyr. It blows with such force that the unwary can't right themselves once dunked. Fortunately, there is an emergency rescue service available courtesy of the Squamish Windsports Society (www.squamishwindsurfing.org). Launch fees at the spit are currently $20 per day or $75 for a season's pass.

At the very tip of the spit is the launch area. You can drive to a drop-off point beside it, unload your board, then park if you're here for sport. If you just want to watch, come out by bicycle to avoid the inevitable congestion, though be warned: the surface of the dike is loose gravel, not the best material on which to ride.

Kiteboarders are the new kids on the spit, and these high flyers are turning heads and rapidly attracting converts from the ranks of windsurfers, wakeboarders, snowboarders, and even motocross riders. They've also created controversy. That's because laying out the lines of one kiteboard prior to launch takes up the same amount of room that *six* windsurfers need, and space is already at a premium on the spit, which boasts more high-performance sailing days than almost anywhere else in North America.

Out on the spit, due west of the Stawamus Chief, kiteboarders take wind sports to new heights—literally. These latter-day Icaruses enjoy what are arguably the biggest and best views in the entire Sea to Sky corridor: Shannon Falls, the Stawamus Chief, Sky Pilot Mountain, Goat Ridge, Mamquam Mountain, Atwell Peak, and Mount Garibaldi—all revealed in one 360-degree panorama. Far below, the dike in summer is lined with pink Douglas spirea, or hardhack, which at a glance can be mistaken for fireweed.

There are often a hundred or more vehicles parked on the shoulders of the spit on summer afternoons. But don't let that stop you from checking out the action. Find a spot on the bank to watch where you're not in the way, then marvel at these aerialists as they ride the wind high above the waves.

> **SQUAMISH ADVENTURE CENTRE** &

Access: Turn east off Highway 99 just north of the Cleveland Avenue intersection (38551 Loggers Lane; 604-815-5084; www.adventurecentre. com)

Squamish styles itself as the outdoor-recreation capital of Canada, and that's what its boldly designed, almost 3,000 square-meter (9,500 square-foot) Adventure Centre silently proclaims to passersby on Highway 99 at the entrance to the city's downtown core. Designed to emulate a bald eagle spreading its wings, the soaring glass structure is composed of 210 panels of half-inch tempered glass, one of the few building materials not sourced locally. The building's main columns were milled from Douglas fir, which, along with the crushed basalt granite pad, came from the Squamish Valley.

The center promotes the joys of kayaking, river rafting, mountain biking, eagle viewing, windsurfing, kiteboarding, skateboarding, camping, and above all else, rock climbing, a sport that first put Squamish on the adventure map in the 1960s. Guided outdoor-adventure trips can be booked here while you enjoy a snack at the center's Pause-Cafe or shop for guidebooks, maps, and souvenirs. As well, a series of carved wooden panels details the history of Squa-mish, particularly the events of the twentieth century.

> **THE INSIDE TRACK**

> *Camping:* Valhalla Pure Outfitters for equipment rentals (1-877-892-9092; www.squamishgear.com)

> *Cycling:* Corsa Cycles (604-892-3331; www.corsacycles.com) for parts and service; Tantalus Bike Shop (604-898-2588; www.tantalusbikeshop.com)

> *Fishing:* River's Edge Sportfishing Outfitters for licenses, gear, guided tours, and tips on where the fish are biting (604-898-5656)

> *Rock Climbing:* Climb On Equipment (604-892-2243; www.onsightequipment.com), Squamish Rock Guides (604-892-7816; www.squamishrockguides.com); Vertical Reality (604-892-8248)

> *Skateboarding and Snowboarding:* Sequence Board Supply (604-892-6314)

> *Tourist Information:* 604-815-4991 or 1-866-333-2010; www.tourismsquamish.com

> *Whitewater Rafting:* Sunwolf Outdoor Centre (1-877-806-8046; www.sunwolf.net); Canadian Outback Adventures (1-800-565-8735; www.canadianoutback.com)

DIAMOND HEAD

Garibaldi Provincial Park

.   .   .   .   .

> LOCATION: 76 km (47 mi) north of Vancouver, 16 km (10 mi) east of Squamish, 41 km (25 mi) south of Whistler, 78 km (48 mi) south of Pemberton

> ACTIVITIES: Camping, cross-country skiing, hiking, mountain biking, nature observation, picnicking, snowshoeing

> HIGHLIGHTS: Fall colors, lava fields, panoramic views

> ACCESS: Take the exit marked "Diamond Head (Garibaldi Park)" east from Highway 99 on Mamquam Road, which runs 16 km (10 mi) east to the parking lot at the trailhead. This access road is one of the pleasures of visiting Diamond Head; it lets you do much of the initial climbing by car. The first 4 km (2.5 mi) is paved, passing through the southern outskirts of Garibaldi Estates. The remainder is along the good gravel-surfaced Mamquam Road, which climbs gradually above the Mamquam River valley. The mountainside rises steeply, with dense stands of second-growth forest concealing the view on both sides. Once you've left Highway 99, you won't catch sight of the peaks again until you're walking the Diamond Head Trail.

At the 12-km (7.5-mi) mark, the road divides. A large sign points left towards the park boundary. A notice next to it reminds visitors that pets are not permitted in Garibaldi Provincial Park, of which this part is the Black Tusk Nature Conservancy Area. The final 4 km (2.5 mi) of road covers a series of switchbacks. Only at the last one does the view of the Squamish Valley open up. This is a good place to stop and look south to Howe Sound and the Stawamus Chief. Across the valley to the west is Cloudburst Mountain, and south of that is the broad body of glaciers around Mount Tantalus.

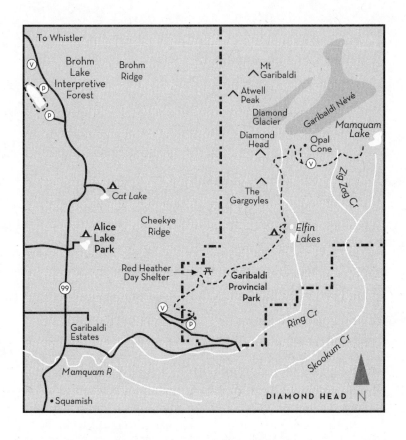

To Whistler

Brohm
Lake
Interpretive
Forest

Brohm
Ridge

Mt
Garibaldi

Atwell
Peak

Diamond
Glacier

Garibaldi Névé

Mamquam
Lake

Diamond
Head

Opal
Cone

Cat Lake

The
Gargoyles

Zig Zag Cr

Alice
Lake
Park

Cheekye
Ridge

Elfin
Lakes

Red Heather
Day Shelter

Garibaldi
Provincial
Park

99

Garibaldi
Estates

Ring Cr

Skookum Cr

Mamquam R

Squamish

DIAMOND HEAD N

WHETHER I'M on snowshoes or wearing my hiking boots, I gravitate year-round to one of the most easily accessible subalpine regions in the Sea to Sky corridor in Garibaldi Provincial Park's southwest corner: Diamond Head, a fortresslike ridge that rises above the Cheakamus River valley. Accompanied by craggy Atwell Peak (Mount Garibaldi's south tower), Diamond Head makes a bold statement about the height of the mountain range here. As you travel north of Squamish on Highway 99, look straight ahead and up—these two imposing features dwarf all else on the skyline. But you'll be surprised at how quickly you can get a close look at them.

The well-worn Diamond Head Trail is a testament to the

generations of hikers who have made their way into the south-west corner of Garibaldi Park, often under arduous circumstances. Before anyone ever considered building the Sea to Sky Highway, members of the Vancouver Natural History Society caught boats from the city's inner harbor to the Squamish waterfront. From there, they hired wagons to bring them as close to the ridges below Mount Garibaldi as possible; hikers then continued upwards on foot. Thanks to the society's persuasive vision, a broad swath of high-elevation peaks—from Squamish to Pemberton—was set aside as parkland in the 1920s. Their feat was remarkable because, back then, it took as much persistence as it does now to convince politi-cians of the need to protect such wild spaces, and that future genera-tions would follow in even greater numbers.

> **RED HEATHER AND ELFIN LAKES TRAIL**

Access: On foot, allow 75 to 90 minutes to reach Red Heather, 5 km (3.1 mi) from the parking lot. From here, a bypass trail for hikers leads beyond Red Heather and rejoins the road on the ridge above. Allow an additional 90 to 120 minutes to reach Elfin Lakes, 6 km (3.7 mi) beyond Red Heather.
Ability Level: Intermediate to expert

An air of profound silence envelops Diamond Head. Few birds sing, no dogs bark. And visitors cross into this zone of tranquility almost as soon as they embark on the old, gently graded road that, in the 1940s heyday of the Diamond Head Lodge, once transported supplies and lodge guests to the Elfin Lakes (see sidebar). BC Parks maintains a winter-only campground plus a day shelter at Red Heather, complete with a wood-burning stove. Believe me, skiers and snowshoers will find this a welcome stop. An elevated outhouse, fronted by a steep staircase, hints at the depth of snow in winter and adds new meaning to the term "throne room."

Beyond here, all sense of time redefines itself en route to the Elfin Lakes. Much like the altered state induced by stargazing, one's mind is drawn into another world, where the rhythms of change occur on a vastly amplified scale. Crevasse-lined glaciers that took millennia to form speak of a time frame that eclipses rational thought. But in the here and now, only in fall and winter will you be safe from the "no-see-ums" (small, biting flies); at other times, come prepared to combat them with repellent, long sleeves and pants, and even a mesh-covered hat.

As the trail rises above Red Heather, the forest thins to groves of deceptively small cypress trees. Their height is restricted because the growing period here is shorter than in the valley; snowstorms can occur here as late as June and resume in August. Ring samples indicate that the mature specimens are at least three hundred years old; some are twice that. This qualifies them for membership in the vaunted "ancient" category of forest appellations.

As you near the Elfin Lakes, the trail levels where it reaches Paul Ridge. The well-traveled route climbs up the mountain in rhythm with the contour of the slope. Walking or skiing it is a pleasure. In any season, the closer you get to Diamond Head, the more colors reveal themselves. What appeared at a distance to be dull gray now shows itself as sandy brown, deep auburn, green, yellow, white, and volcanic black. The rippled surface of Diamond Head's sweeping ridge has been deeply grooved by the retreating glacier that still holds sway on the upper slopes.

The Elfin Lakes appear suddenly as the trail makes its final descent towards the old Diamond Head Lodge. Reduced in size and sagging at the corners, it's still standing, though given the volumes of snow recorded locally in past winters, it's a wonder the structure hasn't fallen in on itself. Sheets of plywood cover the windows. Saggy soffits outline the roof like lipstick applied by a dipsomaniac. Nestled in a meadow beside the twin Elfin Lakes, surrounded by peaks, the old lodge still enjoys one of the most stunning prospects in Garibaldi Park.

A stone's throw away stands the alpine-gothic Elfin Lodge, a two-story, 33-person shelter with bunk beds and kitchen facilities including propane stoves. The chalet, quite cozy inside, is a favorite nest for skiers and snowshoers on cold winter nights. In reality, the Elfin Lakes are little more than two alpine ponds. One is reserved for drinking water, the other for washing. Several picnic tables sit on the open slope next to a small interpretive display. The history of the region is explained simply on several laminated panels that include historical photos.

Elfin Lakes

In an open meadow below and just past the Elfin Lodge is a spacious, 14-site campground with equally superb views. There are outhouses nearby and all-important food caches as black bears frequent the area. Although the campground does not offer much seclusion, there is plenty of room to spread out. Spend a night here and, immersed in the silence of the surroundings, revel in the view of the Tantalus Range to the west when first lit by the early morning light. At that magic hour, you'd think that the sun was pouring forth lava like primordial plasma, the cosmic soup from which matter evolved.

You can hike for hours beyond Elfin Lakes. But if you don't feel like venturing too far, at least take 15 minutes to catch a brief glimpse of this continually changing landscape. The fall color here is not just confined to the trees. The ground cover of red heather interwoven with low-lying blueberry bushes is a riot of scarlets. And six shades of yellow, from gold to pumpkin, climb the banks of small gullies to where scree has tumbled down from Mount Garibaldi's eroding volcanic cone.

Access: A 2-km (1.2-mi) hike from the Elfin Lakes on a well-marked trail that leads uphill and away from the route to the Opal Cone, a short distance north of the Elfin Lakes campground.

Ability Level: Novice to intermediate

You'll discover majestic views from the top of nearby Columnar Peak. (Columnar is the name given to lava formations. Much of Garibaldi Park's landscape was shaped by volcanic eruptions at the end of the most recent ice age.) And it doesn't take long to reach the saddle between several of the spires that constitute the peak. From here you'll get a close-up look at two particularly gnarly formations on Columnar's north flank: dubbed "The Gargoyles," they more than live up to that moniker. In the middle distance, their crumbling facades convey a freakish impression that is almost scary. Up close, they assume cartoonish proportions with glazed expressions, as if they've been kiln-fired in hell.

From the top of one of the spires, which barely affords enough space to accommodate small groups, enjoy the unrestricted

> ## JOANIE GET YER MEN

JOAN MATTHEWS of West Vancouver was a champion slalom skier in the 1930s, who, during the Second World War, mapped out routes in the backcountry north of Squamish. At a ski meet, she met two world-class Norwegian ski jumpers, Ottar and Emil Brandvold, whom she introduced to the Whistler region. After she married Ottar, the three built the Diamond Head Lodge in 1945–46.

The old road used today to reach Elfin Lakes was the approach that brought guests to the lodge. Joan left in the late 1950s, but the brothers operated the chalet for yet another decade, after which it was sold to the province for the park.

Squamish pioneer Rose Tatlow remembered Joan as the driving force behind the Diamond Head project, the one who negotiated the land rights with the provincial government and who worked shoulder to shoulder with the two soft-spoken brothers while displaying the constant cheerfulness that was her hallmark.

panorama south to the North Shore peaks and west to Vancouver Island. Closer at hand, Diamond Head's subtly colored pink ridge links Columnar Peak with a parade of peaks, domes, and ridges that culminates in the lone sentinel of Mount Garibaldi—all it takes to get a closer look at it is more time. When a northern pygmy owl (a very small "earless" owl with a spotted head, frequently heard calling with a mellow "hoo" or seen flying in daytime) alights on top of a nearby subalpine fir, you'll revel in this unanticipated reward.

> ## OPAL CONE

Access: A 6.5-km (4-mi) trail leads north from Elfin Lakes to the Opal Cone. Allow two hours one way
Ability Level: Intermediate

The scale on which formations present themselves in the Pacific Ranges that transect Garibaldi Park is truly astonishing. The Opal Cone is an interesting remnant of an old volcano. At first, much of the trail is downhill. Views of The Gargoyles, the gnarled black rock formations hulking on Diamond Head's south flank, soon appear high above. Mount Garibaldi and The Sharkfin show their profiles north of Atwell Peak. Across the valley to the east, an enormous sheet of glacial ice hangs on the slopes of Mamquam Mountain. Watch for wildlife. Marmots and pikas sunbathe on rocky outcroppings, and if you stop to pick blueberries, you'll probably scare up the occasional grouse.

Past the halfway point, where, in summer months, a bridge crosses boulder-strewn, silt-gray, glacier-fed Ring Creek, you enter a barren landscape. Walking here is difficult because of rock debris recently deposited by the retreating glacier. Perhaps in another century plants will take root, giving fall frosts a chance to color these slopes, too.

The trail climbs towards a ridge beside the Opal Cone. If you want only a view of this ancient volcano, bear left where the trail divides. After 30 minutes on this steep section you will reach a viewpoint of the Opal Cone and the icefields below Mount Garibaldi. If your destination is Mamquam Lake, bear right at the point where the trail divides. The lake, east of the Opal Cone, is a walk of several hours.

Lava is a small, solid-sounding word, one that appears infrequently on British Columbia maps—except for National Topographic

Survey map 92 G/15 (Mamquam Mountain) of the region east of Squamish in Garibaldi Park, where it appears three times. These lava fields lie below the south flank of the Opal Cone, an intriguingly shaped granite plug formed when a spew of molten lava hardened.

Despite its name, the cone is neither conical nor opalescent in appearance. Rather, it squats like a green-gray molar at the foot of Mount Garibaldi's south tower, dagger-nosed Atwell Peak, surrounded by a battleship-gray landscape scoured clean by the retreating Garibaldi and Lava glaciers. As topsoil is scarce, vegetation has yet to take root here. The few traces of flora that do cling to the sides of the cone flourish somewhat mysteriously. At this elevation, above 1400 m (4593 ft), growth is as slow as smoke. But if the lava is rather bland in appearance, it only serves to heighten the intensity of hues in the broader panorama.

> **MAMQUAM LAKE TRAIL**

For those pushing on beyond Opal Cone, the trail leads 4.5 km (2.8 mi) east across a rough and mostly barren landscape, crossing active Zig Zag Creek (fed by the Lava Glacier) and passing the Rampart Ponds on its way to Mamquam Lake. The lake lies hidden until the trail begins its descent to the three narrow but level campsites cleared beside its shore. There are no facilities here, and you can usually count on having the rugged surroundings to yourself. The lake makes a wonderful bowl from which to engage in some intensive stargazing.

> **INSIDE TRACK**

For more information on Diamond Head, go to www.env.gov.bc.ca/bcparks and follow the links to Garibaldi Provincial Park. Note: A parking fee of $3 per day is charged year-round. Those planning to stay at the Elfin Lakes cabin ($10 each per night, $25 per family) or the campground ($5 each per night) must register and prepay at the parking lot kiosk.

3

SQUAMISH AND
PARADISE VALLEYS

. . . . .

> LOCATION: 76 km (47 mi) north of Vancouver, 16 km (10 mi)
  north of downtown Squamish, 50 km (31 mi) south of Whistler,
  87 km (54 mi) south of Pemberton

> ACTIVITIES: Camping, climbing, cycling, fishing, hiking,
  picnicking, whitewater rafting, rock climbing, swimming,
  viewpoints, walking

> HIGHLIGHTS: Eagles, cataracts, swift water

THE SQUAMISH and Paradise valleys are dominated by four
glacial rivers—the Cheakamus, Cheekye, Squamish, and
Mamquam, which converge here before they meet the ocean.
The Cheakamus River, having almost completed its flow south from
Whistler, picks up water from the Cheekye just before it joins the
Squamish near Brackendale. The Mamquam River comes in from
the east to add volume to the Squamish, downstream from Brackendale. As you head along the back roads leading from downtown
Squamish north to the Brackendale neighborhood, then beyond
into the Squamish and Paradise valleys, you'll quickly discover easy
routes on which to walk, pedal, or drive. You can choose to follow a
gentle country road or a river-dike trail, none of which will prove too
lengthy or vertically challenging.

The farms you pass will be small compared to the wide expanse
of the Pemberton prairie to the north. Although the rich agricultural lands here were a powerful lure for the region's first European
settlers, today urbanization is putting the future of Squamish's family farms in jeopardy. Still, a pastoral ambience prevails, making

these back roads a good place to stretch your legs while enjoying seasonal colors, counting eagles, or tracing pioneer byways. The finest hops in the British Empire were once grown here and exported to England for use in brewing beer. Although the market for hops ended abruptly with the outbreak of war in 1914, a reminder of the aromatic crop's glory days in the valley is preserved in the name Hop Ranch Creek, which drains Alice Lake.

As you journey north on Buckley Street from downtown Squamish towards Brackendale, Buckley crosses the BC Rail tracks and turns into Government Road. At the West Coast Railway Heritage Park (39645 Government Road; 604-898-9336; www.wcra.bc.ca), vintage train cars and steam engines such as the *Royal Hudson* are displayed on the grounds and in a large roundhouse. The history of Squamish is interwoven with that of the railway, once the largest employer in town, and the museum has found a receptive home. One of the oldest pieces of equipment on display—and my personal favorite—is the stout-hearted 2-*Spot* locomotive, which went into service in Squamish with the Howe Sound and Pemberton Valley Northern Railway in 1910. Climb aboard and ring its resonant bell.

> ## BRACKENDALE AND CHEEKYE &

Access: Follow Government Road to 7 km (4.3 mi) north of downtown Squamish, or just west of Highway 99 on Depot Road, where a large sign of an eagle is posted.

Once an important relay station on the Pemberton Trail, Brackendale was eclipsed by Squamish when that port began to grow in importance with the construction of a government wharf in 1902. Although Brackendale was located only 7.5 km (4.6 mi) north of the Squamish waterfront, it sometimes took the early travelers who arrived aboard the steamer *Saturna* half a day to make the journey between the two. Today Brackendale is part of the municipality of Squamish.

A large population of bald eagles has called Brackendale home since long before the arrival of Europeans. From November to March, when the tall black cottonwoods stand bare, you can see massive nests high in their branches. The eagles return each year to reclaim their penthouses, repair them, and add new nest material,

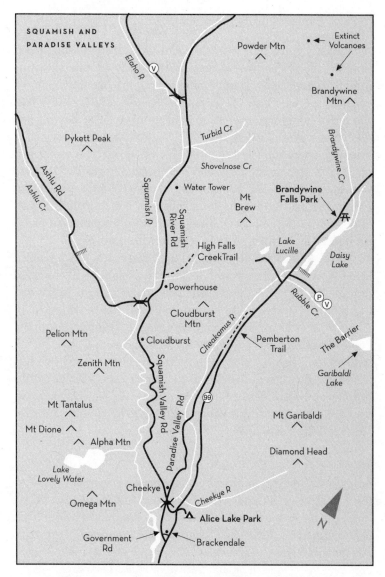

Elaho R

Powder Mtn

Extinct
Volcanoes

Brandywine
Mtn

Pykett Peak

Turbid Cr

Shovelnose Cr

Ashlu Rd

Ashlu Cr

Squamish R

Water Tower

Squamish River Rd

Mt
Brew

Brandywine
Falls Park

Brandywine Cr

Lake
Lucille

Daisy
Lake

High Falls
Creek Trail

Powerhouse

Cloudburst
Mtn

Cheakamus R

Rubble Cr

Pemberton
Trail

The Barrier

Pelion Mtn

Cloudburst

Garibaldi
Lake

Zenith Mtn

Squamish Valley Rd

Mt Tantalus

Paradise Valley Rd

99

Mt Garibaldi

Mt Dione

Alpha Mtn

Diamond Head

Lake
Lovely Water

Omega Mtn

Cheekye

Cheekye R

Alice Lake Park

N

Government
Rd

Brackendale

and every January there is a tally of the birds' numbers. In 1994, a world-record 3,769 bald eagles were counted along the Squamish River, making this one of the largest nesting colonies of these magnificent birds in North America. Thanks to the efforts of community leaders, Brackendale Eagles Provincial Park was created on the site in 1999.

Winter is prime time in eagle country. The best viewing spot is from the top of the dike beside Government Road, directly across from the Easter Seals Camp. From here you may see thirty or more eagles at any one time. (The Squamish River didn't always flow this close. Longtime residents remember when hayfields stretched a kilometer west of where the dike stands. This land was flooded when the river assumed its present channel in 1940.) A wheelchair ramp leads up onto the dike from Government Road. Two benches, whimsically fashioned from driftwood, provide good perches for enjoying grand views of the river, valleys, and mountains. Information kiosks mounted on the dike, including an inspirational Skomish First Nations display, detail the natural history of eagles.

North of Brackendale, Government Road meets the Squamish Valley Road coming west from Highway 99. Signs on Highway 99 indicate the turnoff to Squamish and Paradise valleys. Just as you begin driving west from 99 towards the small Native settlement of Cheekye, also the Squamish name for Mount Garibaldi, one of the best views of Mount Garibaldi's Atwell Peak, Dalton Dome and the red lava ridge below it rises in the east. The best time to catch it is late in the day when the sun lights up the rock face. A bridge crosses the Cheakamus River at Cheekye, and on its far side the road divides into the Squamish Valley Road to the left and the Paradise Valley Road to the right.

> ## SQUAMISH VALLEY ROAD

Access: 12.5 km (7.8 mi) north of downtown Squamish via Government Road; 4 km (2.5 mi) west of Highway 99 on Squamish Valley Road. On the west side of the Cheekye Bridge the road divides. To the left, the Squamish Valley Road continues northwest while to the right the Paradise Valley Road heads north. Check your gas gauge before exploring the Squamish or Paradise Valley roads. The nearest gas station is in Brackendale.

Reasons for making the journey up the Squamish Valley are plentiful. In early summer, daisies, elderberries, and thimbleberries color the roadside while glaciers cloak the surrounding peaks, from the expansive Tantalus Range at the valley's southwest corner north to the aptly named Icecap Peak and Powder Mountain, a reminder that parts of B.C. are still emerging from the most recent ice age. In July, the broad Squamish River, augmented by creeks strung like shoelaces from the receding snowline, gets low enough to entice experienced paddlers and rafters. As the water levels drop, sandbars appear, creating soft campsites for stargazers. Given that the valley rises steeply beside the road, hiking trails are few—though you can explore the well-marked High Falls scenic route, a short distance north of Cloudburst.

Partnered with the Squamish River Forest Service Road, the Squamish Valley Road runs northwest for 40 km (25 mi), winding through shady stands of tall broadleaf maples towards a small settlement informally known as Cloudburst. The Squamish River accompanies the road in places but is hidden for the most part, and this is an easy place to cycle. There's also a particularly good viewpoint of Tantalus and Zenith mountains from the one-lane bridge across Pillchuck Creek, about 13 km (8.1 mi) from the Cheekye River Bridge.

The valley is a narrow floodplain with rarely a cleared homesite. When you do spot a house, it typically sits atop large raised earthen pads or on stilt supports, which provide incomparable views of Mount Tantalus and its companion peaks. A tantalus is a stand on which crystal decanters are displayed, and Mount Tantalus certainly displays the frozen crystals on its slopes to best advantage. Tantalus is also the name of a mythological Greek king, and the names of adjacent peaks here, including Alpha and Omega, also reflect this.

Much of the first 19 km (11.8 mi) of the road passes through a series of Squamish First Nation reserves, which are posted as private property.

> ## SQUAMISH RIVER FOREST SERVICE ROAD
Access: 17.5 km (10.6 mi) from the Cheekye River Bridge

Just past the farmyards of Cloudburst (watch for cattle on the road) is the gateway to Tree Farm 38. The Squamish Valley and the Squamish River widen here for the next 20 km (12.4 mi). By July, when water levels have usually dropped to their seasonal lows, sandbars appear and provide excellent picnicking, camping, and fishing

Squamish River

spots. Dolly Varden char and cutthroat trout run in the silty gray river, which never warms up enough for more than a quick plunge, even on the hottest days.

Just north of Cloudburst a bridge spans the Squamish near its confluence with Ashlu Creek. Rough picnic and camping spots dot the far bank. The creek is one of the few major tributaries that feed the Squamish from the west.

Beyond Ashlu Creek on Squamish River Road, granite walls rise above the east side of the Squamish River, forcing the road to hug the slopes. You soon pass BC Hydro's Cheakamus powerhouse. It receives water pumped through a tunnel from Daisy Lake—a reminder of how interconnected this valley is with Whistler.

Cars are often parked near a water tower north of the powerhouse. This is a good spot to begin a hike of the High Falls Creek Trail or to launch a raft, kayak, or canoe. In summer the current here is often ideal for a leisurely paddle downstream. If you're traveling with a group, leave one vehicle at the tower and another at one of several locations along Government Road, or even at the Squamish Spit, for when you pull out of the river. You can then drive back with a partner to reclaim the vehicle at the water tower.

> HIGH FALLS CREEK TRAIL

Access: 20 km (12 mi) from the Cheekye River Bridge
Ability Level: Intermediate

Picture yourself standing beside a towering torrent of water falling with such force that the ground shakes like the boxcars coupling in the Squamish railway yards. Welcome to High Falls, one of the most powerful places I've ever visited around Whistler—which says a lot.

From the well-marked trailhead just north of the powerhouse, the High Falls Creek Trail follows the north side of the creek from which it takes its name. On busy days, parked vehicles line the shoulders of the road at this popular location.

This is a challenging four- to five-hour hike (best undertaken May through October), though hikers can make use of fixed ropes as they scramble hand-over-hand across outcroppings on the steepest stretches of the rock-and-root trail. The trail is not recommended for young children. Viewpoints of the falls, the Tantalus Range to the northwest, and the Squamish River as it braids its way through the valley below await you along the 6-km (3.7-mi) route. Some require short detours to reach. In places, signs warn of treacherous footing and steep drop-offs. That said, the greatest threat along this well-worn trail is dehydration.

The canyon into which High Falls Creek cascades is so steep and narrow that what lies above and below is not revealed at any viewpoint—only a slice of white effervescence endlessly repeating itself as plummeting water shatters into millions of droplets. The hydraulic motion is so hypnotic that you'll be hard-pressed to pull yourself away.

Expect to catch your first good look at the falls after an hour of steady climbing. The higher you hike, the better the views. Eventually, the trail leads away from the falls into a forested zone of welcome quiet before connecting with the Branch 200 Road. Rather than retrace your steps, you may well decide to descend along this open road that leads 4.5 km (2.8 mi) to the Squamish River Forest Service Road. From there it's a 1.6-km (1-mi) ramble south back to the trailhead. Along the way you'll be rewarded with some of the best views of the Squamish Valley seen all day.

> ELAHO RIVER
Access: 39 km (24.2 mi) from the Cheekye River Bridge

Almost year-round, one of the Squamish Valley's most compelling sights is the hundreds of small glacier-fed waterfalls that pour off the mountains on the western side. The silty waters of Shovelnose and Turbid creeks, cascading down off the slopes of Mount Cayley, Mount Fee, and Brandywine Mountain above, pass beneath the road as it nears the northern end of the valley. Stop at one of several bridges for panoramic look-arounds in the area. The ragged crest of Mount Cayley is particularly distinctive.

A bridge leads across the Squamish next to its confluence with the Elaho River. Here, at last, a half-hour drive from Cloudburst, are easily reached sites along the river for picnicking and camping. A short, steep, rocky access road descends to riverside beside the bridge. (Check from the bridge for a good place to park and spread out.) Above, vast icefields spill down the slopes of the Pykett and Icecap peaks to the west.

The Elaho main road climbs, in dramatic contrast to the mostly level road you've just traveled from Cheekye. Look down into the canyon of the Elaho River and you'll understand how it got its reputation for danger. One mistake in a raft or kayak can lead to serious trouble. Drive slowly as you climb through this section of the canyon. Park and explore on foot for a better look. Interestingly, views of mountains and glaciers in the Squamish Valley are best when traveling south versus north. Make sure you stop and take in the big picture.

The road continues to climb above the Elaho canyon until it passes over Blanca (Maude Frickert) Creek, then enters a long level valley. The most interesting part of your journey is behind you now. Heavy logging has cleared the forest right to the banks of the Elaho in places, accounting for much of the debris that jams up the canyon—and for the scarcity of wildlife, which once thrived here. Only the moose in a protected herd farther up the valley by Sims Creek have stayed in any numbers. The southern boundary of Clendenning Park, a rugged 30,330-ha (74,946-acre) undeveloped provincial park set aside in 1997 as part of the proposed Randy Stoltmann Wilderness Area, lies nearby. Together with Upper Lillooet Headwater Park (see chapter 25), these two massive swaths represent a major portion of the land that Stoltmann sought to preserve prior to his death in 1994 (see sidebar, page 205).

To the northwest are the glaciers of Mount Ralph, which feed the Elaho. Over the icy peaks to the west, a short distance by air, is Princess Louisa Inlet. To the north, the Pemberton Icefield leads up towards Mount Meager. Looking back to the east, you can finally see the glaciers of the Pacific Ranges on the tops of Callaghan, Powder, and Brandywine mountains—three of the extinct volcanoes that molded this region.

BEST SWIMMING HOLE

Levette Lake—wildly popular with cyclists who have pumped their way up from Squamish. The shoreline plunges quickly; to swim, hop off logs into bathtub-warm heaven.

> **PARADISE VALLEY**

Access: 4 km (2.5 mi) west of Highway 99 off Squamish Valley Road; 12.5 km (7.8 mi) north of downtown Squamish via Government Road. See page 60 for a detailed map of this area.

A narrow stretch of land that was carved by the Cheakamus River, Paradise Valley is flanked by high ridges on either side. Highway 99 climbs above the valley to the east, a series of small lakes lies hidden from view on the west side, and the BC Rail line charts a careful course between them. Although less than half as long as nearby Squamish Valley, Paradise has a quiet beauty all its own.

Take the right-hand road north from the bridge at Cheekye and you will be traveling on Paradise Valley Road. Paved for much of its 11.3-km (7-mi) length, the road is level—making for easy cycling, at least until you reach the Pemberton Trail. Along the way are several good picnic and fishing spots on the banks of the Cheakamus River, where fishing is strictly catch-and-release. The historic Pemberton

Trail, now used as a hiking and biking trail through the Cheakamus Canyon, takes over where the road ends.

About 2 km (1.2 mi) beyond Cheekye, you pass an ecological reserve to the west and, across the road, the North Vancouver Outdoor School, where students study the environment. (The school's conference center is available for use by other groups in summer; 604-980-5116; www.nvsd44.bc.ca) The land on which the school stands was homesteaded by Jim Levette, who named Paradise Valley and gave his own name to a nearby lake. Several old fruit trees from his orchard still flourish on the school's grounds. Evidence of the Pemberton Trail can be seen on the scree slope nearby.

Directly across the road from the school, a road leads up to Evans and Levette lakes. Evans is a private lake, but Levette has a public—albeit small—side to it. A 4-km (2.5-mi) road leads past Evans to Levette. Although paved as far as Evans, the road past that can be rough and muddy at times, but is graveled as it climbs towards Levette. Many visitors opt to leave their vehicles at the pullout near Evans Lake and continue on foot. The 11-km (6.8-mi) Skyline/Levette Lake Loop intermediate hiking trail leads uphill from here, at first following the road, then branching through the forest. A detailed trail map is prominently displayed. Conditions at points along this trail have deteriorated to where caution is strongly advised. Decide for yourself whether the trail's excellent views of Tantalus, Diamond Head, and Squamish Valley are worth the risk.

If you opt to drive to Levette Lake, bear right until confronted by a deep ditch, which some drivers consider a personal challenge to navigate; others opt to park and walk the remaining few meters. On the far side of the ditch, a boulder-strewn road leads uphill on the right to Hut Lake, a 90-minute hike one way.

Levette Lake has an open spot for picnicking and swimming at a Forest Service recreation site that has seen better times. There are primitive campsites beside the lake and an outhouse nearby. But a lack of garbage containers (and a general disregard for the principles of no-impact camping) contributes to the trashiness of what was once a pretty little campground. Views of Omega Mountain to the west, hidden by the forest at lakeside, greet those who make the effort to get out on the water.

Just beyond the North Vancouver Outdoor School, Paradise Valley Road crosses the Cheakamus River, then Midnight Way. Local rafting companies as well as anglers launch or cast from the easily accessible riverside beside the bridge. (Midnight Way is named after the Midnight family, who homesteaded here). From here it's possible to drive north for another 7 km (4.3 mi), but the road narrows and becomes quite rough for the last stretch. If in doubt, park beside the BC Hydro tower and walk beside the Cheakamus. The river is frigid even in the dog days of August, which is the best time to spread out on a sun-drenched gravel bar; whitewater kayakers favor this location as a put-in spot.

As it flows through Paradise Valley, the Cheakamus River is a clear emerald color dotted with stretches of whitewater. Water levels in the river are controlled by a BC Hydro dam farther upstream on Daisy Lake, near Whistler. By agreement, an even flow is supposedly guaranteed for the health of fish stocks in the river (a debatable point with local anglers). There's good freshwater action on the Cheakamus River almost year-round, though it's strictly catch-and-release, as is all fishing on rivers and creeks in the Squamish region. Anglers cast from the banks of the Cheakamus for coho salmon in October and November, for steelhead from late February to April, and for Dolly Varden char anytime. Best access to the banks is from the north end of Paradise Valley Road.

> **THE PEMBERTON TRAIL**
Access: 11.3 km (7 mi) north of Cheekye. The Cheakamus Canyon section of the trail from the north end of Paradise Valley Road to Highway 99 is about 5 km (3.1 mi) one way.
Ability Level: Intermediate

The rock walls on each side of the Cheakamus River close in at the north end of Paradise Valley. From here the old Pemberton Trail once led travelers up one of the valley's steepest sections, where traces of the route are still evident. Most cyclists find that the rocky road climbs here too steeply for them to maintain traction for long. You'll have to dismount and push for much of the way until you reach the BC Rail tracks. From here the going is much better heading north. You can also get some good views of the Cheakamus Canyon if you walk along the trail to where it intersects with the railway. Cross the tracks to pick up the trail again. Follow along for another 15 minutes and you'll find that even better views present themselves just north of Starvation Lake (a much prettier lake than its name suggests).

Hut, Levette, and Evans lakes lie hidden across the valley, screened from view by rolling ridges. The Tantalus Range is to the west, with Omega Mountain most prominent. Basalt rock formations beside the railway tracks remind visitors of the volcanic heritage of the region. Another good view of the canyon occurs just as more of the Tantalus peaks begin to appear. The long stretch of river that is now visible below is a jade-green color that instantly turns to white froth when the river drops and encounters one of the numerous boulder gardens. The best view of all is to be had here. And even though the tracks and trail are perched high above the canyon, the ground trembles from the force of the Cheakamus as it splits into two cascading waterfalls.

Follow the Pemberton Trail north until it meets Highway 99 and you will have covered one of the most well-preserved sections of the historic route. This is also the opening segment of the epic Cheakamus Challenge mountain bike race held in September between Brackendale and Whistler (www.cheakamuschallenge.ca).

> ## BEST BEAK SPOTTING

NO MATTER what time of year you adventure here, Brackendale's Art Gallery Theatre Teahouse, just north of Depot Road, makes a good stop to learn more about bald eagles (41950 Government Road; 604-898-3333; www.brackendaleartgallery.com). Open weekends and holidays from noon to 10 PM, this birders' hot spot hosts a variety of artistic, musical, and dramatic productions and serves up steaming bowls of soup—perfect on a frosty morning. Sculptor Thor Froslev, who began building this sprawling space in 1969, is also responsible for publicizing Brackendale as the winter home of the bald eagle and helping to develop the park. The dramatic wooden signs on Highway 99, dominated by the profile of an eagle, are his creation.

> *Camping:* Squamish Valley Campground (16.5 Mile Squamish Valley Road; 604-898-1145; www.campsquamish.com); Paradise Valley Campground (Paradise Valley Road; 1-800-922-1486 or 604-898-1486; www.paradisevalleycampground.net)

> *Flightseeing:* Black Tusk Helicopter (Squamish Municipal Airport, 46041 Government Road; 604-898-4800; www.blacktuskhelicopter. com)

> *Kayaking:* The Sea to Sky Kayaking School in North Vancouver conducts tours of the Cheakamus River and other whitewater sources around Squamish (604-898-5498; www.squamishkayak. com).

> *Rock Climbing:* Slipstream Rock and Ice (5010 Paradise Valley Road; 1-800-616-1325 or 604-898-4891; www.getclimbing.com) operates a private climbing center at Paradise Valley Crags.

> *Trail Riding:* Sea-to-Sky Stables (Paradise Valley; 1-866-898-3934; www.seatoskystables.com) offers trail rides, guided hikes and eagle watching tours.

> *Whitewater Rafting:* Those in search of a lively river experience should experience rafting the Squamish when its water levels and those of a trio of its major tributaries—the Cheakamus, Cheekye, and Mamquam rivers—are on the rise, fed by snowmelt from the local mountains. Here, each May, Canadian Outback Adventures (1-800-565-8735; www.canadianoutback.com) ramps up for another season. In operation since 1992, COA has an enviable record not only for safely guiding rafting trips but also as a training center for aspiring river guides. (COA also runs special rafting trips for families with young children.) Their river of choice is the Cheakamus, which flows past COA's base on Squamish Valley Road. Rafters are bused from base camp to a put-in location farther north in Paradise Valley, where the river broadens after its long run through the narrow Cheakamus Canyon. The Sunwolf Outdoor Centre, situated beside the Cheekye River Bridge, offers a variety of year-round adventure tours of the region, including eagle-watching and rafting. Sunwolf also has cabins available for rent (1-877-806-8046;

604-898-1537; www.sunwolf.net).

From out on the river, views of the Squamish and Paradise valleys open on all sides. This is a remarkably scenic location, dominated by peaks in both Garibaldi Park to the east and the Tantalus Range to the west. Whistler River Adventures (1-888-932-3532; www.whistlerriver.com) also offers guided rafting on the Cheakamus, Elaho, and Squamish rivers.

4

ALICE LAKE
PROVINCIAL PARK

. . . . .

> LOCATION: 72 km (44.6 mi) north of Vancouver, 12 km (7.4 mi)
north of downtown Squamish, 46 km (28.5 mi) south of Whistler,
83 km (51.5 mi) south of Pemberton

> ACTIVITIES: Camping, fishing, hiking, mountain biking,
paddling, picnicking, swimming, viewpoints, walking

> HIGHLIGHTS: Pocket lakes, wide trails, surprise views

> ACCESS: Turn east from Highway 99 at well-marked Squamish
Valley Road.

WARM FRESHWATER lakes are as delightful a discovery as
you can make when exploring the Sea to Sky countryside
in summer, with Alice Lake the largest of a nest of four
such spots just north of downtown Squamish. A popular escape long
before it became a provincial park in 1956, Alice Lake was named
for the wife of pioneer logger Charlie Rose. He was one of the first
settlers to arrive in the Brackendale region in the 1880s and homesteaded where the park is located.

The park is a study in contrasts for first-time visitors. The formal
landscaping at the lake's eastern end—a delightful reminder of the
Rose legacy—is just one example. Groomed lawns roll gently down
to Alice Lake's two beaches, a cushion of comfort for those timid
souls who have yet to discover the wild green heart of the park. But
explore the park more and you'll find it a welcoming place to stretch
your legs, perhaps while getting your feet accustomed to a new pair
of runners or trying out a birthday bike. Walk or cycle to the ridge

above it where I always enjoy the panoramic view of the Squamish Valley, Howe Sound, the Tantalus glaciers, and the Cheakamus River cutting its way through a granite gorge.

> ALICE LAKE &

Access: *Signs at the park entrance direct visitors to Alice Lake's day-use facilities and parking areas at both its northern and southern ends, and its 108 vehicle-access campsites on the northern side.*

Families have thronged Alice Lake each summer for generations. Given Squamish's growth, that's not about to change. Fortunately, by September, a hush prevails over the lushly forested campground, in part due to the thick canopy of western hemlock that shelters much of the park. Hot showers and flush toilets, essential amenities for many campers, make for a pleasant stay. And if you're lucky, one of the sites near both the lake *and* the hot showers will be vacant. Bear right at the entrance to reach these successive rows of pleasantly spaced campsites that spiral up the hillside from the lake.

Given the park's popularity, especially on long weekends from May to August, be prepared to walk several minutes from the far corners of the parking lots to reach the beach. If you're just stopping for a swim on a sunny day, it's still worth the effort. Rows of tables ring the shore, each with its own barbecue. Or look for a grassy place to spread your blanket and prepare to enjoy some serious people watching. The setting, with its manicured tranquility, is enormously restful.

Lakeshore Walk, shaded by cedar groves that thrive on the moisture provided by the lake, links the picnic areas on the north and south sides of the lake. The view from the lake's northern end of the peaks in Garibaldi Park's Diamond Head region is the best in the park—short of the vista granted by climbing nearby DeBeck's Hill. At night, when the stars reflect off the lake's still surface, the finest viewing of the open sky and its cosmic wonders—such as a moonrise over the peaks in nearby Garibaldi Park—is gloriously viewed from the beach, or, even better, from a boat in the middle of the lake.

Of the four lakes in the park, Alice is the one most suitable for paddling. (Motorized boats are not permitted on any of the lakes.) It's not unusual to see pods of kayakers and canoeists taking lessons

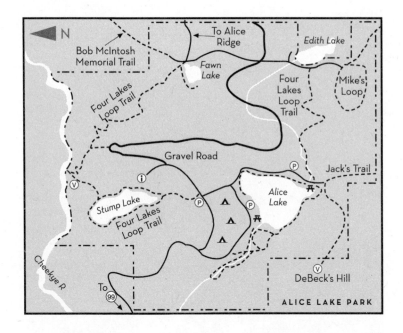

at one end while anglers quietly troll at the other. There's ample room for both, with a pier to fish from at the southern end and launch sites at each end of the lake beside the picnic areas. And while freshwater lake fishing from a dock may not be everyone's thing, there is a chance you'll hook a trout in these stocked waters, particularly in May and June.

> ### FOUR LAKES LOOP TRAIL

Access: The 6-km (3.7-mi) Four Lakes Loop Trail links all four of the park's lakes: Alice, Stump, Fawn, and Edith. The best places to begin are at either Alice or Stump lakes. Allow two to four hours to complete the round trip on foot, depending on how many stops you make along the way. All of the trails are well marked, with both directions and distances indicated.

Ability Level: Novice

Stump Lake. The name conjures up images of decrepitude, so it's a pleasant surprise to discover that the only stumps in sight are beside the trail, not in the lake. Logged over several decades before

Alice Lake

being designated a park, the area does have some impressively wide stumps.

The smooth trail divides as it rounds the small lake. On one side it's quite level; on the other it climbs the hillside. Looking down you may see anglers casting for rainbow, cutthroat, and brook trout. Unlike at Alice, there are no lawns or beaches here—or at Fawn and Edith lakes. You'll find the occasional blowdown on which you can walk out from the shore to see skunk cabbage blooming in spring and water lilies in summer, with Alice Ridge high above. To the north, Atwell Peak, Mount Garibaldi's south tower, is visible.

From Stump Lake's northern end, the trail winds close beside the Cheekye River for a time, then climbs gently towards Fawn Lake. Year-round, the forest floor here is thick with ferns. In spring, delicate wildflowers such as white trilliums and dusty-rose bleeding hearts appear in clusters. Beneath several old-growth cedars is an especially pretty viewpoint overlooking the river.

If you are walking with young children, this may be as far as you care to go on the Four Lakes Loop Trail. Instead of continuing farther, take the short connector to an old logging road that leads back to Alice Lake. Gradually, the trail climbs away from the river, leaving the sounds of rushing water behind, to be replaced by only an occasional birdcall in the silence of the forest. In the 20 to 30 minutes it takes to reach Fawn Lake on foot, there's plenty of time to listen to your own thoughts.

Fawn Lake is smaller and shallower than its companions, and its shoreline is not as accessible as those of Stump and Alice. But the water is warm (and full of tadpoles fidgeting below the surface) and it's possible to swim from the banks of a small clearing. Which is exactly what many cyclists do here in summer after a long ride on nearby bike trails. (Note: From May to September, cyclists must approach Fawn and Edith lakes along a former logging road that snakes through the park and beyond towards Alice Ridge.) A rough trail circles part of the lakeshore and then disappears in a shallow, marshy section. The surrounding woods are surprisingly open in places, with little undergrowth aside from the forest floor's carpet of deep moss.

East of Fawn Lake, the Four Lakes Loop Trail merges with an old logging road for the 10- to 15-minute walk to *Edith Lake*. The road is lined with tall trees, the sound of the wind high in their branches. An occasional train whistle is heard from the valley below. Ravens fly by, the *whoosh* of their beating wings like an owl's hoot.

From Edith Lake's northern end there are good views of Goat Ridge above Shannon Falls and other snowy slopes in the distance. Unfortunately, although there is one rough approach to the lake from the road, most of the waterfront is not within the park boundary. Mike's Loop Trail, an intermediate-level mountain bike trail, and an abandoned logging road lead south of the park towards the Squamish neighborhood of Garibaldi Highlands. Another bike trail, the so-called Tracks from Hell, leads southeast to link with a succession of other bike trails that parallel the park's eastern boundary. (See chapter 5 for more details.)

The turnoff from the logging road to the *Alice Lake* section of the trail is well marked. This leg takes 20 minutes to complete on foot. At midpoint are some steep stretches where the trail keeps company with a small creek flowing from Edith to Alice, and simple wooden bridges span the creek in several places. Close to where the creek spills out into Alice Lake, a charming little stone channel built into the hillside carries the water its final distance. From here, the trail loops around Alice Lake through stands of sheltering cedars and passes through the picnic areas and campground.

> ### DEBECK'S HILL

Access: The trailhead lies at Alice Lake's southern end.

If a steady hill climb that rewards with panoramic views is your idea of fun, tackle DeBeck's Hill. The former logging road begins its relentless ascent just past a large yellow gate. Allow 30 minutes to reach the top on foot and not much less by bike. Just before you reach the summit, you will pass an old logging donkey sitting high on its log skids. The smell of grease hangs in the air still, decades after the donkey was last used. By contrast, at the very top of the hill is a telecommunication station.

During spring and summer, you may find yourself fending off persistent bugs, but the cool breeze that usually blows across the

> ### BEST PADDLE VISTA

WHEN THE stars reflect off Alice Lake's still surface, the finest viewing of the open sky and its cosmic wonders—such as a moonrise over the peaks in nearby Garibaldi Park—is most gloriously scoped from a canoe or kayak in the middle of the lake.

summit dissipates the insects. You'll get the complete picture of the local geography from up here.

> *Camping:* A parking fee of about $3 per day/$1 per hour is charged for day visitors. An overnight camping fee (about $24 for drive-in sites, $19 for walk/cycle-in sites) is charged mid-March to October. Camping reservations, particularly for holiday weekends from May to September, should be made in early March with Discovery BC (1-800-689-9025; www.discovercamping.ca).

> *Cycling:* Although encouraged year-round in the park, cycling is not permitted on the Four Lakes Loop Trail from May 1 to September 15.

> *Hiking:* If you're here for a quick visit, take the left turn at the park entrance towards the park headquarters. Park beside the public telephone next to the Stump Lake trailhead, then follow the Four Lakes Loop route clockwise.

5

SQUAMISH BIKE ROUTES

· · · · ·

Y EAR-ROUND, CYCLISTS in search of both mellow cross-country and challenging technical trails head for Squamish. The three following locales are synonymous with both serious and casual bike action found along more than 122 trails.

> ## CHEEKYE FAN

Access: If you journey here by car, park in the vicinity of Bracken-dale Eagle Provincial Park on Government Road (see chapter 3). Head north on Government past the Brackendale Gallery, cross the BC Rail tracks and enter the well-marked Farmers' Institute Trail, which begins on the east side of the road. (See map, page 60.)
Ability Level: Novice to intermediate

If you're new to mountain biking, one of the best places to begin is the forested trail system in the Cheekye Fan, a boulder-studded zone near the mouth of the Cheekye River in the Brackendale neighborhood. The wide, hard-packed *Farmers' Institute Trail* meanders through several clearings and into a second-growth forest. In some places, paved sections as well as a segment of the historic Pemberton Trail augment it.

At Ross Road, the trail joins up with the Cheekye Fan trail system. Head west on Ross Road to reach one of the trail entrances where a map is posted. From this point a series of interconnected trails, some made more challenging by intentionally placed logs and rocks, loops through the fan. This is a good introduction to technical cycling with a minimum of steep terrain. Chose from a half-dozen single- and double-track routes, such as *Reefer Rip* and *Cracked Patella*. Or, if you're looking for something more laid back, try the paved trails in the Brackendale Family Bike Park on Ross

Paul Ridge, Diamond Head

Road, just east of Don Ross Secondary and Brackendale Elementary Schools.

The main Cheekye Fan route, the *Ray Peters Bike Trail*, circles around the Fan beside Government and Squamish Valley roads. You'll frequently see vehicles parked at a series of entrances to the main trail and its offshoots, such as the *Rusty Pail Trail* off Squamish Valley Road, where the trailhead is marked by a corroded coffee can suspended from a tree. Rusty Pail offers a carefree ride with fewer rocks and roots to deal with than elsewhere on the Fan. It's a spongy trail that twists through a sheltered stand of Douglas fir; the forest floor is carpeted with moss and sword ferns and studded with cedar stumps, evidence of the old-growth forest's glory days.

Signage in the Cheekye Fan is sparse, but some trails are marked with colored ribbons. It's up to you where to turn when the trail divides. The trails cover a relatively small, contained area, so getting lost isn't likely, particularly if you have a copy of the *Squamish Trail Recreation Map.* A cleared BC Hydro right-of-way crosses the Fan and Farmers' Institute trails. Following the trail and service road that leads through this land reserve will return you to a main road no matter which direction you choose. The joys of cycling the Cheekye Fan include more than just the fun of twisting your handlebars. The sheltering forest also offers cool relief on hot days in summer and a dry ride on wet ones.

> ### ALICE LAKE PROVINCIAL PARK
Access: For directions to Alice Lake, see chapter 4.
Ability Level: Novice to intermediate

Bike trails around Alice Lake (see map, page 49), on the east side of Highway 99 opposite the Cheekye Fan, are wider, smoother, and less technical. They also enjoy more daylight. The most popular is the *Four Lakes Loop Trail,* open to cyclists from September to May.

Jack's Trail is one of the best intermediate routes on which to experience the joy of mountain biking locally, as it rolls and winds

> ## BEST TWO-WHEEL BLAST

ONE OF the homegrown pioneers of B.C.'s cycle revolution, mountain-bike designer Paul Brodie (brodiebikes.com), staged the province's first Test of Metal endurance mountain bike race (www.testofmetal.com) on the Sunshine Coast in 1988; the race was moved to Squamish in the mid-1990s. Reflecting North America's ever-growing passion for mountain biking, today's 67-km (41.6-mi) Test of Metal is the highlight of the three-day Squamish Mountain Bike Festival, held mid-June. In all, an astounding 800-plus riders line up for the races each year, including The Mini-Metal for aspiring young rippers and the spectator-friendly Rockstar invitational downhill contest.

between Alice Lake Park and the Garibaldi Highlands area. This 5-km (3-mi) trail—from which more numerous and demanding routes, including *Mid-Life Crisis* and *Crouching Squirrel Hidden Monkey*, branch off—begins at the southern end of Alice Lake. The well-marked trailhead lies adjacent to the gravel road that leads up DeBeck's Hill (a demanding workout in its own right, with a broad view of Squamish and Howe Sound from the top before a barrelhouse descent).

Elsewhere in the park, at Edith Lake's eastern end, two options present themselves. *Mike's Trail* loops south of the park towards Garibaldi Highlands, where several short trails lead west and link with Jack's Trail for a return journey to the park. Alternatively, *Tracks from Hell* leads southeast from Edith Lake and connects with a succession of bike trails such as *Ray's Café*, *Don't Tell Jude*, and *Cliff's Corners*, all of which run parallel to the park's eastern border. If you're in need of a port to wait out a storm, watch for a shelter along this route. These trails eventually connect with the *Bob McIntosh Memorial Trail*. This gentler route heads uphill out of the park from Fawn Lake and past a string of power lines to a succession of trails, including *Deadend Loop*, *Made in the Shade*, *Rock 'n' Roll*, and *Ed's Bypass*. Follow this trail system south beneath the power lines to Rob's Corners and Cliff's Corners. From there, you can link up with Tracks from Hell or the *Mashiter Trail*, then return to the park on the ever-popular Jack's Trail.

TRAIL TIP

Best way to make sense of the Squamish trail system is the *Squamish Recreation and Trail Map* (Taiko Publishing), available at local bike stores and the Squamish Adventure Centre.

> **ELFIN LAKES** (GARIBALDI PROVINCIAL PARK)
Access: Take the exit marked "Diamond Head (Garibaldi Park)" east from Highway 99 on Mamquam Road. Drive 16 km (10 mi) to the parking lot at the trailhead, the last 4 km (2.5 mi) on rough road. Ability Level: Intermediate

Get out the granny gear, at least for the first third of this 22-km (13.6-mi) subalpine gut check. One of only two sanctioned bike routes in Garibaldi Park (Cheakamus Lake Trail is the other), this well-worn wagon road has drawn generations of visitors, most recently on two wheels. Fresh air as thick and sweet as cake will fuel the initial grunt as you power your way 5 km (3.1 mi) to Red Heather Meadows (see chapter 2). Above here the views expand exponentially with every pedal stroke. Diamond Head's lava ridge rises in a palette of pastels towards the tip of Mount Garibaldi, which pokes above the northern skyline. Just past Paul Ridge (which often holds snow from one year to the next) lie the twin Elfin Lakes. From a meadow beside these waters, surrounded by peaks, one of the most commanding viewpoints in Garibaldi Park opens wide before you, reason enough to pump your way up here before milking every drop of satisfaction from the suspension-testing descent back to Squamish.

> **THE INSIDE TRACK**

> *Bike Parts and Service:* Corsa Cycles (604-892-3331; www.corsacycles.com); Tantalus Bike Shop (604-898-2588; www.tantalusbikeshop.com)

6

CAT LAKE AND BROHM LAKE INTERPRETIVE FOREST

. . . . .

> **LOCATION:** 86 km (53.3 mi) north of Vancouver, 26 km (16.1 mi) north of downtown Squamish, 32 km (19.8 mi) south of Whistler, 69 km (42.8 mi) south of Pemberton

> **ACTIVITIES:** Camping, cycling, fishing, paddling, picnicking, swimming, walking

> **HIGHLIGHTS:** Summer swimming holes, shaded biking and hiking trails, rewarding viewpoints

AS HIGHWAY 99 wends north of Brackendale towards Whistler, it passes between two small lakes, Cat and Brohm. Many visitors are drawn here in summer but leave the lakes almost entirely undisturbed the rest of the year. During daylight hours, their warm waters are the main attraction.

While Brohm Lake is strictly day-use, Cat Lake hosts walk-in campers around its shore. Both are worthy of an hour's break from the traffic—or as a destination in themselves. As at all great swimming holes, leaping in to one of them is like discovering an oasis in the desert, especially if you work out on the trails that surround the two lakes before "indulging."

> **CAT LAKE** &

Access: Cat Lake is best approached when driving north on Highway 99. The turnoff from the highway is marked by a large green Forest Service sign about 14 km (8.7 mi) north of the Alice Lake Provincial Park exit. Watch for a marker reading "Whistler 42 km," then a bridge over a small creek. Take the next right, turn onto a dirt Forest Service

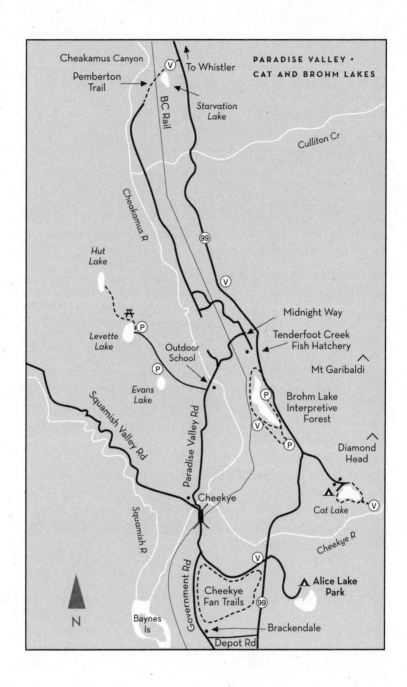

Cheakamus Canyon

Pemberton Trail

To Whistler

V

BC Rail

Starvation Lake

PARADISE VALLEY •
CAT AND BROHM LAKES

Culliton Cr

Cheakamus R

99

Hut Lake

V

Levette Lake

P

Outdoor School

Midnight Way

Tenderfoot Creek Fish Hatchery

Mt Garibaldi

P

Evans Lake

Paradise Valley Rd

P

Brohm Lake Interpretive Forest

V

P

Diamond Head

Squamish Valley Rd

Cheekye

V

Cat Lake

Squamish R

Cheekye R

Government Rd

V

Cheekye Fan Trails

99

Alice Lake Park

Baynes Is

Brackendale

Depot Rd

N

road on the east shoulder. Note: When you leave, all vehicles must turn north onto Highway 99 towards Whistler. If you wish to head south towards Squamish, proceed to the parking lot at Brohm Lake where you can then turn around.

This sweet little lake has managed to maintain its charm despite years of logging nearby. Each spring, its clear, deep-green waters are stocked with fish, primarily rainbow trout from the nearby Tenderfoot Creek fish hatchery in Paradise Valley.

Almost immediately after you turn off Highway 99, the road to Cat Lake passes an open area where vehicles with trailers for ATVs, dirt bikes, and snowmobiles often park. The road from here climbs gently for 2 km (1.2 mi), with several side roads feeding off at intervals. Just before the road reaches the lake, there is a small parking area and a gate that bars vehicles, requiring visitors to walk in. The Brohm Ridge Forest Service Road leads up a steep hill to the left of the gate, testing both cyclists and walkers just long enough to heighten their appreciation for the little lake when it suddenly appears.

There are 36 campsites scattered around the lake, each with a sturdy picnic table and fire rings. My favorites are numbered 1 to 4, a short distance from the parking lot on a handicap-access trail and above a small beach and dock that serve the needs of anglers, young children, and non-swimmers. There are a few shallow approaches elsewhere on the shore, with more docks tethered in strategic spots, making good diving platforms. Handicap-accessible toilets have been thoughtfully located at the parking lot and above the beach.

Connected by a narrow trail around the lake are numerous forest campsites, though most have limited access to the lake. Part of the trail is actually an old logging road. (A circuit on this trail is an easygoing warm-up on a mountain bike.) A short trail at the eastern end of the lake leads to a fenced promontory high above the Cheekye River. From here you look south across Alice Lake Park towards Sky Pilot Mountain and Goat Ridge above Shannon Falls. Elsewhere on Cat Lake, there are good views of the peaks in the Tantalus Range rising above the treetops to the west. The open bowl of sky above the lake fills with stars in the evening.

Access: *The main entrance to Brohm Lake is located 1.6 km (1 mi) north of the Cat Lake turnoff on the west side of Highway 99. An alternative way to the trail network on the steep ridge above the lake is from a gated entrance on the western side of the highway. Drive 1 km (0.6 mi) south of the lake. For safe access, approach in the south-bound lane. Although there are no road signs indicating this approach, there's plenty of room to pull off Highway 99. The trailhead itself is marked by a large brown Forest Service sign with a detailed trail map.*

Brohm Lake is deceptive. When viewed from Highway 99 it appears to be little more than a diminutive, reed-filled pond. But if you park at the well-marked day parking lot and explore the ridge that shields most of Brohm Lake from view, you'll discover a lake that's much larger than it first appeared. Brohm Creek flows into the lake's northern end and drains out of the main lake into a much smaller and more visible pond to the south. In summer, reeds choke the waterway between the two; a wooden footbridge links with the western shoreline.

Historically, the main approach to Brohm was from the pond, downstream from the main body of the lake's southern end and the site of an old logging operation. Some anglers still use the roadside pullout here, but this is not recommended. Much better access to the most open part of the lake is from the large well-marked parking lot, with a walk-in launch spot for small hand-carried boats.

There is no real beach on Brohm Lake. The shoreline drops away sharply on all sides, so keep an eye on small children. To find the best swimming spots, walk the short Rock Bluff Loop Trail, which

> ## BEST TARZAN SWING

· · · · · · · ·

Brohm Lake. Grab one of the ropes that hangs from the substantial branches of several old-growth cedars, then cut loose with you best Tarzan yell. The rock walls of the basin holding the lake create a great echo effect—amplifying your whoops several times over. (Beware of jumping into the lake from the ridge, as there are hidden obstacles that make this treacherous.)

Cat Lake

leads beside the lake from the parking lot. Granite outcroppings appear almost immediately.

Travelers who stop at Brohm Lake with more than a swim in mind discover an extensive 11-km (6.8-mi) network of trails running through the 400-ha (988-acre) forest to the south and west of the lake. Quick access to the trails is available from the recreation site parking lot via a wooden pedestrian bridge, which spans the southern end of the lake a short 0.5-km (0.3-mi) walk along a shoreline trail.

There's probably more ground to cover than you can explore in one visit, which makes the Brohm Lake Interpretive Forest an ideal destination for repeat forays. Although the lake itself is the main attraction, the more remote trails have a quiet charm of their own. The majestic forest muffles traffic sounds from the highway, and in several places the well-signed trail divides, offering visitors a choice of directions. For example, the High Trail leads north to Brohm Lake, while the Cheakamus Loop Trail leads west onto a ridge.

The 3.5-km (2.2-mi) lakeside trail that rings Brohm is more challenging than the level route around Cat Lake, leading past several rough picnic sites on the lake's western and northern sides. Much of the lake is hemmed in by steep rock cliffs, but there are several level spots at its marshy north end where the water is somewhat shallower. For a good two-hour workout, tie in a walk around the lake with a side hike to the Tantalus Viewpoint above the lake's western side.

Within an hour's walk from the south parking lot, starting on Alder Trail and then branching onto the Cheakamus Loop trails, you reach two viewpoints that look across Paradise Valley to the glacier-clad Tantalus Range. Staircases assist visitors up the steepest stretches to the Tantalus Viewpoint (as mentioned above). Here, on a rocky outcropping next to and below a covered fire-spotting shelter, are my favorite picnic spots. The Cheakamus River flows past unseen below, the Squamish waterfront is visible in the distance, and Shannon Falls' white scarf stands out beside Stawamus Chief Mountain. All of the peaks in the Tantalus Range—including the Tantalus, Zenith, Pelion, and Serratus—are revealed. Lake Lovely Water Creek drains from the lake of the same name, hidden in the bowl between Alpha and Omega mountains. Bonus: A breeze blows here most days, which helps keep the bugs at bay.

WHISTLER

> 7

BLACK TUSK AND
GARIBALDI LAKE

Garibaldi Provincial Park

. . . . .

> LOCATION: 99 km (61.4 mi) north of Vancouver, 39 km
  (24.2 mi) north of Squamish, 19 km (12 mi) south of Whistler,
  56 km (34.8 mi) south of Pemberton

> ACTIVITIES: Camping, cross-country skiing, fishing, hiking,
  paddling, picnicking, snowshoeing, swimming, viewpoints

> HIGHLIGHTS: The prettiest lake in the Sea to Sky corridor,
  dominated by the region's most recognizable landmark.

> ACCESS: The turnoff to Black Tusk and Garibaldi Lake is
  just south of Daisy Lake. (Watch for the BC Parks signs on
  Highway 99.) This paved road runs 2.5 km (1.6 mi) east to a
  large parking area beside Rubble Creek. A 9-km (5.6-mi)
  trail to Garibaldi Lake begins here. Note: Dogs and domestic
  pets are not allowed in Garibaldi Park.

THIS IS really two destinations in one. In fact, the trail to Garibaldi Lake and the Black Tusk offers so many choices for adventure that I expect to revisit the area for years before exhausting the possibilities. Still, Black Tusk is the magnet that has been
attracting attention since the first mountaineers arrived to explore
it in 1912. With the exception of Stawamus Chief Mountain (see
chapter 1), no other rock formation in the surrounding fortress of
coastal peaks is as noticeable or as readily identifiable in a region
that's a living lesson in geological history. We know, for example,
that the pillar of volcanic rock we see today is the remnant of a

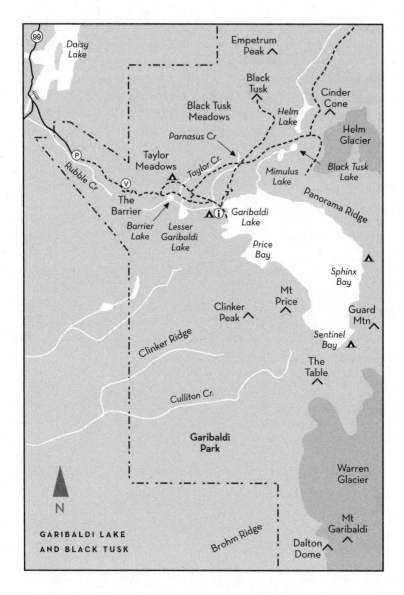

GARIBALDI LAKE
AND BLACK TUSK

much larger lava flow that vented on these slopes, though the reason for its unusual shape is still not well understood. However, geologists are almost certain that Black Tusk predates the climax of the most recent ice age, which ended 12,000 years ago.

Access: Easily viewed from the parking lot or a hike to the "6 km" point on the Garibaldi Lake Trail
Ability Level: Novice

Even if I don't intend to walk the trail to Garibaldi Lake, I often drive the short distance in from Highway 99 to the parking lot to enjoy the wide-open view of The Barrier, the rock wall rising above Rubble Creek. (Due to the wall's instability, there is a ban on overnight camping in a wide area below the parking lots.)

The broad face of red volcanic rock is especially appealing when lit by the setting summer sun. It's a unique formation in this region, the result of a flow of molten lava coming face-to-face with a glacier that once occupied what is now Rubble Creek. The ice cooled and hardened the lava, forming the thick rock face that holds back the jeweled waters of Garibaldi Lake, a basin that filled as the surrounding glaciers melted and retreated.

> The Barrier's most recent slide, in 1855, blocked the flow of the Cheakamus River and created Daisy Lake. Water levels in the lake rose even higher after BC Hydro dammed it in 1964.

The name Rubble Creek says it all. Owing to the area's geology, the creek's banks are lined with boulders left from the last great slide and the steadily eroding features of The Barrier. And the waters of the creek are frothy-white year-round and especially in late summer when the snowmelt is at its highest. For these reasons it's often difficult to approach the creek to refresh yourself. An old overgrown trail follows the creek towards the apron of talus rock at the foot of The Barrier.

Encouraged by the rushing sound from Rubble Creek, you can hike from the parking lot to the "4 km" sign in an hour along a smooth trail that switchbacks up the mountain. The Douglas firs and western red cedars lining the beginning of the trail are smaller in girth than those higher up, since the great landslide wiped out much of the forest at lower levels. Only trees that weren't in the slide path predate 1855. The ones lower down have all taken root in the years since then. For the most part, this is a welcoming forest with an open, moss-carpeted understory. Brightly-colored trail markers affixed high on tree trunks flanking the trail attest to the depth of the annual snowpack. Snowsport trekkers rely on them as much as hikers.

With one or two exceptions, there are few distant views from the trail until just prior to and past the "6 km" marker. A map of the area posted here helps decide which way to head. The trail to the left leads up to Taylor and Black Tusk meadows, and beyond there to the Tusk itself as well as a host of other destinations. The trail to the right leads immediately to the viewpoint you've been waiting for. Pick a flat rock and start gawking. Next to you rises the red-and-gray streaked Barrier. In the morning light, hues streaking the rugged face are muted, a subdued sight compared to its visage later in the day. To the southwest you can see a panorama that takes in the broad white swath of the Tantalus Range rising above the Squamish Valley and around to peaks above the Callaghan Valley.

> **GARIBALDI LAKE**

Access: 9 km (5.6 mi) from the parking lot; 3 km (1.9 mi) from The Barrier viewpoint
Ability Level: Intermediate

Depending on when you visit, water may or may not be flowing out of either Barrier or Lesser Garibaldi lakes, and ice and snow may or may not cover their steep-sided surfaces. The outflows occur only in late summer, when water levels are at their highest. Year-round, the waters from Barrier, Garibaldi, and Lesser Garibaldi lakes percolate down through a layer of scoria—porous volcanic rock—venting into Rubble Creek through a series of springs at the base of The Barrier. This explains how water levels in the creek can be so high beside the parking lot despite the modest proportions of the outflow feeding it from the lakes. Bottom drainage also accounts for low water levels in the three lakes during spring and fall months.

The best time to enjoy the visual delight of the three lakes is in August and September; not only are water levels at their highest, but this is when their color is most intense. This vivid blue is a result of sunlight reflecting off the very fine sediment in the water. Earlier in the year, the particles washing into the lakes from the winter snowmelt are larger, resulting in pallid, cloudier shades.

Just around the corner from the viewpoint, the scene is astonishingly beautiful. Barrier Lake spreads like a table before you, with fish often jumping in full profile. In summer, without turning your head, you can see whitewater entering and leaving the small lake at each end. When you look back along the trail, you'll catch Cloudburst Mountain framed by the notch at the lake's western end. You'll have a bounce in your step as you walk the mostly level trail around Barrier Lake to Lesser Garibaldi Lake, because it feels so good to be here after the steadily uphill, two-hour hike. Near the bridge over Taylor Creek, watch for an approach to the lakeside that anglers in search of rainbow trout will find helpful. (Ensure you have a valid freshwater fishing license when the ranger comes calling.) The trail narrows as it rings the lake on the hillside above and offers little other access.

Past the lake, the trail enters the forest once more, dividing again just before the "8 km" sign. The trail to the left is one of several that lead to the Taylor Meadows campground. You are now cloistered among the evergreens, 15 minutes from Garibaldi Lake, in preparation for the screamingly grand views awaiting at the big lake. From the bridge over Parnasus Creek, which feeds Lesser Garibaldi, you may see other hikers taking in the view from a bridge over the outflow creek from Garibaldi Lake, framed in a notch of red volcanic rock and evergreens with the white of the glaciers behind them. By this time you may be wondering whether your nervous system can handle the volume of visual stimuli being fed to your brain.

Cross the bridge and walk (or wade) around to the Garibaldi Lake campground. Three-dozen campsites are scattered across the hillside above the lake, some with wooden platforms on which to pitch a tent—helpful when the ground is wet. There are four sturdy shelters for day use in summer and heated for bivvying in winter, with picnic tables situated both inside and in front of them. Campers must pack in their own cooking equipment. Note: On summer weekends, camping spots at the lake and nearby Taylor Meadows are in high demand. I recommend you arrive as early in the day as possible to claim one.

Just offshore are the Battleship Islands, a string of small rocky outcroppings. Several are lightly forested. You can walk out to them

Black Tusk

when water levels are low enough; otherwise you'll have to wade or swim. Water temperatures in the big lake are rarely hot enough to be enjoyable, but if the sun is shining it will help warm you up once you emerge. Benches are conveniently placed on the largest island and along the lakeside trail, where a sign lets you know that you've reached the "9 km, Elev. 1470 m" mark. It's a treat just to sit here and look out over the landscape, trying to put a name to the many peaks and icefields. Picking out the Black Tusk is the easiest.

Given that the trail around the lake runs only a short distance past the campground to the ranger station, you'll meet the occasional visitor carrying paddles and an inflatable boat. Paddling is one way to visit parts of Garibaldi Lake that would otherwise take some serious hiking or trekking to reach. Wilderness camp shelters at several locations near the south end of the lake, including the Varsity Outdoors Club's Butler/Sphinx hut, receive more visitors in snow months than summer. The classic 30-km (18-mi) Garibaldi Névé ski traverse typically includes overnight stops here, bookended by the Garibaldi Lake shelters and the Elfin Lakes hut (see chapter 2).

> TAYLOR MEADOWS

Access: 7.5 km (4.7 mi) from the trailhead/parking lot

As you pass through Taylor Meadows, the Black Tusk towers above while Garibaldi Lake is hidden from view. The western skyline predominates in this open area. A network of boardwalks leads through the campsites here, helping to protect the delicate alpine soil from the many pairs of feet that walk through each year. The meadows' old log cabin, now used to house park equipment, once quartered a crew of hydrologists dispatched in the 1930s to investigate the energy-generating potential of the region. There is a covered cooking shelter nearby.

An amazing number of visitors are attracted to Black Tusk and Garibaldi Lake. I recommend you go on a weekday when you will have the area more to yourself. On weekends, the wide trail back to the parking lot at the end of the day can be as congested as Highway 99 —just be patient and revel in your new memories.

> BLACK TUSK

Access: 15 km from the parking lot; 6 km (3.7 mi) north of Taylor Meadows or Garibaldi Lake. Allow two hours one way.
Ability Level: Intermediate to advanced

For many, the most obvious direction to head from Garibaldi Lake or Taylor Meadows is towards Black Tusk, even if they don't plan to climb to the summit. A trail from Garibaldi Lake ascends through the forest above the lake, meeting up with the trail from Taylor Meadows after 30 minutes. Along the way it passes a series of small mountainside ponds where the views from the open meadows change constantly as you gain altitude. Very few peaks emerge from the Sphinx Glacier predominant in the east, which is a vast névé, or permanent icefield. (Not all glaciers are in retreat. At higher elevations they may even be growing larger as unmelted snow accumulates from year to year. Over time, as old snow is covered by new, the compression creates glacier ice.)

Below, Garibaldi Lake unfolds, revealing the full extent of its long contour. It is so large that parts of its surface lie undisturbed while others are patterned by the play of the wind. Up here, the meadows are more spacious than in almost any other part of Garibaldi Park, with the possible exception of the Diamond Head; parallel tracks can be followed up to them. Years ago, packhorses bringing supplies to large camps in the Black Tusk Meadows wore these deep ruts, which have eroded further with each spring's runoff. Restoration work continues to repair the delicate tundra.

In summer, squadrons of small butterflies accompany you as you make your way to the trailhead marker in the Black Tusk Meadows. Climbers already on top of the Tusk look like clusters of insects. You have a choice of several trails: to the Black Tusk, 3 km (1.9 mi) above, or to Helm Lake and Panorama Ridge, closer by. The Helm Creek Trail leads north to Cheakamus Lake, 14 km (8.7 mi) distant through a distinctly volcanic zone (see chapter 11). If you are not prepared to go the distance, you should still explore the area—about 15 minutes around the lake and glacier. From Panorama Ridge, 3 km (1.9 mi) farther, you get unlimited views around Garibaldi Lake, with features that were hidden at lower altitudes now revealed in detail. To the south, Mount Garibaldi's 2678-m (8786-feet) peak rises higher than all others.

The trail to the Tusk now climbs steadily towards a nearby ridge. Take time to enjoy your surroundings, as little streams run across or

> **THUNDER CITY**

. . . .

BEFORE THE coming of the Europeans, Black Tusk was known by First Nations as the landing place of the Thunderbird. Their mythology taught that the magical bird lived on top of the Black Tusk, flapping its wings to cause thunder and shooting lightning bolts from its eyes at anyone who came too close.

parallel to the trail. It's worth going at least a short distance farther to get a view of Garibaldi Lake. From late July to mid-August the meadows on all sides are blooming with blue lupine, red heather, Indian paintbrush, and yellow cinquefoil.

If you persist, in 60 minutes you will reach the ridge. Now nothing stands in the way of Black Tusk's south face, as the last of the alpine firs is passed and the barren expanse of broken granite revealed. A dusty trail leads across the flats and up to the Tusk—still another hour away. But from the ridge you can see every place from which you've ever viewed the Tusk, and then some.

You'll have to psyche yourself up to accomplish the last stage of the journey to the top. The going isn't easy. Although many visitors eschew wearing helmets, it's prudent to sport one when making the final ascent; the terrain is unstable. Or you may be content to take in the views from the shelter of a nearby grove while you picnic. You can now see Mimulus Lake and Black Tusk Lake below. The trails to Helm and Panorama Ridge pass beside them. Even at this exalted altitude you'll find hummingbirds keeping you company. If you have a brightly colored piece of clothing with you, spread it on the ground and sit quietly nearby. A hummingbird will soon be along to check out this strange flower.

> **THE INSIDE TRACK**

> *Camping:* There are campgrounds beside Garibaldi Lake and in nearby Taylor Meadows, 9 km (5.6 mi) and 7.5 km (4.7 mi), respectively, from the parking area. Along the way, the elevation gain is 810 m (2657 ft) to the lake and slightly more to the meadows. The popularity of the Garibaldi Lake and Black Tusk trails makes for a full parking lot every weekend between May and October. Vandalism here is an unfortunate problem; leave nothing of value in your car if you're planning to be away overnight.

BRANDYWINE FALLS PROVINCIAL PARK

. . . . .

> LOCATION: 107 km (66.3 mi) north of Vancouver, 47 km (29.2 mi) north of Squamish, 11 km (6.8 mi) south of Whistler, 48 km (29.8 mi) south of Pemberton

> ACTIVITIES: Camping, cross-country skiing, cycling, hiking, picnicking, snowshoeing, swimming, viewpoints, walking

> HIGHLIGHTS: Historic trail, high falls, Tusk views

MUCH IS hidden of Brandywine Falls Park as traffic hurries by on Highway 99, with most motorists eager to cover the winding distance between here and Whistler as quickly as possible. But pull in and peek behind the scenes at this provincial park, leaving the sounds of the highway behind you as you hike into the surrounding forest. Impressive firs quickly buffer you from all but Brandywine Creek's gurgling, and in minutes, the sound of the creek gives way to the roar of the falls.

It's a 10-minute walk from the park entrance to the falls on a well-marked trail, which begins at the parking lot and immediately crosses a bridge over Brandywine Creek. A sign posted on the bridge's far side points left for the trail to the Cal-Cheak recreation site (part of the Sea to Sky Trail, see chapter 27) or right to Swim Lake and Brandywine Falls. Bounded by Highway 99 and the BC Rail line, this is an extremely popular park on summer weekends. For more information, visit the BC Parks website: www.env.gov.bc.ca/bcparks.

> ## SWIM LAKE

Access: 0.5 km (0.3 mi) northeast of the parking lot

As you make your way towards the falls, a secondary trail branches left to Swim Lake. Aptly named, Swim Lake is one of several small ponds skirted by the trails between Brandywine and Cal-Cheak, and the most approachable. The short route to Swim Lake climbs the hillside away from the falls trail beneath some massive trees. Lakeside, there are several clear areas from which to enter the lake but very little shallow water in which to stand. The geometrically shaped basalt rocks on the hillside display telltale signs of the volcanic activity that has given the Whistler area its distinct geological character.

> ## BRANDYWINE FALLS

Access: 0.5 km (0.3 mi) east of the parking lot

The main trail to the falls leads from the forest into a clearing where the BC Rail tracks are located. Once you've crossed these, the trail re-enters the woods beside Brandywine Creek and quickly leads to a wooden observation platform. From here, visitors are treated to a hypnotic display: the creek relentlessly spilling over the rim of the falls to the canyon below. (The creek may look benign, but don't be fooled—that's a strong current. Children should be discouraged from playing on the smooth banks near the platform, for there are few handholds along the edge of the stream.)

The water tumbling 66 m (217 ft) into the gorge below creates a spray that nourishes the canyon wall's lush growth of ferns and moss. Years ago, divers explored a deep pool directly beneath the falls, though they found nothing for their efforts. Bottles of brandy and wine were long rumored to be at the bottom, having been wagered in a contest to guess the falls' true height. The name of the falls derives from this bit of surveyors' lore. Nearby Daisy Lake takes in the waters from the creek and elsewhere, but it lies far below the observation platform. Venture a short distance farther for an even better view of the lake and the Black Tusk high above.

> ## THE PEMBERTON TRAIL

Access: The Pemberton Trail branches north from the trail to

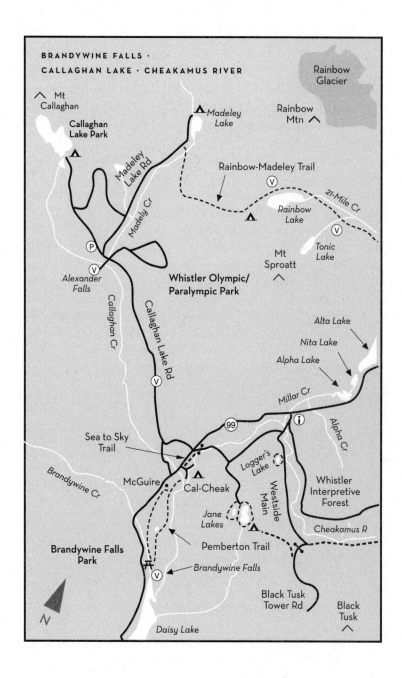

BRANDYWINE FALLS ·
CALLAGHAN LAKE · CHEAKAMUS RIVER

Rainbow
Glacier

Mt
Callaghan

Callaghan
Lake Park

Madeley
Lake

Rainbow
Mtn

Rainbow-Madeley Trail

21-Mile Cr

Rainbow
Lake

Tonic
Lake

Alexander
Falls

Whistler Olympic/
Paralympic Park

Mt
Sproatt

Alta Lake

Nita Lake

Alpha Lake

Callaghan Cr

Callaghan Lake Rd

Millar Cr

Alpha Cr

Sea to Sky
Trail

Logger's
Lake

Whistler
Interpretive
Forest

Brandywine Cr

McGuire

Cal-Cheak

Westside Main

Cheakamus R

Jane
Lakes

Brandywine Falls
Park

Pemberton Trail

Brandywine Falls

Black Tusk
Tower Rd

Black
Tusk

N

Daisy Lake

Brandywine Falls east of Swim Lake and before the railway tracks and leads 4.3 km (2.6 mi) to the Cal-Cheak campground. Allow 90 minutes each way.

Ability Level: Novice

Two routes link the park with the Cal-Cheak Forest Service Recreation Site. No matter which you choose, you'll cross the historic Pemberton Trail.

At Brandywine Falls Park, you must decide on your route as soon as you cross the bridge over Brandywine Creek. If you're on foot, you can make a loop by going to Cal-Cheak via one trail and back to Brandywine by way of the other. Though this is not a difficult route, there are some parts that climb and descend rock outcroppings and staircases; young children may find it challenging, so be prepared to carry them for part of the way.

Cyclists following the Sea to Sky Trail should turn left (west) after crossing the creek and stick to the Brandywine Trail, a 4-km (2.5-mi) scenic cruiser route. In winter, snowshoers and cross-country skiers alike will also enjoy this approach. The trail's one challenging

> ## HERITAGE HIKE

. . . .

TWO HISTORIC routes trace the Whistler region: the Gold Rush Trail (Harrison Lake to D'Arcy) and the Pemberton Trail (Squamish to Pemberton). In a frontier land with little evidence of a past beyond the rare traces left by pictograph painters in the Lillooet Lake region, these are important souvenirs.

When Europeans arrived in the mid-1800s, they named the ancient trading route linking the First Nations of the coast with those in the mountain valleys the Pemberton Trail. Unfortunately, there are few sections of it left to enjoy. A neglected trail soon becomes overgrown; all it takes is the passing of a generation for the old to be forgotten. But a section between the former BC Rail whistle-stop at McGuire and the provincial park at Brandywine Falls is still navigable. You can hike it round trip in a half-day, from the park or from the Cal-Cheak recreation site near McGuire.

section appears at the beginning, where it climbs steadily for a short distance before leveling off and following a BC Hydro right-of-way to the whistle-stop of McGuire. (Be cautious when making the descent down this steep section on your return to Brandywine, particularly on skis). Trail markers placed high up on the trunks of trees help snow trekkers find their way. This route joins the Pemberton Trail at McGuire for the remaining short distance to Cal-Cheak. Alternative parking to link up with this trail, particularly in winter, is east of Highway 99 at the Brandywine Forest Service Road turnoff, about 3.5 km (2.2 mi) north of Brandywine Falls Park.

The Brandywine Trail's north terminus lies a short distance from the railway tracks west of McGuire, towards Highway 99 on a gravel road. Pick up the trail on the south side beneath the hydro poles.

> ## CAL-CHEAK RECREATION SITE

Access: Watch carefully for the Cal-Cheak Forest Service Recreation Site and Whistler Bungee sign beside the railway tracks where a dirt road crosses going east, 4.3 km (2.7 mi) north of Brandywine Falls Park. Coming from Whistler, it's the first major road on the left south of Callaghan Lake Access Road.

Cal-Cheak takes its name from the two streams that converge here, Callaghan Creek and the Cheakamus River. There are actually three sites in one at Cal-Cheak: a day-use picnic area on the banks of Callaghan Creek and 47 drive-in campsites split between the north site on the Cheakamus River and the south site where the two waterways meet. At present, an overnight camping fee of $10 is charged May to October. The forest around the picnic area and the south site is particularly imposing.

Good picnic spots are always a welcome find. The one at Cal-Cheak is hidden from view just around the first corner of the road. Five sturdy tables—several with barbecues—are located here. There is an outhouse but no drinking water. (If you use water from the creek or river, boil it first for at least 10 minutes to purify.)

There are also good picnic spots at the other two campsites. To find them, continue along the road. A sign points left to the north site and right to the south site. (The logging road that runs past the recreation sites continues south for 3 km/1.8 mi to the Whistler

Brandywine Falls

Bungee jump site—604-938-9333; www.whistlerbungee.com—and continues on for quite a distance, eventually climbing towards Empetrum Ridge.) At the north site there's a place for children to wade in the backwater of the Cheakamus if water levels aren't too high. The road through the south site runs in a semicircle past numerous tables set back in the woods.

When occupancy is high and tents and RVs crowd the campground, you may have trouble at first finding the path to the suspension bridge across Callaghan Creek that links with the Pemberton Trail. Watch for the graveled approach that runs farther back into the forest than the approaches to other campsites. A signpost beside a short set of stairs that descends to the bridge indicates a section of the Sea to Sky Trail that skirts the campsites and follows the creek north to the day-use site.

In late spring and well into summer, Callaghan Creek runs strong with the overflow from four lakes—catch-buckets for the melted snow. Mount Callaghan also sends water down to blend with the Cheakamus River. McGuire lies just west of here, linked to the recreation site by a suspension bridge. The bridge is well fortified and screened on both sides, so there is no fear of sacrificing small children or pets to the waters rushing below, but two persons walking across it in cadence will set it bouncing and swinging giddily.

Once across the bridge, stay to the left. Within minutes you'll reach the railway tracks. From here, Brandywine Falls lies 4 km (2.5 mi) away via the Pemberton Trail. This is an important spot geographically. Nearby, three bridges cross Callaghan Creek. Without them, travel of all kinds—rail, vehicular, and pedestrian—would come to a halt. Log pilings from an abandoned span can still be seen west of Highway 99 on Callaghan Creek.

> 9

CALLAGHAN VALLEY

. . . . .

> **LOCATION:** 113 km (70 mi) north of Vancouver, 53 km (32.9 mi) north of Squamish, 6.5 km (3.1 mi) south of Whistler (Function Junction), 40 km (24.8 mi) south of Pemberton, on the Callaghan Valley access road

> **ACTIVITIES:** Camping, cross-country skiing, cycling, driving, fishing, hiking, paddling, swimming, viewpoints

> **HIGHLIGHTS:** Fresh-whipped powder snow, soothing waterfall, magic lake

> **ACCESS:** The Callaghan Lake access and Forest Service Roads lead 15 km (9.3 mi) northwest from Highway 99. The Whistler Olympic/Paralympic Park and Alexander Falls Forest Service recreation site lie 9 km (5.6 mi) uphill on pavement; from there, a rough Forest Service road continues 6 km (3.7 mi) to Callaghan Lake Provincial Park. Note: Snow often persists on its upper sections until the beginning of summer.

THE CALLAGHAN Valley, site of the Vancouver 2010 Olympic Winter Games Nordic ski events, lies southeast of Whistler, well within sight of Whistler Mountain's west side. Parts of the valley have been logged, but much of the old-growth forest at higher elevations remains intact. Rising above the valley on its west side are the snowy summits of Brandywine, Cayley, and Powder mountains. Callaghan Creek flows down to join the Cheakamus River, close to Highway 99, from its headwaters—a turquoise jewel of a lake at the foot of Mount Callaghan.

> **CALLAGHAN LAKE ACCESS ROAD**
The road to Callaghan Lake provides an excellent vista of the mountains on the west side of Whistler Valley, but perhaps the most

Callaghan Valley

compelling reason for traveling even partway up is the view on the descent. To the east is Black Tusk, which stands alone before you as you descend back into the valley—a view comparable to those from the summits of Whistler and Blackcomb. This is one of the most panoramic vantage points from which to admire this snaggletooth.

The road climbs along the north side of a spacious valley past a series of clear-cuts. Just before the road crosses a small bridge over Madeley Creek at the 10-km (6.2 mi) point, a turnoff to the left leads to a small recreation site beside Alexander Falls with a captivating viewpoint of the falls and valley. On the west side of Callaghan Lake access road sits the Nordic center. One of my favorite times to stop here is near sundown, when the evening light plays over the snow domes of the Pacific Range peaks to the west: Brandywine Mountain at the southern end (the highest at 2227 m/7300 ft), Mount Cayley in the middle, and Powder Mountain to the north. This range separates the Squamish Valley from the wide Callaghan Valley spread out below. Best views of the Black Tusk occur just beyond the Madeley Creek bridge at the junction of the Madeley and Callaghan East Forest Service roads.

Access: Whistler Olympic/Paralympic Park lies 10 km (6 mi) above Highway 99 on a paved access road 6.5 km (4 mi) south of Whistler and 115 km (69 mi) north of Vancouver.

From what I've seen, the Whistler Olympic/Paralympic Park may well prove to be the most significant legacy of the 2010 Winter Games. Not only does the site provide a companion venue for cross-country skiers to Whistler's Lost Lake trails (see chapter 13), come summer the 50 km (31 mi) of trails do double-duty for mountain bikers as well. Don't be scared away by the fact that the park has been built for world-class athletes. When it comes to recreation, these trails offer a variety of challenges suited to all ability levels. Simply exploring them on foot or snowshoes may be all the activity you need.

The park also includes two chairlift-serviced ski jumps and a 4-km (2.5 mi) biathlon course complete with a shooting range that is open for guided tours in summer as well. In addition, thanks to the profusion of wildflowers in summer blossom, the park has quickly

> ## BEST WINTER SLEEP

. . . .

TUCKED AWAY in the shadow of Powder Mountain, the Solitude Glacier, and Mount Callaghan is Callaghan Country Wilderness Adventure's backcountry lodge (604-938-0616; www.callaghan-country.com), accessed by a 12.5-km (7.8-mi) trail that leads from the Alexander Falls area. At an elevation of 1370 m (4495 ft), walled in by snowfields and glaciers, the upper Callaghan Valley enjoys a reputation as an icebox in winter—a sure-fire guarantee of dry, fluffy powder snow, ideal for snowshoeing, cross-country skiing, and alpine touring. The lodge—so invitingly tucked away in the woods to the west of Callaghan Lake that on approach it always seems to spring unannounced from the landscape—epitomizes the unique architectural style that has evolved locally since the 1940s. Whistler's Alta Lake Hostel in Whistler and the Diamond Head Lodge in Squamish are other fine examples of this striking architecture.

developed a reputation as the easiest—and safest—place to observe black bears around Whistler (see Bear Advisory, page 3). For full details on the park, including a regularly updated web cam, visit www.whistlerolympicpark.com.

> **MADELEY LAKE**

Access: Just north of the Madeley Creek Bridge, the rough 4-km (2.5-mi) road to Madeley Lake branches to the right from Callaghan East Forest Service Road. If you make the journey on foot it will take you a leisurely hour one way, slightly less by bike.

Exploring on foot or by bicycle, snowshoes or skis up the Madeley Lake road is worthwhile, as there are many sights you may miss driving it, including unbeatable views of the Black Tusk at the road's outset. Be prepared for a little hike-a-bike on steeper sections. In heavy snow years it's not unusual for this road to be blocked by the occasional blowdown.

Halfway to the lake a logging road branches to the left and eventually leads back to Callaghan East Forest Service Road, higher up the mountain. Along the way this second road passes beside a small lake, one of several that dot the slopes of Mount Callaghan. Close to this junction, views begin to open up through the brush with better views of chatty Madeley Creek (spelled Madely on some maps). Fat marmots sunning themselves on the rocky hillside above the road may whistle at you—their loud calls are sure to catch you off guard. As you journey along, views of the summits of both Callaghan and Rainbow open up before you. The road curves around Madeley Lake. The best access point is from the north end where there are several rough campsites.

The western terminus of the 15-km (9.3-mi) Rainbow-Madeley Trail lies just south of the lake. Originally brushed out decades ago by renowned forest ranger Jack Carradice, the Rainbow-Madeley Trail more recently received a face-lift courtesy of forester Don MacLaurin and a group of Whistler Rotary Club volunteers, with help from the Resort Municipality of Whistler. Budget a full day to complete a round-trip to Rainbow Lake or a point-to-point trek to Alta Lake Road (West Side Road) in Whistler. Note: Bikes and dogs are not permitted on the trail from Rainbow Lake to

Whistler (see chapter 18). The section between Madeley and Rainbow is rougher though the elevation gain isn't as great as the stretch from Rainbow Lake to Whistler.

> ## CALLAGHAN LAKE PROVINCIAL PARK
Access: *Callaghan East Forest Road climbs beyond Alexander Falls. Six km (3.7 mi) past you reach a large cleared parking area on Callaghan Lake's south side. The road ends here at the provincial park entrance.*

Fishing for rainbow trout is a major attraction here, though the stunning views warrant bringing a boat, kayak, or canoe simply to experience the setting. Rising directly above is Mount Callaghan, the headwaters for the lake, which drains into the Cheakamus River, cutting through the valley below. Cool winds blow down the mountain's slopes, even in summer. Camping is limited to the parking lot on the shores of this cold, modest-sized lake. BC Parks staff have closed off the delicate underbrush and put the former lakeside sites in rehab.

For the observant, nature continually exhibits cues to the changing seasons. Towards the end of summer and with the approach of the autumnal equinox, one of the most colorful of these signs— even preceding the turning of the leaves—is the shift of the mountain lakes' hues. Their intense coloring at this time of year is a result of sunlight reflecting off the very fine sediment in the water. In the Whistler region, this phenomenon can be witnessed most profoundly at Callaghan Lake.

Unlike the opaque tones of nearby mountain lakes such as Wedgemount and Lillooet, Callaghan is a sublimely clear shade of emerald green. It's handy to have a small craft in which to explore the lake, but you can look deep down into the water from a number of locations along the shoreline. Follow the rough trail that leads west from the parking lot around a series of small bays to where Callaghan Creek flows from the lake. If you're tempted to dive in, keep in mind that even when the water is at its warmest, the highest reading is still a numbing 16°C (61°F).

Those who bring a canoe, kayak, or small boat are in for the best views. As soon as you move away from the shoreline and get out far enough to see above the trees, the skyline is filled with an immense expanse of mountains, almost all them snow-clad. Closest at hand is Mount Callaghan, which rears its rocky head above the lake's northern end. A long, snaking waterfall drops noisily down Callaghan's lower slopes before it splashes into the lake. This is one of a half-dozen streams that feed the lake with runoff from the surrounding ridges. Nearby to the north, taller Rainbow Mountain is almost as dominant. Looking west across the broad, densely forested Callaghan Valley, you'll see the ample white snowcap atop aptly named Powder Mountain, though on a clear day the icefields of Powder Mountain and its neighbor, Brandywine Mountain, are reflected on the surface of the lake so perfectly that you need not even raise your eyes to appreciate them.

Callaghan Lake is perched about 1250 m (4100 ft) above sea level; the more distant features to the southeast are increasingly visible as you move towards the center of the lake, including a panorama that runs from Whistler Mountain across to Black Tusk to end at Mount Garibaldi, its north face almost entirely cloaked by the Warren Glacier. Short of scaling one of the nearby ridges, you'd be challenged to find more spectacular vistas than those presented here. And you'll be in good company: that of dark-eyed juncos and red male crossbills and their yellow mates. So caught up are these birds in their incessant search for food that they'll come right up to you with no sign of fear.

After exploring the Callaghan Valley, you'll have a new perspective on the Whistler area. Instead of regarding it, as I once did, as a remote, inaccessible, confusing jumble of names, you will have a mental picture of how this region links up from one peak to the next, from one valley to the other. And looking west or south from Blackcomb or Whistler Mountain, you'll find it much easier to identify other peaks by name.

10

CHEAKAMUS RIVER
AND THE **WHISTLER**
INTERPRETIVE FOREST

. . . . .

> **LOCATION:** 118 km (73 mi) north of Vancouver, 58 km (36 mi) north of Squamish, 4 km (2.5 mi) south of Creekside in Whistler, 37 km (23 mi) south of Pemberton

> **ACTIVITIES:** Camping, cross-country skiing, fishing, hiking, kayaking, mountain biking, picnicking, snowshoeing, swimming, viewpoints, walking

> **HIGHLIGHTS:** A rushing river, shady trails, cool lakes, and a volcanic rim walk

> **ACCESS:** East of Highway 99 across from Whistler's Function Junction intersection. (See map, page 97.)

As THE Cheakamus River charges to the sea between Whistler and Squamish, its frothy course mimics the volcanic turbulence that shaped this landscape millennia ago. In late summer, dagger boats play in the whitewater kicked up as the Cheakamus beats its way past stubborn granite outcroppings. Mountain bikers and hikers on trails that parallel the river and web the hillsides both hear and feel the subtle rumbles and tremors of submerged boulders that the pugnacious river punches along in its path.

Flowing northwest out of Garibaldi Park, the Cheakamus then hooks south towards Daisy Lake to pass through the Whistler Interpretive Forest. Here you'll find dozens of riverbank picnic spots for relaxing, either before or after a ride or walk, which might include a visit to the nearby Jane Lakes. If you're searching for solitude, there's

Squamish Harbour and the Stawamus Chief

Shannon Falls, Squamish

High Note Trail, Whistler Mountain

Tantalus Range from Diamond Head

Piccolo Summit, Whistler Mountain

High Falls Trail

Callaghan Valley

Rainbow Park, Whistler

Ancient cedars, Cougar Mountain

Hanging Lake, Rainbow Mountain

Red-breasted sapsucker

Whistler Mountain, Symphony Bowl

Pemberton Valley

MacLaurin's Crossing

plenty here as the throaty river wraps its wall of sound around your mind.

> ### WHISTLER INTERPRETIVE FOREST

Crisscrossing both the Eastside Main and Westside Main roads, the Whistler Interpretive Forest trails have garnered a reputation as some of the best built and, therefore, most enjoyable rides in Whistler. In addition, they are well marked, with signs indicating time, distance, and elevation gain.

A suspension bridge links the trails on both sides of the Cheakamus. Named MacLaurin's Crossing, it lies several kilometers upstream from the entrance to the forest. Paired with BC Parks' Helm Creek Trail Bridge, about 6 km (3.7 mi) farther upstream in Garibaldi Park near Cheakamus Lake (see chapter 11), the bridge allows for adventuring along both sides of the river.

A good place to begin is on the 4.5-km (2.8-mi) *Riverside Trail*, which runs along both sides of the Cheakamus. It's easy to find and, aside from several short, steep stretches, suited to all ability levels, whether you're exploring on foot or by bike. You can pick up the trail at any number of points along its route, starting beside the large trail sign kiosk just east of Highway 99, at the beginning of Cheakamus Lake Road. One drawback is that on the trail's eastern side there's only limited access to the fast-flowing river, which frequently channels through steep-sided granite walls—best appreciated from midspan on MacLaurin's Crossing.

Other trails include the moderately challenging *Ridge Trail*, a 3.4-km (2.1-mi) route beginning at Westside Main's pruning display, a short distance south of the Cheakamus River Bridge on the west side of the road. After climbing an open ridge, it links with a network of former logging roads that surround Logger's Lake, then heads south to the Crater Rim walking trail to link with the Basalt Valley Spur Road.

> **WESTSIDE MAIN**

Access: This is the companion to Cheakamus Lake Road (also known as Eastside Main). Make the well-marked turn from Highway 99 onto Cheakamus Lake Road at the south entrance to Whistler. Follow along the paved road and stay right until you reach a wooden bridge over the Cheakamus. There is a pullout on the other side where you can stop for a look into the gorge. After crossing the river, the road divides again. Stay left. Logger's Lake lies slightly less than 3 km (2 mi) past the bridge. (The road to the right goes to the Olympic Village. From there the Sea to Sky Trail links with the Jane Lakes Trail and Sugarcube Hill road, also discussed in this chapter.)

As the Cheakamus River tumbles out of Garibaldi Park, its course widens west of the Helm Creek Bridge (see next chapter). But no matter what you have in mind, the best way to reach the river is from the numerous well-marked approaches along Westside Main. Five are favored as put-in/take-out spots by kayakers. They also provide open places where those on foot can best appreciate the river's power and the ruggedness of the surroundings. There are many challenging sections that only experienced river runners should attempt, particularly the 1-km (0.6-mi) "Wow" stretch, upstream from the Westside Main Bridge. On average, water levels remain high through August. As a result, September and October are the prime paddling months on the Cheakamus. After the ice breaks in early spring, seasonal low levels allow beginners to try their hand. If you go early enough in the year you may even be able to launch into the river from a snow ramp.

> ## LOGGER'S LAKE

Access: Parking and trailhead lie 2.5 km (1.6 mi) east of Highway 99 via Westside Main.
Ability Level: Novice to intermediate

As Westside Main follows the Cheakamus River towards Logger's Lake, there are multiple turnoffs to the left. The first goes in a short distance to a water-gauging station by the river. Farther along, another leads to a kayak launching spot marked by several large storage containers. You can park here and follow an old trail a short distance farther to the edge of the river. From here, Westside Main turns rough for a short distance as it climbs uphill. The turnoff west to Logger's Lake is well marked. Park off the road in the cleared section. The walk from here to the lake is an easy 10 minutes.

You can stay beside the lake to try your luck fishing for rainbow trout from several good spots or walk the 2.5-km (1.6-mi) Crater Rim

> ## BEST INTERPRETIVE PEDAL

IN THE 1990s, forester Don MacLaurin (whose wife, Isobel, painted many of the signs around Whistler's Valley Trail; see chapter 13) spearheaded the Whistler Interpretive Forest development. This is a joint project of the B.C. Ministry of Forests and the Resort Municipality of Whistler as well as other players from both government and industry. Highlights of a managed second-growth forest, including geological data, are displayed at pullouts along the Eastside and Westside Main roads, which run through the forest on both sides of the Cheakamus River. The Whistler Interpretive Forest's major recreational feature, however, is its extensive 13-km (8-mi) network of narrow trails, which are particularly suited to mountain biking.

Trail that, together with the mixed-use 3.4-km (2.1-mi) Ridge Trail, loops high above the lake. One end of the trail begins beside the road before it reaches the lake. It is well marked. (Plan on taking between 90 minutes and two hours to complete the round trip.) By going this way and walking clockwise around the lake, you may find the going slightly easier on the steep section above the lake's southern end.) The other option is to follow along Westside Main past the first trail marker and bear right where the road divides at the lake's southern end. This leads in five minutes to the other end of the loop trail and its marker. Logger's Lake itself lies nestled in the cone of an ancient volcano, one of the most interesting and easily accessible sites in the Whistler region.

A close examination of the forest floor reveals a number of exotic botanical features, including fleshy orange fungi and delicate red fuchsia look-alikes with bell-shaped flowers.

The first entrance to the trail will get you to the lake more quickly than the road does. From lakeside, for several minutes the trail climbs steadily to a viewpoint above the north end of the lake. Beside this trail, an especially big conifer stands out among the many old-growth firs that cling to the moss-covered scree. The branches of the trees here are heavily laden with trailing moss, a sign of how much moisture this region receives. As the trail crests the ridge, it provides good views of sections of the winding Cheakamus River below. Logger's Lake passes from sight for the next while.

The curved shape of the rim that rings the lake suggests it was once a volcanic cone. As the trail climbs through the forest, several good viewing areas near the rim reveal unique geological formations. There are three rustic wooden benches along the trail. One has a view to the southeast of Empetrum Ridge; another looks west towards Mount Brew and the Metal Dome; the third is among the trees beside the trail, perfectly suited for sitting quietly while watching and listening to nature.

The descent from the ridge at the lake's southern end is steep and rough compared to the rest of the trail. You may wish to retrace your steps rather than attempt it, especially in wet weather. Be careful here. You'll have to cross a section of scree near the bottom of the trail; watch for the orange trail markers to reappear beside a dense stand of alder. From here an old road leads around to a trailhead marker. Stay right at this point. Logger's Lake is only a few minutes beyond. Along the way you will pass a smaller, less accessible lake. Stay left on the road once it reaches Logger's Lake and it will lead you back down to Westside Main.

> RIVERSIDE TRAIL

Access: Off Westside Main a short distance past Logger's Lake turnoff
Ability Level: Novice

Westside Main is in good shape for another 3.5 km (2.2 mi) south past Logger's Lake. One of the best access points to the upper Cheakamus River is on the left side of the road, a short distance past the Logger's Lake turnoff. There is room for several cars to park here. A trail leads down to a rock shelf jutting into the river—one of my favorite picnic spots on the Cheakamus.

Riverside Trail runs both ways along the riverbank. The trail leads north to the Logger's Lake turnoff past several more picnic spots or south across a good fishing stream, meeting up with Westside Main a short distance beyond. The forest along the river is quite lush, and this trail is a short, pleasant walk.

> BLACK TUSK TOWER ROAD

Access: 5 km (3.1 mi) east of Highway 99 on Westside Main
Ability Level: Novice

Several more roads lead off Westside Main. The first one, on the right past Logger's Lake, is the Basalt Spur Road, which leads back to the Olympic Village. Farther along, Westside Main divides at a point where it begins to climb uphill. A BC Hydro sign points right to Black Tusk Tower Road, 7 km (4.3 mi) of rough switchbacks (best suited to four-wheel-drive vehicles). Permanently gated at the 6km mark, the road ends on a ridge below the Black Tusk where a microwave tower stands.

The road to the left, now little more than a pathway, deteriorates rapidly and becomes quite overgrown with alder. Several unruly creeks and rockslides have rearranged it in places. This route is also the Helm Creek biking trail. Much of its distance is for serious, well-prepared bushwhackers only. With time, trail builders may extend the route farther south of Helm Creek, where it now terminates, to link up with the Helm Creek hiking trail in Garibaldi Park (see chapters 7 and 11).

> ## JANE LAKES

Access: 8.5 km (5.3 mi) east of Highway 99 via Westside Main and Black Tusk Tower Road
Ability Level: Novice to intermediate

The three small but interesting lakes called the Jane Lakes are nestled on the slopes of Empetrum Ridge, just outside the boundaries of the Whistler Interpretive Forest. They can be reached on foot or by mountain bike via two separate routes. The easiest way to reach the trailhead is to follow Westside Main south to its junction with Black Tusk Tower Road, where it's advisable to leave your vehicle if you've driven in this far. From here it is a 45-minute walk uphill along the pleasant road to reach the trailhead, which may or may not be marked. Watch for a pullout beside a small stream that flows through old-growth forest. The trail begins just beyond here. If you go much farther, the road straightens and enters a meadow with an open view of Black Tusk, an indication that you should retrace your steps to the trailhead. The Jane Lakes Trail leads 1.5 km (0.9 mi) west across the stream on several fallen logs and through forest to serene East Jane Lake.

The silence as you make your way along this gently undulating trail is remarkable. After 30 minutes, you'll be rewarded with secluded campsites—and perhaps a rainbow trout if you've brought your fishing gear. The trail continues around East Jane's shoreline and leads to West Jane Lake, where you'll find several rough campsites. The hillside around West Jane is quite steep. A path leads down to a large dock across from a small island. The forest surrounding the lake has been left undisturbed, though logging has cleared much of the nearby hillsides.

A trail circles West Jane Lake. Aside from the slope beside the dock, the lakeshore is rough and rather inaccessible. From the lake's southern end, another trail with orange markers leads off to an unnamed smaller lake nearby. The path is soft underfoot as it winds through a lovely stand of old-growth evergreens. Below it, a scree slope drops to the eastern shore of the lake. The trail skirts the scree, leading to several very large trees at the lake's southern end. When you're exploring, watch for these special microclimate areas—they return the energy that nature invests in them a thousandfold.

You'll have to pick your way down the scree at the lake's southern end for a short distance before the trail resumes its forest flavor at lakeside. Here, it makes a jog to get around a small, boggy finger of the lake. Balancing on two logs that have been laid side by side, you walk through tall ferns and skunk cabbage as high as your waist. If the logs are overgrown by greenery, look for the orange markers posted on the trees on either side of the bog. Just past here is a small clearing at lakeside, and the water is surprisingly warm.

The trail ends nearby at a marker on a side road. At this point you are just downhill from West Jane Lake. Follow it a short distance to an old logging road, an alternative way to the Jane Lakes from West-side Main via the Olympic Village along the Sea to Sky Trail, the preferred route for those on mountain bikes.

> **THE INSIDE TRACK**

> *Cycling:* Evolution Bike Service (604-932-2967; www.evolutionwhistler.com); FanatykCo Ski and Cycle (604-938-9455; www.fanatykco.com); Katmandu Whistler Sports (604-932-6381); Wild Willies Ski Shop (604-938-8036; www.wildwillies.com) for rentals, trail maps, and repairs

> *Maps:* Information on outdoor activities as well as detailed recreation maps of the Whistler Valley, including the Whistler Interpretive Forest are available in print or by download from the Whistler Visitor Info Centre (4230 Gateway Drive; 604-932-5528 ext. 17; www.whistlerchamber.com) and the Whistler Activity Centre (4010 Whistler Way; 1-877-991-9988 or 604-938-2769; www.tourismwhistler.com); Whistler Area Topographic and Street Map (Talisman); Whistler Trail Map (Terrapro); Whistler Mountain Biking (Quickdraw)

> *Whitewater Kayaking:* For kayak services on the Cheakamus River, contact the Captain Holidays Kayak and Adventure School (604-905-2925; www.kayakwhistler.com).

11

CHEAKAMUS LAKE

Garibaldi Provincial Park

. . . . .

> LOCATION: The trailhead lies 8 km (5 mi) east of Highway 99 at Function Junction, 126 km (78 mi) north of Vancouver, 66 km (41 mi) north of Squamish, 45 km (28 mi) south of Pemberton.

> ACTIVITIES: Camping, fishing, hiking, mountain biking, paddling, picnicking, viewpoints, walking

> HIGHLIGHTS: Old-growth forest, a welcoming trail, a turquoise lake ·

> ACCESS: To make your way to the Cheakamus Lake trailhead parking lot, follow the BC Parks signs east of Highway 99 onto Cheakamus Lake Road, which begins across from Whistler's Function Junction industrial neighborhood. Note: Dogs are not permitted in Garibaldi Park.

> ABILITY LEVEL: Novice

ONCE YOU'VE journeyed to this aqua jewel ringed with glaciated peaks, you'll never forget the soft feeling of the forest floor on the trail that leads to the shores of Cheakamus Lake, or the way that branches high above in the old-growth forest lend shelter from the rain and sun. Unlike the rapid pace of change in Whistler, little more than the seasons has altered here since the early 1900s. If you're looking for an easy outing, walk in or steer a bike along the humpty-dumpty 3.5-km (2.2-mi) path. This is not the first trail novice riders should attempt, but if you've been around Lost Lake's trails (see chapters 13 and 18), you can handle this one.

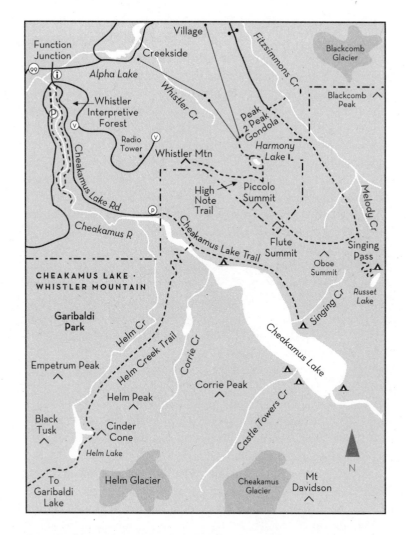

During the rainy season, you may have to dismount and walk for short distances around some mucky sections.

Cheakamus Lake Road is initially paved, then turns to dirt and gravel. On the way to the lake parking lot, the road passes through the Whistler Interpretive Forest (see chapter 10), where various aspects of a managed second-growth forest are explained at pull-outs along the road. The interpretive information extends beyond silviculture to include geological data. Drive or ride carefully here, especially on the narrow sections. The road is mostly uphill for the first 3 km (1.9 mi), then levels out and climbs gradually until near the end. There are usually several riders having a go at it; the reward is written on their smiling faces when they soar downhill on their way home.

At the parking lot you'll find a large map of the trail. The boundary of Garibaldi Provincial Park is close by; from here on, logging has not affected the appearance of the surroundings.

The trail to Cheakamus Lake does not rank as a true hike because most of the distance covered is over level terrain, but its length qualifies it as an energetic walk, with a hilly section in the beginning that overlooks a steep embankment to the noisy Cheakamus River below. The trail is well established and slightly spongy underfoot, the forest open, without the jungle of secondary growth found in areas outside the park boundary. It's the kind of trail on which you can set your own pace, one where the kids can run ahead and still be heard among the tall trees. The wind blows down off the glaciated peaks, the sunlight is diffused as it filters through the large branches overhead, and moss grows in a dozen shades of green on all sides of the tree trunks. Take along an extra layer of clothing to avoid getting chilled.

From the parking lot to the south end of the lake is a one-hour walk or a 45-minute bike ride through magnificent stands of cedar, Douglas fir, and western hemlock. Almost as soon as you enter the forest, the rich smell of balsam greets you.

A bridge spans the Cheakamus River near its outflow from the lake. The wood-and-steel structure provides hikers access to the Helm Creek Trail, which begins on the opposite bank and eventually leads to Garibaldi Lake. It's an all-day excursion to the small lake on the slope high above Cheakamus Lake, suitable for summer and early fall hiking, and a four-hour climb along the trail from the Cheakamus River to Helm Lake—tucked high in the alpine. Helm Creek eventually ties in with the Black Tusk Trail (see chapter 7), and with adequate preparation you can climb the entire length in one or two days, coming out at Highway 99 south of Daisy Lake.

A very rough route leads west from Helm Creek on the opposite side of the river from Cheakamus Lake Road. This trail is eroded by runoff, overgrown by alder, and covered by rockslides, and BC Parks has posted warning notices beside the bridge. The trail is in much better condition near its junction with Black Tusk Tower Road (see chapter 10).

The Cheakamus River catches your ears and eyes as soon as you start on the trail. Once you enter the forest it fades from view but never from earshot, and by the time you reach the Helm Creek turn-off it is visible again through the trees at the bottom of the steep slope. The river flows at a brisk rate here, particularly from May through July. Along the trail during these months there are many streams feeding into the lake and river. Small wooden boardwalks and bridges carry you across the wettest sections of the trail.

At the lake's western end, the first of several clearings provides a wide-open view out past the thick trunks of the forest. Overlord and Davidson mountains are the dominant peaks to the east. Directly across the lake, Corrie Creek can be heard rushing down from little Corrie Lake, which is hidden high up on the slopes. The Cheakamus River flows quietly northwest out of the lake as it gathers momentum, then begins to raise its voice around the first corner.

> ## BABE IN THE WOODS

ON ONE visit to Cheakamus Lake in the 1980s, I noticed an aluminum marker the size of a business card on an amabilis fir beside the trail. It was engraved with the name of a baby born on this isolated ground to a hiker. Each time I walked the trail since then I looked for the marker, but without success. I slowly began to doubt my memory and wondered if the story were too good to be true. Then, in 1998, I found it again, the inscription all but faded.

In recent years, a new sign has replaced the old: it reads: "Matthew Wayne Cormack, July 20, 1985. Thanks to all Whistler EMS & Search+Rescue." Look for the plaque on the north side of the Cheakamus Lake Trail, about 2.5 km (1.5 mi) from the trailhead, just west of a prominent creek crossing.

Cheakamus Lake Trail

There are some large logs along the shoreline from which anglers can cast, with pan-sized rainbow trout and Dolly Varden char swimming in these clear green waters. There's more to catching them than just dangling a lure under their noses, however. They seem to have an ample selection of food already. As you walk the shoreline, several varieties of ducks will emerge, most traveling in pairs. In spring, mother mergansers appear to have their ducklings strung on an invisible towline behind them.

A small boat that belongs to BC Parks is tied up on the shore beside a small beach—a reminder that it's worth the effort to portage a boat in to Cheakamus Lake, not just for the fishing but to explore unique features you would otherwise miss. The headwaters of the Cheakamus River lie deep within Garibaldi Park, and waters from the massive icefields of the McBride Range feed the river and its tributaries as they wind their way down to the lake's eastern end, creating a braided, silted delta where they converge.

Soon after you sight the lake, several rough campsites appear. Open fires are not permitted in the park, so bring your own stove. (Of course, pack out all your garbage and, as a salute to the beauty of the setting, maybe even a little left behind by a less appreciative visitor.) Just beyond the first campsites is a cathedral-like grove of trees that for many visitors will crown their journey. For the scale of the forest at Cheakamus is imposing. There is a hush here found only at exalted elevations.

> ## SINGING CREEK
Access: The 7-km (4.3-mi) trail from the parking lot to Singing Creek takes about two hours each way.
Ability Level: Novice to intermediate

Trees shelter the trail for two-thirds of the distance to Singing Creek, though the woods occasionally open into thickets of blackberry and alder where small creeks flow down from the ridge of Whistler Mountain. Modest meadows are also evident above natural clearings around each creek. At one noticeable spot, the trail crosses the hillside above the lake where the embankment plunges steeply. This is a wildflower rock garden. It has such an orderly appearance that you might imagine someone had labored to plant the wide variety of brightly colored ground-hugging plants that bloom here. These small but brilliant patches of vivid orange paintbrush, wild tiger lilies, stalks of white valerian, and blue lupine climb up the hillside in summer. A small overhang here with a shading tree is a refreshing spot to stop in summer and enjoy the mountainside and lake stretched out before you. With the first frosts, much of the foliage changes hue, and the quiet is uncanny in September and October as the lake awaits its first snowfall. Autumn is my favorite season to visit here.

There are no easy access points to the lake once you pass the rock garden on the way to Singing Creek. For the next 20 to 30 minutes, the trail climbs and falls, crossing many little creekbeds, as the old-growth forest rears skyward. During spring runoff and after summer rainstorms, the waters flowing down from the Piccolo, Flute, and Oboe summits high above on the south flank of Whistler Mountain mingle in these creekbeds, singing harmony with the wind blowing in the treetops. Added to this musical score is the deep bass voice of Castle Towers Creek, carrying across the lake.

In spring the earth is damp in many places, the ground cover just beginning to show, and lush ferns thickly carpeting the slopes above the lake, vividly green in the forest twilight. In several places rockslides have cut paths down from the southern ridge of Whistler Mountain. In others, the trail is so overgrown with nettles you'll want long pants for protection. The weeds also hold the dew or raindrops; brushing past them can quickly soak a pair of jeans.

The farther along the trail you go, the more the views to the east and west open up. Brandywine Mountain is northwest in the distance; the Overlord group, hidden by forest for the most part, is behind you to the east; the McBride Range is to the southeast. Whistler Mountain is to the north and west, very evident as a long ridge above the trail. The Cheakamus Glacier covers the near side of the mountains at the southwestern end of the lake; a cool wind is always blowing off its slopes.

When you reach Singing Creek, you will find a particularly good campsite perched above a small beach, where families of merganser ducks summer and share the lakeside. There are very few spots with a beach along the trail, so this is a welcome respite.

Because Cheakamus Lake is fed by numerous creeks that originate in the surrounding glaciers and snowfields, the water is chilly year-round. Don't expect to do more than give your feet a refreshing soak to revitalize them for the return trip.

With its splendid alpine views and the stillness of its original-growth forest, this walk will encourage you, your family, and friends to return time and again.

> ## CHEAKAMUS DELTA

Access: 3 km (1.9 mi) portage from trailhead, then 5-km (3.1-mi) paddle

If you go to the trouble to transport a canoe or kayak out to Cheakamus Lake, the most challenging portage will be at the outset, where you may have to bob and weave like a prizefighter. Keep in mind that you will be able to explore areas not accessible by any trail—you'll also have almost the entire lake to yourself. It helps if your imagination is fueled by a prior visit on foot and memories of peaks and snowfields in the distance from the lake's northern shore. A similar view of the lake and its surroundings from the top of Whistler Mountain while skiing in winter can stoke your determination to try paddling here.

The most colorful time to paddle Cheakamus Lake is in late summer and early autumn, when the fall color in both forest and lake—its pale hue deepens by September to a milky turquoise—harmonize in a swath of greens and blues. You can reach the small campground at the mouth of Singing Creek, several sites at the mouth of Castle Towers Creek, or those just east of Castle Towers on a small beach in less than an hour. From each campsite, you can then set off to explore a remote corner of the lake.

In contrast with much of Cheakamus's thickly forested shoreline, a broad stretch of sand washed down from its headwaters in the wild heart of Garibaldi Park defines the lake's southeastern side. On its soft surface you'll usually find a host of fresh animal prints, including bear and deer. The most impressive of all are made by fishers, supremely elusive members of the weasel family who only exist in deep, untouched wilderness.

Stroll among the tall black cottonwoods that in September display brilliant golden foliage. Watch as a dipper, a gray bird that can "fly" underwater, walks the shoreline while almost entirely submerged. Magical experiences like these endear the lake to me.

> **THE INSIDE TRACK**

> *Camping:* Check www.env.gov.bc.ca/bcparks for details on campsites at both the Cheakamus River's outflow and at Singing Creek.

> *Canoeing or Kayaking:* A canoe or kayak cart offers a less taxing alternative to portaging when realizing your Cheakamus Lake paddle dreams. In Vancouver, Mountain Equipment Co-op (www.mec.ca) rents trolleys.

12

WHISTLER MOUNTAIN

. . . . .

> **LOCATION:** Whistler Village, 127 km (78 mi) north of Vancouver, 67 km (40 mi) north of Squamish, 28 km (17.4 mi) south of Pemberton; and Creekside, 122 km (75.6 mi) north of Vancouver, 62 km (38.4 mi) north of Squamish, 33 km (20.5 mi) south of Pemberton

> **ACTIVITIES:** Hiking, mountain biking, skiing, snowboarding, snowshoeing, walking

> **HIGHLIGHTS:** Alpine bowls and musical trails

> **ACCESS:** Year-round, the Whistler Village gondola carries visitors up the north side of Whistler Mountain from the Skier's Plaza in Whistler Village; the Creekside gondola operates from November to April from the Creekside base on the mountain's west side.

THE ALMOST century-old growth of recreation in the Whistler Valley has been focused around Whistler and Blackcomb mountains—far beyond what was originally anticipated. Today more than two million skiers and snowboarders come calling each year; from May to October, more than 100,000 mountain bikers alone ride the Whistler Mountain Bike Park trails (www.whistlerbike.com).

For the first half of the twentieth century—the golden age of the lodges on Whistler's Alta Lake—summer was the high season in Whistler. But with the decline of the lodges in the mid-1960s, May marked the beginning of the quiet months following the hectic ski season. Then in the 1990s, with the advent of the valley's golf courses and the growth of mountain biking, summer came back into its own here, drawing outdoor enthusiasts to new walking trails, the open waters of the lakes, and a host of festivals such as Crankworx (www.crankworx.com), a multi-day mountain bike extravaganza.

Piccolo Summit

> WINTER TRAILS

Creekside (elevation 653 m/2140 ft), at the south end of town, is the site of the original Garibaldi Lift Company operation. The Creekside gondola runs up the west side of Whistler Mountain to Midstation (elevation 1300 m/4265 ft). From here, skiers and snowboarders make their way even higher up the mountain on the Big Red Express chairlifts or head back downhill to either Creekside or Whistler Village. The Whistler Village gondola runs to the Olympic Station at midmountain (elevation 1019 m/3346 ft), site of the Whistler Blackcomb Adaptive Ski Program for disabled skiers and the Children's Learning Centre, and continues up the north side of Whistler Mountain to the Roundhouse Lodge (elevation 1850 m/6069 ft) from where the new Peak 2 Peak gondola connects with Blackcomb's Rendezvous Lodge (see chapter 15).

In the midst of all the new additions on the slopes below the peak of Whistler Mountain stand my favorite lifts, the resort's original two T-bars, which still hum along, probably the all-time best investment made by the Garibaldi Lift Company. Lift lines may form elsewhere, but you can still catch a ride on the T-bars almost as soon as you cruise up to them. These simple lifts access some of the best and least-tracked powder snow on the face of the Headwall run, T-Bar Bowl, and even parts of the Whistler Glacier.

Pause for a moment at the top of the T-bars to read the plaque affixed to a rock. It pays tribute to Franz M. Wilhelmsen, Whistler Mountain Ski Corporation's first president (1960–63), for whom the original Franz's Run was christened. Until the Peak chairlift enabled skiers to reach the 1530-m (5020-ft) level in 1988, Franz's Run, from the top of the T-bars to the bottom of Whistler Creek, boasted the greatest vertical fall of any ski trail in North America. Today, with the Peak chairlift on Whistler and the T-bars on Blackcomb's Horstman Glacier, skiers have longer descents than forty years ago, but the runs don't get any better than the one named for Wilhelmsen. (Another of Whistler's longest runs is the Dave Murray Downhill, one of the world's premier downhill racecourses and site of the men's downhill race at the 2010 Winter Games.)

What sets Whistler Mountain apart from Blackcomb is an extensive network of beginner runs plus its series of wide alpine bowls: the Bagel, West, Whistler, Harmony, Symphony, Sun, Burnt Stew, Flute, and the more recently opened Symphony Amphitheatre bowls

TWO DIFFERENT editions of the *Ski and Snowboard Guide to Whistler Blackcomb*—one written for advanced/expert, the other for intermediate level snow sport enthusiasts—help make sense of the hundreds of runs on each mountain. At present, only a dozen or so routes leading from Piccolo Summit to the base of the Symphony chairlift have been officially named. Once ski patrollers develop a more intimate knowledge of the amphitheatre's alpine contours and forested glades, they will begin to assign further designations, as much for the purpose of search-and-rescue operations as for generating new material.

define the upper reaches of the mountain. Because they are tucked away at high altitude, it's difficult to appreciate their magnificence from the valley.

Flute Bowl: Almost from the moment that Whistler Mountain opened, Flute Bowl has been sought out by skiers—and more recently snowboarders—confident in their abilities to deal with avalanche hazards. On a clear day, the wide chalice that opens below Flute Summit lies well within sight of the groomed runs east of Whistler's Harmony and Symphony chairlifts.

At 3 square km (1.2 square mi) in size, the terrain around Flute Summit—including an arching cornice of snow that forms on the northwest side like an eyebrow below the mountain—is vast. Winter storms often fill the big basin with blowing snow carried by wind currents rising uphill from Cheakamus Lake, which lies far below on the summit's south side. With few landmarks for clues, visibility during such storms drops dramatically as the rolling alpine whites out. Even though Flute Bowl zone is patrolled, the element of danger can never be entirely mitigated. Despite the controls, those who venture here should still come prepared to deal with any eventuality.

Each day during winter months, patrollers clear potential snow hazards before skiers and snowboarders are allowed access to this region. (Whistler Mountain is divided into four such zones.) Increasingly, once the bowl is open, Flute is seen as a training area for those who wish to push farther afield. Although avalanche transmitters, shovels, and probes aren't mandatory accessories for those looking to adventure here, it is well worth carrying them to become better experienced in their use.

It doesn't take long for the novel effect of a backcountry hike to hit home. Within minutes of setting out on the 30-minute slog to the summit, with equipment slung over your shoulder or strapped onto your pack, and with your heavy boots digging into snow, it quickly becomes apparent that this approach to trekking is a far tougher workout than one would typically experience on skis or boards.

The ridge you ascend rolls out like a sheet on an unmade bed. Instead of dwelling on the distance ahead, you find other ways to occupy your mind, such as imagining what it must be like to traverse the entire Musical Bumps route (see Chapter 17), a far more daunting task in winter than during a summer day trip on foot.

No matter which season you choose to hike Flute, the scenery never loses its appeal. Far below, frozen Cheakamus Lake appears whitecapped from one end to the other. Higher above to the south, diminutive Corrie Lake rests like a moonstone inset on the flank of Corrie Peak. With sights like this to remark on, conversation with fellow hikers swirls like spindrift. All are of one mind: a superb run lies ahead and there's more than enough powder to go around.

At the bottom of the bowl, after carving many a well-earned turn, your reward is admiring the curved lines you improvised on Flute's face. Not to mention the occasional *sitzmark* where you might have bitten into more powder than you could handle.

Prepare yourself for a surprise. From this point the hiking resumes once again, particularly for snowboarders. One of the benefits of being on skis is that at least you have poles to propel yourself along the flat Flute Hike Out trail that leads—eventually—to civilization, in this case the Harmony Express chairlift. In the lift line, the chatter among many hooked-on-the-feeling backcountry hikers revolves around whether there's enough time to play the Flute refrain one more time.

Following the success of luring adventurers to Flute, the Symphony Express chairlift made its debut in late 2006. Word of yet another new chairlift at a B.C. resort is hardly unusual. What makes the Symphony Express special is its high elevation—1525 m/5003 ft—as well as the 400 ha (1000 acres) of alpine terrain below Piccolo Summit. By definition, alpine zones are delicate ecosystems. With this in mind, building the chairlift was one of the greenest projects ever undertaken at

HIKING TIP

In summer, the air temperature on top can be cooler than in the valley—a relief on a hot day, but still an invitation for a bad chill if you're not prepared. The persistent breeze helps moderate body heat generated while hiking and certainly keeps bugs away, but pack along some repellent and heavy sunscreen (minimum SPF 15) as well as a wide-brimmed hat.

Whistler. Chairlifts require power to operate—and that energy has to come from somewhere. In this case, electricity is generated from a micro-power station located on nearby Flute Creek. And for the first time since chairlift construction began at Whistler in 1964, no access road was cut to truck in construction materials. Everything associated with the $9.2 million project was transported by helicopter to mitigate any future impact.

Along with the new terrain come new rewards. The Piccolo Amphitheatre, as this area is now called, is a unique environment to either Whistler or Blackcomb mountains. The high alpine bowl is accessible to intermediate skiers and snowboarders. It doesn't have the typical double-black diamond runs found elsewhere.

> **SUMMER TRAILS** &

From May to October, Whistler Mountain's Village Express gondola ferries passengers, including those with mountain bikes and wheelchairs, from the village to the mountaintop on a non-stop 20-minute ride with an elevation gain of about 1160 m (3800 ft). Many options for exploring present themselves once you arrive, including catching the Peak chairlift to Whistler's summit, but before you get going remember that the weather can be much cooler—or perversely warmer—in the alpine than in the valley. Conditions also change quickly, so come prepared for the worst while expecting the best.

If you're planning to climb into the high alpine, take sturdy, waterproof footwear. The going is fairly easy even if there is still snow, but a cold dampness will set in after awhile. As you emerge from the Express into the Roundhouse Lodge, take a minute to enjoy the view of Whistler Mountain's peak before anything else. The later in the summer you go, the more of its geological makeup will be revealed by melting snow. A rocky red apron spreads out below the peak, flanked by the browns, grays, and blacks of the wide bowl. Whistler Glacier on the north face of the mountain has shrunk considerably over the years that the mountain has been operating commercially.

From the Roundhouse Lodge visitors can explore a dozen or more scenic walking or hiking routes that spread out from the terminus of the Express in a network of well-marked roads and trails.

Complimentary guided tours are available several times a day. These are detailed in a brochure available at the Express ticket office or on the Roundhouse's Adventure Deck. In lieu of a tour, you can choose to walk one of the easier pathways, such as the *Paleface Trail* (1 km/o.6 mi round trip), for views of the valley on the Whistler Creek side of the mountain. Across to the west are the round tops of Mount Sproatt and Rainbow Mountain (see chapter 16). The Paleface Trail descends below the Roundhouse Lodge, winding its way around and under the Express in a loop that will bring you back to the lodge in 30 minutes. Along the way are benches on which to relax while enjoying the views. By August, much of the mountaintop is covered with wildflowers. Whistler Mountain's gardening staff seed many of the open slopes with grasses that turn gold as summer yields to fall. Come September, low-lying berry bushes turn crimson. The colors of the rock formations and the vegetation combine to form such a pleasing vista that you can't help but slow your pace as you pass by in wonder.

Many visitors opt to climb the open slopes above the Roundhouse. A short loop trail leads around nearby Harmony Lake (3.5 km/ 2.2 mi), which, depending on how early or late in the summer you arrive, may still be hidden under snow and ice or may already have been reduced to pond size by its runoff into the Fitzsimmons Creek valley far below. The *Harmony Lake Trail* requires more stamina than the Paleface Trail, as there is a steeper descent to get to the lake.

If you're feeling spry, ride the Peak chairlift to its 2128-m (6982 ft) summit. Take a good look around. A 1.6 km (1 mi) interpretive trail loops around the summit. This vista of the Black Tusk and the heart of Garibaldi Park will stick in your memory. When you return to the valley, imagine seeing yourself standing on the peak, a time-honored technique for being in two places at once.

If your legs are really fresh, tackle the 5.1-km (3.2-mi) *High Note Trail* that leads east to its junction with the Musical Bumps Trail near Garibaldi Park's boundary. Budget five hours to cover the well-marked, single-track route that winds its way to-and-fro across the south face of Whistler Mountain through intermittent stands of subalpine fir on the rock-strewn slopes above Cheakamus Lake. It's impossible to overstate the captivating beauty of the lake's polished

Peak 2 Peak Gondola

turquoise surface (see chapter 11). Fortunately, it's your companion during much of this hike, which eventually leads to the saddle
between Piccolo and Flute summits, two of a trio of "musical bumps."
At this point, either head west to the gondola via Harmony Lake
along the Musical Bumps Trail or continue east along this same trail
towards Singing Pass (see chapter 17). The sunnier the weather, the
more you'll be lured to scramble up Flute and beyond to Oboe Summit. With Cheakamus below and a wall of Spearhead Range peaks,
including Blackcomb, to the north, there's no finer place to appreciate the alpine.

13

VALLEY TRAIL

. . . . .

> LOCATION: Whistler Village and surrounding neighborhoods

> ACTIVITIES: Birdwatching, cross-country skiing, cycling, fishing, in-line skating, paddling, picnicking, snowshoeing, swimming, viewpoints, walking, windsurfing

> HIGHLIGHTS: Parks, lakes, river, and creeks linked by a sinuous recreational pathway

> ACCESS: It's difficult to say where this trail throughout Whistler begins and ends. There are numerous entry points in almost all neighborhoods between Spring Creek Function Junction on the south and Emerald Estates on the north.

WHEN IT comes to getting around town without a vehicle, Whistler is a model community. Almost all the neighborhoods between Spring Creek and Emerald Estates are connected by an extensive network of pathways. For recreationalists and commuters alike, the almost entirely paved Valley Trail functions as a green alternative to the traffic on Highway 99, as it passes beside seven parks, five lakes, a river, and several creeks, with Whistler Village at its hub. In summer, the 35-km (21-mi) Valley Trail is a cycling and in-line skating path and a walkway; in winter it's primarily a cross-country ski trail, though with a good pair of snow boots you can tramp along it quite comfortably. The beauty of the Valley Trail is that you can get onto it easily from almost anywhere in Whistler. And each year it gets longer, keeping pace with the resort's growth.

Before you start out on the Valley Trail, decide whether you are going to do the entire loop or make one of the parks or lakes your destination. On foot it will take three hours to complete the loop; by bike, half that or less. But you don't have to go the whole distance in order to enjoy the trail.

Approaching from Whistler Village, you will find the Valley Trail on the west side of Highway 99. Next to the conference center, take the underpass that leads to the Whistler Golf Club, where you can link up with the main section of the trail—detailed in a large map. Or, before you cross Highway 99, take the short section of trail that leads south past the Tantalus Lodge to the Brio neighborhood. Cross the highway at the stoplight here to get on the main trail beside the 16th hole of the golf course.

The other option from the village is to join up with the Valley Trail as it heads north towards Lost Lake. Cross Blackcomb Way, following the signs to the Lost Lake trailhead just north (to the left) of the intersection of Valley Gate Boulevard and Blackcomb Way. The trailhead, beside a large parking lot, is well marked; a map posted here will give you a detailed look at the trail system. Just down the trail is Fitzsimmons Park, with the Whistler Skateboard and Trials Park as its centerpiece. Nearby, Rebagliati Park provides a mellow picnic spot on a semi-forested point of land above Fitzsimmons Creek. Alternatively, on Blackcomb Way just south (to the right) of this same intersection, cross at the traffic light to get to Fitzsimmons Creek. Take the covered wooden bridge across the creek, then stay to the left on a trail beside the creek rather than heading uphill to the Blackcomb Wizard Express chairlift. Both the Lost Lake section of the Valley Trail and the Fitzsimmons Creek Trail follow the creek for a short distance north before a bridge links them. A network of cross-country ski trails around Lost Lake, suited to walking, cycling, or even horseback riding in summer, begins from this point.

> **LOST LAKE PARK**

Access: The easiest approach is via the Valley Trail at the well-marked Lost Lake parking lot (lot 6) on Blackcomb Way, across from the municipal offices.

I remember a time when Lost Lake used to be just that: remote, difficult to find—its warm waters a rare haven for swimmers. But with the rise in summer visitors, Lost Lake, tucked on the bench-land beside the Chateau Whistler golf course, has become a much more sought-after destination. Many of the trails around the lake are

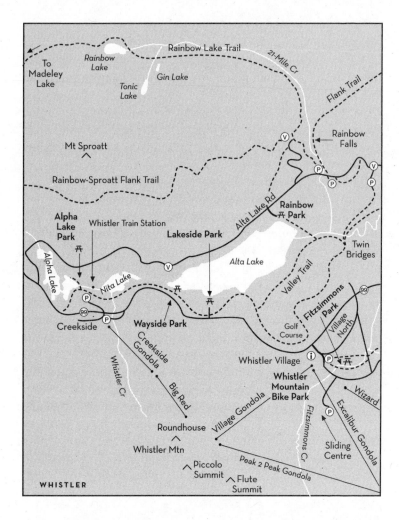

marked with interpretive signs to help you assess their level of difficulty—graphic illustrations of the ups and downs you'll encounter. The steeper the curve on the sign, the more effort required on the trail. (These graphics are effective not only during winter months, but also in summer, when the trails are used for mountain biking.) Note: Not all the trails lead directly to Lost Lake—stay right at all points for the quickest approach to the beach. Centennial, Old Mill Road, and Panorama are the major trails, but a warren of narrower

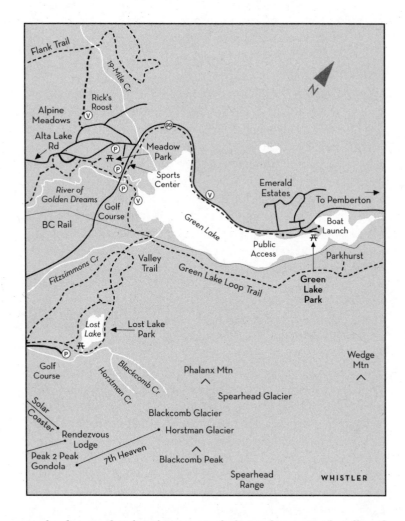

tracks also crosshatches this area, including a forest nature walk and the mixed-use Tin Pants Trail. A wide, dirt road circles the lake. In winter it accommodates both track- and skating-style cross-country skiing.

A beach has been built up on the east end of Lost Lake. Picnic tables, barbecues, and a smooth lawn lend a very pleasant appearance to the park. The shallow swimming area here is more enjoyable for junior swimmers than the steep drop-offs at other points around the lake. For those who like to sun on a dock, try the ones on the north side of the lake.

> LOOP TRAIL &

From the Whistler Golf Course, you have a choice of two directions in which to head. The loop section of the Valley Trail runs past the village. Following it clockwise, head north past the Whistler Golf Club, along the River of Golden Dreams to Meadow Park and across Highway 99 to Green Lake, then turn south past the Nicklaus North Golf Course to Lost Lake and back into the village. The loop is 10 km (6.2 mi) long, takes 90 minutes to walk, and is mostly level except for the section around Lost Lake. Before it crosses the River of Golden Dreams on the north side of the Whistler Golf Club, the Valley Trail sends out an arm to Rainbow Park on Alta Lake's northwest corner. This section takes 15 minutes to walk one way.

> RAINBOW PARK &

Access: Northwest side of Alta Lake, 5 km (3.1 mi) from Highway 99 intersection with Alta Lake (West Side) Road

It's fitting that one of the prettiest locations on Alta Lake should be a large park, doubly so since Rainbow Park is the site of the original lodge that first attracted recreational visitors to the valley. Rainbow Lodge stood here from 1915 to 1977, when it was destroyed by fire. Ten years later, the municipality cleared the shoreline for a park. It is now a popular place for windsurfers to launch; a section of the beach is reserved exclusively for them and for boaters. A large dock floats offshore for swimmers. A number of old log cabins have been brought to the park from other locations on the lake. These are gradually being restored. You can reach the park via the Valley Trail or you can drive to the entrance of the park via Alta Lake (West Side) Road.

Past the turnoff to Rainbow Park, just after the Valley Trail crosses the railway tracks, a rough trail leads off to the west. It climbs past an old gravel pit (marked as private property; use the trails here at your own risk), and through a wildlife refuge, then connects with Alta Lake Road. The 4-km (2.5-mi) section of the Valley Trail that runs from the railway tracks to Meadow Park is one of the longest stretches of level pavement in the entire trail network. It passes close by the River of Golden Dreams at several points. Yellow skunk cabbages sprout beside the trail in many places. Their unmistakable odor is pervasive in spring, and in later months the size of the green leaves on these plants is astounding.

> ## MEADOW PARK AND WHISTLER SPORTS CENTRE &

Access: *On the west side of Highway 99, 4 km (2.5 mi) north of Whistler Village*

Of all the parks in the valley, Meadow Park is the largest. In addition to six picnic tables with barbecues set up on the banks of the River of Golden Dreams, the park has an extensive system of playing fields and tennis courts, plus an imaginatively designed children's play area. On its north side is the skating rink and swimming pool housed in the Whistler Sports Centre. To drive to the park, take the Alpine Meadows exit west off Highway 99, then turn left off Alpine Way onto Rainbow Drive. Watch for the signs pointing to the park at the intersection of Camino and Rainbow. The Whistler Sports Centre has its own entrance on the west side of Highway 99, a short stretch between the bridge over the River of Golden Dreams and the Alpine Meadows turn. The Valley Trail runs beside the sports center's parking lot, following the River of Golden Dreams.

> ## MEADOW PARK TO LOST LAKE &

North of Meadow Park, the Valley Trail follows the River of Golden Dreams to the south side of Green Lake. From here you have some of the best views on the whole trail. In the cool hours of early morning and again towards sundown, mist rises from the surface of the River of Golden Dreams as it enters the lake. Tall Sitka spruce, black cottonwood, and poplar trees line the riverbank. Birdwatching is good here. Upstream from Green Lake is a viewpoint from which you can see the glacier on the north face of Whistler Mountain.

An observation deck is located beside the Valley Trail on Green Lake. From here you can watch the peaks on the east side of the valley reflect in tableau on the still surface of the water at dawn and sunset. Wedge Mountain is unmistakable. Beyond it is Mount Weart, with the volcanic ridge named The Owls fanned out behind. Mount

Moe and the Hibachi Ridge lead up to the solid mass of Mount Currie. (For more information on Green Lake, see chapter 21.)

The Valley Trail runs along the open shore of Green Lake past the Nicklaus North Golf Club and Whistler Air's summer seaplane base (1-888-806-2299; 604-932-6615; www.whistlerair.ca). A branch of the trail follows a tree-lined lane that quickly leads out to the mouth of Fitzsimmons Creek. In summer, as water levels in Green Lake drop to their seasonal lows, I enjoy heading out onto the hard-packed fan that stands revealed for wide-open views of the surroundings.

From Green Lake, the Valley Trail crosses the railway tracks and heads uphill to a bridge over Fitzsimmons Creek. A short distance above here, a trail marker directs you back into the forest past the hydro lines. From this point you may choose from a variety of trails that skirt Lost Lake. Keep left at any junction if your immediate destination is Lost Lake, a 15-minute walk away. Past Lost Lake, the Valley Trail loops back to Whistler Village.

> ### ALTA LAKE &

Access: 3 km (1.9 mi) south of Whistler Village on the west side of Highway 99

South of the trail map kiosk at the Whistler Golf Club, the Valley Trail borders the east side of the golf course to the Blueberry Hill neighborhood. Watch for a good view of Rainbow Mountain in the west at one open point. The trail leads downhill on St. Anton Way to Archibald Way and then south onto Lakeside Road. It is well signed at each turn.

There is a small point of public access to Alta Lake at the foot of Carleton Way off Lakeside Road where it winds south towards Lakeside Park. This is a good location for boats or windsurfers to launch. There is no parking at this launch, but there's plenty of room for vehicles at *Lakeside Park*, one block past here.

Lakeside Park is an open area on the southeast side of Alta Lake. A lawn runs down to the beach, where there are two L-shaped docks. The park has six well-spaced picnic tables, most with their own barbecues. There is no lifeguard, and dogs are not allowed on the beach. In summer you may rent boats and windsurfers here;

guided tours of the lake and the River of Golden Dreams can also be arranged (see chapter 14).

The Valley Trail climbs the hill behind Lakeside Park, rounds the corner past Alta Vista Point, then reaches *Wayside Park* after a short descent through the trees. This is a smaller park than Lakeside. Four picnic tables, each with its own barbecue, sit on a sloped hillside overlooking the south end of Alta Lake. There is a modest beach with an open lawn above for sunbathing. A dock is moored just far enough offshore to make swimmers appreciate hauling up on it after a chilly plunge.

As the Valley Trail heads south of Wayside Park, across from the Nordic Estates and Whistler Highlands neighborhoods, it passes the south end of Alta Lake. A handful of old cabins nestled beside the railway tracks are a reminder of the time before 1965 when the only access to Whistler was by train.

BEST SKINNY-DIPPING

Lost Lake features a discreet clothing-optional dock and several semiprivate locations at the northeast end for swimming sans bathing suit.

> **NITA LAKE**

Access: West of Highway 99 in the Creekside neighborhood, 4 km (2.5 mi) south of Whistler Village

The Valley Trail rounds the rocky corners of Nita Lake, crossing Whistler Creek on its east side. There are two picnic tables here and a small gravel beach built up by the annual freshet in the creek when the snow melts on the mountainside. A seasonal dock for launching small boats is moored at the foot of Drew Drive behind the Husky gas station. This lake is a popular spot for fly-fishing.

At the south end of Nita Lake is the Whistler train station, hidden behind a small evergreen ridge and the Nita Lake Lodge. Black cottonwoods beside Jordan Creek, which drains south from Nita Lake, offer shelter on warm summer afternoons. The view from here is of the famous Dave Murray Downhill course, site of the 2010 Winter Games men's alpine ski race, on Whistler Mountain's west face. A small trail runs behind the train station over to Alpha Lake Park.

> ALPHA LAKE

Access: West of Highway 99 in the Whistler Creekside neighborhood, 5 km (3.1 mi) south of Whistler Village

Alpha Lake Park is beside one of the oldest neighborhoods in the valley, Whistler Creekside. Squaw Valley Crescent and Lake Placid Road are two of the original streets in modern Whistler.

The park features some whimsical architecture, including a hobbit-sized playhouse and swing for young children and a bridge of yellow cedar over Jordan Creek. (Similar Art Nouveau–style wood-work creations around Whistler include the kids' play area in Village North and on Franz's Way adjacent to Whistler Mountain's Creek-side base.) A tennis court, volleyball courts, canoe and dinghy rentals, and the Taylor Nature Walk augment the beach, picnic tables, and barbecues.

Alpha Lake is very irregularly shaped, making it enjoyable to explore by boat. Circle around the island, on which stands one of the most admired cottages in all of Whistler, linked to the mainland by a private bridge.

> BEST MIDNIGHT GLIDE

A SIDE FROM trails in the Callaghan Valley (see chapter 9), the finest cross-country action in Whistler takes place on the 32-km (20-mi) network of packed and tracked trails around Lost Lake—designed for both skate- and classic-style skiers of all skill levels. Water stations, a warming hut, and friendly volunteers ensure a dreamscape experience by day. If you're into skiing by moonlight, gliding the trails with a headlamp translates into a truly magical midnight ride. A detailed map of the Lost Lake trail system is posted beside the Valley Trail (itself a designated ski route) as it leads from day parking lot 3 beside Black-comb Way in Whistler Village towards Lost Lake. Free maps of the Lost Lake Trail system are available from Cross Country Connection (604-905-0071; www.crosscountryconnection.ca), where skis can be rented or repaired and advice obtained. Day passes range from $8.50 for children, $17 for adults, and $34 for families.

The Valley Trail ends at Alpha Lake. If you wish to go farther, follow the rough trail and the train tracks around the west side of Alpha Lake until they link with Alta Lake Road, or ride out through the Baseline neighborhood to Highway 99 and around onto Alta Lake Road. The road into Whistler originally came from Function Junction at the town's southern end, then divided at the southern end of Alpha Lake. The old road to Function Junction now serves as a bicycle path. It crosses Millar Creek, which drains out of Alpha Lake's southern end.

> ## ALTA LAKE (WESTSIDE) ROAD

Access: *West of Highway 99, 1 km (0.6 mi) south of Whistler Creekside*

Although not a part of the Valley Trail, Alta Lake Road links Alpha Park with Rainbow Park and the Valley Trail at the northwest end of Alta Lake, which are 5 km (3.1 mi) apart. The road runs along the west side of the valley, giving limited access to Alpha Lake before climbing the steep ridge above it and Nita Lake. North of Rainbow Park, the road runs 5 km (3.1 mi) to the neighborhood of Alpine Meadows, changes its name to Rainbow Drive for a short distance, then rejoins Highway 99.

Paddlers should head for Pine Point, at the south end of Alpha Lake, where there's parking and a little dock for fishing. It's the best place to launch a boat directly from your vehicle onto the lake. To reach it, drive around from Highway 99 on Alta Lake Road until you reach the railway crossing. The turnoff is just to the right of the tracks before you cross them.

If you're not stopping at the park, continue across the tracks to where the road climbs steeply up Cardiac Hill. Running off to the left of the pavement is a rough gravel road that leads to popular climbing routes as well as several mountain bike trails on Cardiac Bluff. This road continues north above the hydro lines, rejoining Alta Lake Road opposite the entrance to Rainbow Park.

Where Alta Lake Road reaches the ridge above Nita Lake there is a fine viewpoint with a pullout beside the road. An interpretive sign, beautifully painted by local artist Isobel MacLaurin, details some of the highlights of the view across the valley, with Whistler

Lost Lake

Mountain as the centerpiece. Similar interpretive signs are posted at many other scenic locations in the valley, including one farther along Alta Lake Road.

South of Rainbow Park on Alta Lake Road is the former site of the Whistler Hostel (www.hihostels.ca). Years before, it operated as Harrop's Lodge; in the late 1960s it housed the first ski instructors employed by the Whistler Mountain Ski School. The lodge, whose design typifies an architectural style that has evolved since the 1940s, was purchased by Hostelling International Canada in 1972. After many season's use, HI-Canada sold the property to the Resort Municipality of Whistler in 2009 in exchange for new quarters in the Olympic Village once the 2010 Winter Olympic and Paralympic Games conclude. Designated as park, the site occupies a choice point of land on the lakeshore, one of two public waterfronts on the west side of Alta Lake. To reach it you must descend a staircase and cross the railway tracks. Here at Cypress Point is one of the best views on the lake.

If you wish to make a round trip of the Valley Trail and Alta Lake Road by bike, I recommend this approach: take the Valley Trail out to Rainbow Park, follow Alta Lake Road south to Highway 99, swing around north on the highway for a short distance, then hook up with the Valley Trail at Alpha Lake. The reasoning is simple: near the south end of Alta Lake Road there is a great downhill run that will be more enjoyable than climbing uphill in the opposite direction.

North of Rainbow Park, Alta Lake Road follows the ridge above a wildlife refuge towards 21-Mile Creek. (There is no access to the refuge, which is a large wetland for nesting birds.) Along the way there is another pullout and an interpretive sign. A short distance uphill on the opposite side of the road is the Whistler Cemetery. This quiet spot is the resting place of several Whistler pioneers, including Myrtle Philip and her sister, Jean Tapley. Dave Murray, who achieved so much on behalf of amateur skiers after a successful career representing Canada on the World Cup alpine circuit, is also buried here.

The well-marked trail to Rainbow Falls begins just up the road from the cemetery. There is a parking lot for visitors. You can make a quick circuit by taking the trail up to the falls, then descending the gravel road that comes out onto Alta Lake Road next to the cemetery (see chapter 16). Just before Alta Lake Road enters the Alpine Meadows neighborhood, there is a well-marked entrance to the Valley Trail on the east side of the road. Meadow Park is a short distance north of here.

> **THE INSIDE TRACK**

> *Maps:* Information on outdoor activities as well as detailed recreation maps of the Whistler Valley, Whistler Village, Lost Lake, Whistler Mountain, Whistler Mountain Bike Park, and the Whistler Interpretive Forest are available in print or by download from the Whistler Visitor Info Centre (4230 Gateway Drive; 604-932-5528 ext. 17; www.whistlerchamber.com) and the Whistler Activity Centre (4010 Whistler Way; 1-877-991-9988 or 604-938-2769; www.tourismwhistler.com).

14

RIVER OF GOLDEN DREAMS

Alta Creek

. . . . .

> **LOCATION:** Links Alta and Green lakes, 4 km (2.5 mi) north of Whistler Village

> **ACTIVITIES:** Birdwatching, cycling, paddling, picnicking, viewpoints

> **HIGHLIGHTS:** Valley-to-peak views of Whistler from the quiet vantage point of a canoe or kayak

> **ACCESS:** From Rainbow Park on Alta Lake Road (Westside Road), Lakeside Park on the east side of Alta Lake beside Highway 99, or the dock beside the Valley Trail on the east side of Highway 99. Turn onto Nicklaus North Boulevard, then left on Golden Bear Place and follow to the parking lot beside the trail and dock.

WHISTLER SITS at the summit of the highest pass between Squamish and Pemberton, where Alta Lake—the name by which Whistler was once known—balances on a geographic fulcrum. Two small creeks drain the lake in opposite directions: one south into Nita Lake and the other north into Green Lake.

In the 1940s, when Whistler's founding father Alex Philip wasn't running Rainbow Lodge on Alta Lake with his wife, Myrtle, he found time to write two novels with western settings. (One, *The Crimson West*, was turned into a screenplay for a romantic Hollywood production.) He also used his literary skills to add a poetic touch to the small stream that flows between Alta Lake and Green Lake, dubbing it the River of Golden Dreams in honor of the honeymooning couples who would paddle it while staying at Rainbow or

River of Golden Dreams and Green Lake

one of the other lodges on the lake. The stream is officially named Alta Creek, but as a tribute to Alex the municipality of Whistler refers to it as the River of Golden Dreams on signs and maps.

Sadly, Rainbow Lodge was destroyed by fire in 1977, though picturesque Rainbow Park (see chapter 13) has risen in its place. And couples—not to mention singles, trios, and quartets—still launch small boats from here or several other spots on Alta Lake to paddle down the creek. It's a leisurely way to spend several hours, drifting with the current, hardly having to put your paddle in the water in order to glide along.

Once on the lake, the entrance to the River of Golden Dreams lies in a small bay at Alta Lake's northern end. There is no sign of the channel that flows out of the lake until you have almost reached the shore, where tall reeds form the perimeter of the bay. Just when you think you should have taken another approach, perhaps closer to the lake's northeastern side, a narrow opening leads you into a winding channel. (See pages 114–15 for a map of this area.) This is the beginning of the River of Golden Dreams; its waters will eventually reach the Pacific via the Fraser River. Drink in the great view to the west of Rainbow Mountain's peak. In spring and early summer, dozens of birdcalls serenade paddlers; some species nest in the reeds beside the channel. As you pass by you may startle them into performing a distress routine, hoping to distract your attention from their young.

Near the outset of the narrow, sinuous channel stands a pleasant little dock with racks of canoes next to a private condominium development. Paddle under the wooden bridge nearby. (The path that crosses the bridge is part of the Valley Trail to Rainbow Park.) Just beyond this point you must lift your boat over a knee-high concrete weir, built to compensate for a sudden drop in the river. This is easily negotiated, as the builders kept river travel in mind when they designed it.

From here, the river parallels the BC Rail tracks for a straight shallow stretch before merging with the outflow of water from 21-Mile Creek. In spring, water levels in the channel are high enough to allow passage. Later in the year you may have to get out of your canoe or kayak for part of the distance if it bottoms out. With this in mind, wear a pair of water shoes so you can hop out if necessary. Alta Creek's bottom is mostly sand, so footing is solid.

The river, augmented by its confluence with 21-Mile Creek, becomes much wider and better defined from here as it does a sharp oxbow north. Be prepared to negotiate several tricky turns for a short distance as the increased volume of water moves along more quickly here. There are no rocky rapids, but an occasional floating snag or submerged branch might catch you momentarily.

Almost as soon as the two waterways merge, you pass under a large pedestrian bridge next to where the Valley Trail crosses the BC Rail tracks, adjacent to a gravel quarry. As the river bends around several corners beside the tracks, the roofs of nearby homes in the Whistler Cay neighborhood appear above the tall growth on the riverbank. North of here the railway and river diverge, with the tracks running off along the eastern side of the valley while the river cuts over to the west. The river widens even more as it passes beneath a series of hydro towers. Blackcomb Peak is prominent to the east as the houses drop from sight and the vista becomes more open. Pairs of yellow warblers and goldfinches flit from branch to branch on the red willow overhanging the banks. In summer you may have to portage over several sturdy beaver dams; high water covers them until late spring, when the water level begins to drop.

The river flows beside the Valley Trail in several places as it moves away from the hydro lines. Thus begins the most pleasant stretch. One of the best views appears as you round a bend: the high vegetation suddenly thins out to reveal a panorama of peaks stretching from Blackcomb to Wedge Mountain and Hibachi Ridge, which runs all the way north to Mount Currie. For the next half-hour the current carries you gently onwards with this mountainscape rising before you.

Picnic tables and fireplaces at riverside announce Meadow Park's appearance on the west bank. Just past here, pilings from an old wooden bridge stand as a reminder of a time when it was the principal means of crossing.

You are close to Green Lake now. If the water levels in the river are high, prepare to take your boat out at either Meadow Park or, after you pass under Highway 99, at the boat dock below a wooden footbridge on the Valley Trail. Otherwise your only other take-out option is Whistler Air's float dock. The beach beside Edgewater Lodge is reserved for lodge guests and those with the Whistler Outdoor Experience Company (see The Inside Track, next page).

The current picks up as the river approaches Green Lake. Early in summer you'll find it challenging to work your way back upstream; by August, water levels have usually dropped to the point where you can paddle to Green Lake and back upstream without a fight.

The river serpentines through several final turns before it reaches the lake, with tall Sitka spruce lining the banks. This last section is special; don't pass it up unless you are really pressed for time. Reaching Green Lake triggers a great feeling of release. As the river enters the lake, its color deepens from clear gold to green. Much of this change occurs before your eyes as you paddle over the gravel bar deposited by the River of Golden Dreams.

Green Lake lies open before you, inviting exploration. Depending on which direction the wind is blowing, it may take as much as an hour to reach Green Lake Park at the lake's north end (see chapter 21). If you visit the lake in early spring or late fall, you may be treated to the sight of white trumpeter swans. The swans spend several days here while on migration. You can mark the seasons by their arrival here on their way north, as the ice goes out in April; they return on October 30, almost always to the day.

Directly beside the boat dock is a large parking area and public phone. If you are not planning to paddle back to Alta Lake, this is a good place to arrange to be picked up. Another option is to leave a bicycle here before you start; drive your vehicle and boat over to either of Rainbow or Lakeside parks, paddle downstream to the boat dock, then ride back along the Valley Trail to reclaim your vehicle, returning to retrieve your boat. (This may sound long-winded but it can make for an enjoyable round trip.)

> **THE INSIDE TRACK**

> *Canoeing or Kayaking:* Backroads Whistler (604-932-3111; www.backroadswhistler.com) offers guided and independent canoe and kayak trips on the River of Golden Dreams with the option of a pedal ride back; the Whistler Outdoor Experience Company (1-877-386-1888 or 604-932-3389; www.whistleroutdoor.com) offers canoe and kayak rentals and guided tours at Lakeside Park on Alta Lake and the Edgewater Lodge on Green Lake.

15

BLACKCOMB

. . . . .

> LOCATION: Whistler Village and Upper Village

> ACTIVITIES: Nature observation, skiing, snowboarding

> HIGHLIGHTS: Terrain parks, glacier summer camps

> ACCESS: From the heart of Whistler Village (elevation 675 m/ 2215 ft), the Excalibur gondola links with the Excelerator Express chairlift on Blackcomb. The Wizard Express quad-chair runs from the Blackcomb Day Lodge in the Upper Village (elevation 685 m/ 2247 ft) and connects with the Solar Coaster Express quad-chair to take skiers, snowboarders, and sightseers to the Rendezvous Lodge (elevation 1860 m/6102 ft).

UNQUESTIONABLY, BLACKCOMB'S commitment to deliver more services than visitors expect was—and still is—a major factor in Whistler becoming North America's number one winter resort. Along with the money both mountains have pumped into infrastructure (hundreds of millions since Blackcomb first opened in 1980, in direct competition to Whistler Mountain until 1997), Blackcomb has perfected the soft touch of a polished proprietor. For example, its Mountain Hosts service is still the best way for those with intermediate and advanced skills to begin the ski and snowboard season when you want to check out what's new. It's like having a coach ski with you for a couple of hours. Since most hosts are long-time Whistler residents, it's also a guaranteed way to touch base with those in the know locally.

Free 90-minute tours are offered daily at 11:30 AM on both mountains. Meet up at the Guest Satisfaction Centre at the top of the Solar Coaster chairlift on Blackcomb or under the light board at the top of the Whistler Village gondola on Whistler. On Blackcomb, explore trails in tucked away places such as Seventh Heaven and Blackcomb Glacier, both of which originate in the high alpine. Revel in the views from the south-facing slope on the Seventh Heaven side of the mountain; the sight of the craggy spires in the Spearhead Range, of which Blackcomb Peak is a prominent member, is always a balm for tired urban eyes. The runs on the slopes of Whistler Mountain farther south appear to feed into Blackcomb's, while the white apron of the Overlord Glacier on the western flank of Mount Fitzsimmons dominates the view.

Elsewhere on Blackcomb, a dozen lengthy treed runs have been designed for those who love powder. You're almost guaranteed to find it below Crystal Ridge and the Expressway Trail, even on the busiest days. When the groomed runs are buzzing, there's usually shelter and solitude in the trees.

Blackcomb and Whistler mountains have an array of ski and snowboard zones draped about their respective slopes. While once visitors could traverse most of each mountain during a day's visit, many of these areas have become so developed that you may well be content to explore just one or two at a time. Consider Blackcomb's

> ## BEST SKI AND SNOWBOARD SCHOOL

SINCE 1984, thousands of skiers and snowboarders from around the world have traveled to Whistler for the Whistler Blackcomb Ski and Snowboard School's three- and four-day Ski Esprit and Ride Guide camps. Instructors and clients form tight-knit groups that follow a "learn while you move" tempo as they traverse Whistler and Blackcomb mountains, a hugely successful learn-to-ski formula that brings skiers together both on and off the slopes. Each day, groups work on specific techniques assisted by video analysis; touring together helps new skiers familiarize themselves with the 200-plus trails that crisscross the mountains' 3307 ha (8171 acres). Groups are encouraged to try runs that are slightly above their ability level, to build confidence (1-866-218-9681; www.whistlerblackcomb.com).

Terrain Park. When it opened it was a just minor experiment occupying a sidetrack of the lengthy Choker run. Each year since, the terrain park's boundaries have expanded to the point where sculpted jumps now dominate almost the entire run. If you like jumps, you can spend all day getting air in the park without worrying about a conflict with those who prefer constant contact with snow. (If you want to see freestyle snowboarders in action, spend time at the massive Nintendo half-pipe adjacent to the Catskinner chairlift. A medley of languages hangs in the air here, attesting to the international appeal of both the sport and the resort itself, and the presence of a camera will draw riders to perform in the same way an alpine picnic attracts whisky-jacks.)

World freestyle champion Lauralee Bowie's Ski Adventure training program is just one of a burgeoning list of clinics—offered winter and summer—at Blackcomb that includes Masters camps, the Canadian Legends of Ski teaching camps, the Camp of Champions, the Roxy board clinics, Gatebashers, Ski Esprit, and more. In fact, there seems to be a camp for everyone interested in perfecting his or her preferred style of skiing or snowboarding. And all this activity certainly supports the statistics, which indicate more people learn to ski and snowboard on Blackcomb and Whistler combined than any other resort in North America (see page 130 for more details).

> **TERRAIN PARKS**

Rails and rollers. Hits and hips. Tabletops and jibs. Welcome to the world of snowboard and ski terrain parks, where you can ride through an obstacle-strewn course and learn a new vocabulary at the same time. A new generation of snow riders spends as much time tackling human-made obstacles as they do freeriding in the powder-slick action that has caught the attention of filmmakers. Almost every week, Whistler Blackcomb's seven terrain parks host camera crews who come to shoot the rock stars of the sport in action. Made-for-rider videos in turn stoke the interest in terrain parks among a steadily growing urban audience.

I agree that terrain parks can all be a bit intimidating but once you've experienced the adrenaline rush of getting a little air, you'll be back for more. A good starting point is the Whistler Blackcomb

Ski and Snowboard School, where first-timers sign up to learn a specific trick or for an introduction to the park's features. Lessons are most popular with the 25- to 35-year-olds, but a surprising number of parents want to keep up with their kids, learn the lingo, and find out what this style of riding is all about. In fact, the biggest part of what the school does is provide a "new school" link between kids and their parents.

> ### HORSTMAN GLACIER CAMPS

When school lets out for summer, kids usually head for the hills. And on Blackcomb, more of them are doing just that—literally. Paradoxically, just as the weather is really starting to warm up, the hills these students head for means school, but a *new* school—on snow. Just like the new math revolutionized arithmetic in the 1960s, since the late 1990s, new school skiing has reinvented the way young skiers look at the white world: like from upside down, backwards, or both. Up on Blackcomb's Horstman Glacier, class is in session when summer ski and snowboard camps convene from mid-June to early August.

One of the benefits of all the snow that's dumped on the Coast Mountains is that skiing and snowboarding can be enjoyed almost year-round. In summer, all you have to do is go high enough. Today, the Horstman Glacier's Camp of Champions (www.campofchampions.com) is the longest-running summer snowboard camp in Whistler. It helps that, with the exception of similar camps on Oregon's Mount Hood, Whistler is the only place in North America where such summer camps are offered. Demand has increased so sharply that there's a waiting list for space on the Horstman Glacier, where all Whistler camps are held. In fact, the Horstman Glacier is the crucible of the new school of freeskiing technique that, thanks to twin-tipped skis developed by two coaches here, made skiing cool again. New-school style evolved from freestyle skiing as taught at John Smart's Momentum Camps (www.momentumcamps.com). The former Canadian national team member has been teaching mogul-style skiing here—his fame made it easier to organize a camp with World Cup coaches, including Olympic gold medalist Jean-Luc Brassard. Of all the students who have graduated from his camps, Smart is

Mike Michalchuk, Blackcomb superpipe

proudest of Jennifer Heil, who won gold in the moguls competition at the 2006 Winter Olympics in Turin.

For more information on summer ski and snowboard camps offered on Blackcomb, visit www.whistlerblackcomb.com/youth.

> **SPEARHEAD-FITZSIMMONS TRAVERSE**

Access: In winter, Blackcomb sells one-ride lift tickets to Seventh Heaven for alpine-touring skiers. In summer, from Whistler's Upper Village neighborhood, hikers ride Blackcomb's chairlifts and shuttle bus to the bottom of Seventh Heaven Express, where a one-hour trek through alpine meadows leads to Decker Creek below Blackcomb Peak. This approach to the horseshoe-shaped traverse starts high on the Spearhead Range (elevation approximately 2000 m/6560 ft). By the time you reach Russet Lake there's the option of descending back

to Whistler via Garibaldi Park's Singing Pass Trail (see chapter 17) or the Musical Bumps Trail that leads from Singing Pass through the Fitzsimmons Range to the top of Whistler Mountain (see chapter 12).
Ability Level: Advanced, with good route-finding and survival skills

This coveted high-alpine traverse is a trophy route for ski tourers, especially in early spring when the truly super-stoked have been known to cover the 40-km (25-mi) distance in as little as four hours. Allow four *days* for comfort's sake on foot in summer, especially to enjoy some side trips to the U-shaped route's big features, such as 2603-m (8540-ft) Mount Fitzsimmons. Although not technically demanding, the traverse does call upon general mountaineering techniques.

The route crosses a dozen glaciers, where fundamental rope and crevasse rescue skills are prerequisites for a safe journey. As snow in the upper alpine lasts well into July, be prepared to spend the majority of your trek with crampons firmly fixed to your plastic boots. The rewards are camping in fields of yellow avalanche lilies, harbingers of a riotous parade of alpine blossoms that crescendos in early August. You'll have white-tailed ptarmigan for company. Their cryptic coloration—whether white as snow or mottled like lichen on rock—may not catch your eye at first glance. In the impersonal vastness of the alpine traverse, they'll be welcome company.

> ## PEAK 2 PEAK GONDOLA

As if to prove B.C. is indeed the "Best Place on Earth," Whistler Blackcomb has staked out a place in the record books with its Peak 2 Peak Gondola lift. Welcome aboard the longest tram span on the planet. The $50 million tri-national project was two years in the making. The twenty-eight gondola cabins—two with see-through floors—glide 3 km (1.9 mi) between the two Coast Mountains peaks. The big Peak 2 Peak winners will be visitors who want to explore both mountains over the course of a short stay. Sadly, not everyone has the luxury of living with Whistler in his or her backyard. Above all else, the Peak 2 Peak Gondola should help settle the debate as to which of the two companion peaks—Whistler or Blackcomb—skiers and snowboarders prefer most. Local wisdom has long held that when you're in heaven, it hardly matters which side of the street you stroll down. Truer words were never spoken.

> *Snowboard and Ski Rentals:* Whistler Blackcomb operates four Mountain Adventure Centres, where those who wish to test the latest high-performance ski and snowboard equipment can sample a variety of brands. The centers are located in the valley at the Blackcomb Day Lodge, in the Pan Pacific Hotel at the foot of the Excalibur and Whistler Village gondolas, in the alpine at the Guest Infocentre on Whistler Mountain, and beside Blackcomb's Rendezvous Lodge. Once you're set up, drop into any of the four centers and exchange equipment as often as you like.

> *Tubing:* The Tube Park is built above Blackcomb's Base Two area, where the mountain's first lifts were installed twenty-five years ago. Much like at a half-pipe, tubers walk partway up the outside wall of the park then ride a "Magic Carpet," similar to a moving sidewalk in an airport, to the top of the runs. Choose from four runs on the milder side or four wilder banked and curved runs. The area is floodlit for night tubing.

> *Web Cams:* For a panoramic webcam and an interactive tour of Blackcomb Mountain's terrain park, visit www.whistlerblackcomb. com/mountains/parks; to view live conditions visit www.whistler-blackcomb.com/weather/cams.

> *Ziplining:* Ziptrek Eco-Tours (www.ziptrek.com) arrived in Whistler in 2001 and has taken the town by storm. Not nearly as intimidating as bungee jumping, a ride or walk through the snow-draped old-growth forest between Whistler and Blackcomb mountains offers an entirely new perspective on winter.

16

RAINBOW MOUNTAIN

. . . . .

> LOCATION: West side of Whistler Valley, opposite Whistler and Blackcomb mountains

> ACTIVITIES: Camping, fishing, hiking, viewpoints

> HIGHLIGHTS: Prismatic patterned waters, slippery smooth heather slopes, unsurpassable valley views

> ACCESS: The Rainbow Lake Trail begins from Alta Lake Road, 6 km (3.7 mi) north of the road's southern intersection with Highway 99 in Whistler Creekside, or 3.5 km (2.2 mi) south of the Alpine Meadows exit from Highway 99. There is parking on both sides of the road next to 21-Mile Creek. The trail is well marked. (See chapter 13 for a map of this area.)

> ABILITY LEVEL: Intermediate

THE FULL-DAY trek up Rainbow Mountain (elevation 2328 m/ 7638 ft) is the twin to the Singing Pass hike (see chapter 17). The two trails begin on complementary sides of Whistler Valley: Singing Pass in the east and Rainbow in the west. By the time you reach the top of Singing Pass you see Rainbow Mountain in all its glory, and vice versa. Both hikes require steady uphill footwork before the pay-offs of making the effort reveal themselves. One of the chief rewards is the bright displays of colorful ground cover from August though September.

> **RAINBOW FALLS**

If you don't have a day to spend hiking the 15-km (9.3-mi) round trip to Rainbow Mountain in summer, or if snow conditions make it impossible to reach higher elevations, you can still enjoy a view of

Rainbow Lake

Rainbow Falls (over which expert kayakers occasionally hurl themselves) only a 10-minute, 0.5-km (0.3-mi) walk from the trailhead.
At this point, 21-Mile Creek is close to the end of its run down the
mountain. Before it was diverted by construction of the railway, it
emptied into Alta Lake; now it flows into the River of Golden
Dreams (Alta Creek) and from there into Green Lake (see chapter 14).
A smooth trail follows the creek, then climbs through a series of
switchbacks in the original-growth coastal western hemlock forest.
This is a short but pleasantly challenging bike ride. Scramble down
a moderately steep slope to view the falls. Water levels are highest
in late May, making this one of the best times to see the frothing
creek in action. The canyon through which it flows is full of smooth
boulders and thick moss. The relentless, hypnotic sounds of rushing
water shut out all else; you'll come away refreshed from this medita-
tive experience.

Take another few steps to the municipal road above the falls
to enjoy a good view east up Fitzsimmons Valley, which separates
Blackcomb and Whistler mountains. If you walk just a little bit
higher above the pumphouse, you can see Green Lake to the north.
For those on bikes, the 2-km (1.2-mi) Whip Me Snip Me bike trail

runs downhill from here past the Whistler Cemetery towards Rainbow Park on nearby Alta Lake while the epic Flank Trail leads both north and south from this junction (see chapter 18).

> RAINBOW LAKE

Above the pumphouse, Rainbow Lake Trail briefly climbs along an old logging road overgrown with alder. The branches gradually straighten up during summer months after being bowed down by the weight of snow in winter. Occasional openings offer captivating views of peaks grouped above Whistler. Across the valley on Blackcomb's west face you can pick out details such as the Showcase T-bar on the Horstman Glacier. Below it are the distinctive features of the famous Couloir Extreme chute, framed by the shoulders of the canyon above 21-Mile Creek. This is a pretty place.

The trail soon reaches Whistler's watershed boundary. Watershed rules forbid bikes and dogs on the trail as well as swimming, bathing, or camping beside Rainbow Lake. In 15 minutes you leave the lower slopes behind as the trail now enters graceful old-growth forest of Douglas fir and western hemlock, with occasional stands of red cedar. The trail is the well-tracked, rocks-and-roots forest floor supplemented by boardwalks and small bridges of varying degrees of sturdiness, these in turn augmented by fallen logs notched into steps and staircases.

One particularly pleasant spot occurs just past the "4 km" sign, where a new log bridge built by the Resort Municipality crosses an active creek. Above it, a waterfall drops through a canyon off the north ridge of Mount Sproatt. You get a good look at the falls once you've crossed the bridge and climbed up the bank a short distance. If you're here on a summer's morning, position yourself with the sun shining down on you. Look up into the cedars at the backlit spiderwebs strung between the trees, arranged like a totem of dartboards, waiting for flies to hit the bull's-eye. Although the branches seem impossibly far apart for spiders to span, the tiny eight-legged creatures perform like trapeze artists on the end of their silk threads. Moments like this are among the subtle little joys of the Rainbow Lake Trail, particularly on days when a breeze helps keep the insects at bay.

The trail climbs up and down for the next half-hour, with an occasional rare glimpse of 21-Mile Creek below. Berry bushes line the route in summer, followed by colorful fungi in rainy months. Once you've rounded Mount Sproatt, the trail then levels as it crosses a wet meadow on a series of short boardwalks. Some of the best views of Rainbow Mountain on the entire trail now appear on your right, and you can see that, instead of one distinct peak, Rainbow Mountain has a series of crests. In warm months, wild azaleas will be blooming in delicate shades of white beside the trail. (Near Tonic Creek, two trails lead off to the left within a short distance of each other: a rough newer one and an older one in better shape. Both go to Tonic Lake, an interesting detour up an open valley, an hour from the boardwalk.)

Just before the trail reaches Tonic Creek, a perfectly situated viewpoint presents itself. I like to pause here to feed both myself and the gray jays, aka whisky-jacks, while studying the multi-hued flanks of Rainbow Mountain. Steps away lies another new municipal bridge, a springy suspension one that is removed in winter months. If you come on snowshoes, be prepared for a challenging crossing of the narrow canyon below.

In another 1.5 km (0.9 mi) the blue aster-lined trail crosses 21-Mile Creek below a small waterfall that marks the lake's outlet. Climb up beside it and see how Rainbow Lake is naturally dammed at its eastern end, creating this waterfall. As your last steps bring you up to the top of the falls, the lake is suddenly laid out before you. The water near the shore is a clear golden hue, changing to green, then aquamarine, and finally turquoise as the depth increases. By now you'll be looking for a place to relax. For the best views, follow the trail around the north side of the lake. The slope on the south side holds shelves of snow until well into the summer; some years it never completely melts, which accounts for the lake's frigid temperature.

Opinions vary as to why this lake is named Rainbow. Anglers insist it's due to the trout that flourish here. This may well be true—certainly a number of hikers carry fishing rods in their backpacks. But to contemplate another possibility, position yourself on a rock that overlooks the lake. When the sun reflects on the lake bottom, you'll see rainbow patterns. These prismatic effects color the shadows cast by ripples on the lake's surface.

You may be content to rest awhile at lakeside before you head back down. Or you may meet a party coming the opposite way from Madeley Lake with whom you've arranged in advance to exchange car keys. (See chapter 9 for more information.) Or you may climb any of the ridges on either Rainbow or Sproatt mountains within an hour's range of the lake. Both of these mountains have open slopes with relatively easy footing. Their eroded peaks promise more elevated views. It's just a question of having the time to reach them.

If you can, I suggest you take the time to hike a short distance past Rainbow Lake to the pass that separates the lake from the Callaghan Valley. A panoply of peaks is visible from this vantage point: from Brandywine Mountain to Mount Callaghan. A faint hiking trail leads north onto the alpine tundra slopes of Rainbow Mountain. Bear right

> JACK'S THREE FAVORITE TRAILS

THE VIEWS don't get much better than from the Rainbow Lake Trail on Mount Sproatt. Still, there's more to a great hike than bird's-eye vistas—like that springy feeling underfoot as you traverse a trail built up by years of forest canopy mulch. Even under a different name I'd pick Jack's Trail in Alice Lake Provincial Park (see chapter 4) as one of the most satisfying in this regard, whether exploring on foot or by bike (my preference). The same can be said of the Tin Pants Trail, a mixed-use marvel that meanders around the hillside to the west of Lost Lake (see chapter 13). And when it comes to alpine accessibility, no trail is as easy to reach—or as immediately rewarding—as the Joffre Lakes Trail, immediately adjacent to Duffey Lake Road (see chapter 30).

where the trail divides to reach remote Beverly Lake, about 5 km (3 mi) from Rainbow Lake, where you'll find a more secluded—and more picturesque—campsite than at Hanging Lake, 2 km (1.2 mi) farther east along the trail to Madeley Lake (see chapter 9).

> MOUNT SPROATT

Access: A rough trail leads uphill from Rainbow Lake's southern shore.

Ability Level: Intermediate, with basic route-finding skills

. If you make the effort to climb above Rainbow Lake onto Sproatt, you'll feel like you've struck gold. From the ridges near the summit (elevation 1844 m/6050 ft) are superb views in every direction—as many peaks as you can possibly identify, all in one panoramic vista as you look down on several small alpine tarns tucked into the folds of the ridges around Rainbow Lake. As you climb east along several ridges towards the top of Mount Sproatt, you lose sight of Rainbow Lake but can now see Tonic Lake in the valley below. The meadows beside it have an open, inviting appearance. In the distance you can tell where the boardwalk trail runs. If you have several hours to spare, and good weather, you can find your way down off the ridge and back to the boardwalk without having to retrace your steps around Rainbow Lake. You'll have to remove your footwear to cross several creeks. (The red heather underfoot is surprisingly soft if you want to remain barefoot between crossings.) Halfway down, watch for surveyor's tape to show you the way. Stay in the open and you should be fine. There's no need to navigate any rockslides; just follow the natural lie of the land. Let the mountain lead you down from snow patches to the ridges below, which are moderately steep chutes carpeted with berry bushes and heather. Stay in the middle of the valley for most of the distance.

As you leave the ridge, views to the east of Wedge Mountain and the Blackcomb and Horstman glaciers give way to prominent Rainbow Mountain. The late afternoon sun descends and casts a zigzag pattern of light and shade on Rainbow's glacier. Four bumpy peaks mark the mountain's brow. The only drawback can be the presence of pesky helicopters full of sightseers. Rainbow Lake is definitely on the flight plan. I'm sure the passengers look down on this stunning scene and wish they could linger longer. Through your own efforts, you can take as long as you like!

You'll be tired but happy on the way back down along the main trail, where the girth of the trees increases as you trek through an endless network of their roots. Leaving the forest behind, suddenly there are views of Blackcomb's runs; Iago, Fitzsimmons, and Overlord mountains; village rooftops, and Alta Lake too, all at once. It's a release and a relief to feel the end is in sight. If it's sunny, head to Rainbow Park for a quick plunge to freshen up as your final reward of the day.

17

SINGING PASS

Garibaldi Provincial Park

. . . . .

> **LOCATION:** Headwaters region of Fitzsimmons Creek, 125 km (77.5 mi) north of Vancouver, 65 km (40.3 mi) north of Squamish, 37 km (22.9 mi) south of Pemberton

> **ACTIVITIES:** Camping, cross-country skiing, cycling, hiking, viewpoints

> **HIGHLIGHTS:** Alpine flower show, friendly wildlife

> **ACCESS:** The Singing Pass Trail begins at the main bus loop in Whistler Village. BC Parks signs on Highway 99 mark the turnoff to the trailhead at Village Way Boulevard. Follow the boulevard to Blackcomb Way. If you are traveling by car, turn left and park in one of the day lots. If you are planning to camp at Russet Lake, be sure to park in one of the lots (as of this writing, lot 4; summer only) where overnight parking is permitted. Signs point to Singing Pass at the bus loop across from lot 1 as Blackcomb Way approaches the bridge over Fitzsimmons Creek. Follow the dirt service road uphill. Quite soon you pass to the left of a gated private road that leads up Whistler Mountain. (Guidelines for walkers who wish to follow this road are displayed on a large sign.) As the 5-km (3-mi) access road to the Singing Pass climbs steadily uphill, views of the valley and Overlord Mountain open before you. If you are cycling, be prepared for a steady pump. Near the end of the road, much of which is increasingly overgrown, you'll pass an earth slump that first appeared in 1999 and which continues to expand. As a result, the Singing Pass road has been closed to vehicular traffic. Bicycles are not permitted in this part of Garibaldi Park, but you can ride as far

as the boundary, 3 km (1.9 mi) farther up the trail from a former parking lot at the end of the access road. From here an older road leads past an abandoned mine site and across Harmony and Flute creeks. A bike trail descends from the parking lot to Fitzsimmons Creek and links via a bridge with the Mini Spearhead Trail on the north side of the creek, which leads downhill to Blackcomb's Base Two area.

> ABILITY LEVEL: Intermediate

FITZSIMMONS CREEK flows west off the slopes of Overlord Mountain into Green Lake. The wide valley through which it descends separates Whistler and Blackcomb mountains. Whistler pioneer Bill Bailiff ran a trapline here in winter and in summer cleared trails into Singing Pass and around Cheakamus Lake. These days, the road and trail leading to Singing Pass run along the north side of Whistler Mountain, the slope originally intended for ski development in 1965. Outstanding mining claims on the Fitzsimmons side of Whistler Mountain forced a relocation of the proposed site to Whistler Creek, on the mountain's west side. It took a decade to finally settle the claims. Only then did the plan for Whistler Village and the Blackcomb ski facility take shape. Of all the developments since then, none tops the resort's most recent addition, the Peak 2 Peak Gondola (see page 134) linking Whistler and Blackcomb mountains which soars high above the Singing Pass Trail.

> **VILLAGE TO GARIBALDI PARK**

Singing Pass lies within Garibaldi Park. BC Parks has upgraded the trail somewhat since Bill Bailiff's time, though near the top of the pass you can still see his handiwork. (See chapter 11 for a map of this area.) From the former parking lot, the first 15-minute section of the Singing Pass Trail takes you over some of its steepest and roughest parts. Good footwear with upper-ankle support and a non-skid sole will make it easier to negotiate the loose surface. If your shoes are waterproof, so much the better; you will be crossing several creeks without bridges and may even encounter snow. Pace yourself, as you'll be on this trail for three hours going uphill, then half that going down.

Singing Pass

Coming upon the abandoned mine shaft entrance is always a bit of a surprise. Old, twisted tracks exit from a hole in the side of the mountain, dangling in space where a roadbed once was. Wooden beams still support the entranceway; a small stream trickles out. Darkness hides the interior of the shaft, which is partly blocked to keep casual explorers out. Beware low oxygen levels should you consider an in-depth appraisal. (After pumping uphill on the forest trail, cyclists may feel like the whole mountainside is a low-oxygen zone.)

The trail varies from moderate to steep as it rises past Harmony Creek, which you'll have to pick your way across as there is no bridge. A short distance on, a bridge spans a smaller creek between the "2 km" and "3 km" signs. The constant wind coming down off Whistler Mountain blows a fine spray off the whitewater. All of Blackcomb's south face is showing across the valley now. This is the boundary of Garibaldi Park and as far as you can come by bike. The trail divides, with a sign pointing to the left for Singing Pass. The road on the right leads up Whistler Mountain to the base of the Harmony Express chairlift.

A long, moderate, shaded section now begins and leads past small and large creeks. The sounds of Fitzsimmons Creek in the valley are louder here, with an occasional birdcall heard from a junco or varied thrush. Shortly past the "3 km" sign, a good viewpoint to the north opens up where windstorms have brought down numerous tall trees.

A sign announces Oboe Creek. The bridge over it is a good place to rest and watch the sun shining down through the canyon above, illuminating the white water. Moderate but steady climbing brings you to the "4 km" sign; 20 minutes beyond here the trail passes beside a large wooden arrow positioned on an old stump, pointing uphill. Bill Bailiff's old trail leads downhill towards Melody Creek, a pleasant but often wet walk. The newer trail built by BC Parks continues on uphill. The old trail is visible below where it passes through clearings in the forest, which thins out as you gain elevation.

The park trail crosses Melody Creek at the "6 km" marker. You are entering the subalpine zone, and after two hours in the shelter of the forest, it's a relief to reach an open area. The walking for the past 30 minutes has been easy and continues to be so. Above you, the open slopes may hold snow as late as August. Fitzsimmons Creek is out of earshot now, as the trail leads away from it, towards Singing Pass.

Past the "7 km" marker, watch for a trail resembling a small creekbed leading uphill off the main path. This is the turnoff for the Musical Bumps Trail, which leads west across the Oboe, Flute, and Piccolo summits to Harmony Lake and the Roundhouse Lodge's Whistler Express gondola. (See chapter 12.)

An interpretive sign positioned beside the trail lets you know when you've reached the pass. Two small ponds appear on your left, perfect for soaking tired feet while enjoying the views to the west. Don't pass up the chance to climb just a little higher past this point even though the trail inclines steeply towards an open ridge. The best views are only another 10 to 15 minutes beyond. With each step you take, more peaks and glaciers—and even turquoise Cheaka-mus Lake—appear until you are seeing Garibaldi Park in the round. Small groves of subalpine fir offer shelter from the breeze, which can blow cool even on the hottest days. When you see the glaciers that hold the surrounding peaks in their grip, you understand why the wind off the slopes isn't warmer. I always carry a lightweight windbreaker with me, even on days when it's hot in the valley.

In the 1950s, the sound of the wind blowing across the slopes here inspired Ottar Brandvold to christen this Singing Pass—while on a camping trip with his wife, Joan Matthews, and his brother, Emil, owners of the Diamond Head Lodge (see chapter 2).

> **RUSSET LAKE**

Access: 3 km (1.9 mi) beyond Singing Pass
Ability Level: Intermediate

Those who journey to Singing Pass with intentions of camping overnight must carry on to Russet Lake, another 3 km (1.9 mi) beyond the ridge above the pass. If snow conditions or weariness weigh you down, rest in the sheltered grove to the left of the sign that asks hikers to take care when walking on the delicate alpine undergrowth. A rough trail leads to a number of clearings in the grove, with grand views to the west of Rainbow Mountain.

The trail from Singing Pass to Russet Lake is marked by rock cairns. Even if there is still snow you can find your way to the ridge

> **AUTUMN GLORY**

EACH SEASON has its own spectacular highlights, but in the Coast Mountains, autumn is champion in the color category, with the first good frost triggering the greens of summer into shades of red, gold, and purple. From Howe Sound to the Pemberton Valley, the rivers and lakes are flanked by stands of ash, cottonwood, and vine maples in spectacular display. But their leaves turn at a much slower pace than those in the alpine regions, where low-lying shrubs thickly carpet the gullies near the peaks. This is where you want to be. Pumpkin yellow and orange leaves blaze on black huckleberry and oval-leafed blueberry bushes, augmented by an understory of white partridgefoot, green Alaska clubmoss, and pink-tipped Pacific mountain-heather. The only thing missing will be the bugs.

above the lake by following these markers. Occasional red patches on the snow, which look as if they have been colored with dye, are colonies of algae that bloom in summer.

Once you've reached the ridge above Singing Pass, you'll see a red roof beside Russet Lake's northern end. The B.C. Mountaineering Club built this rustic cabin, which is large enough to hold eight visitors. In summer, tents sprout around the perimeter of the lake, one of the few level spots in the vicinity.

Rising above modest-sized Russet Lake are the crumbling maroon-tinted slopes of Fissile Peak. It stands in the way of Overlord Mountain, blocking views of the predominant peak at the east end of the Fitzsimmons Valley. Once you have gotten your bearings, you will be able to distinguish parts of Overlord as they appear to the east of Fissile Peak. Farther east is the Cheakamus Glacier, veined with crevasses, on the slopes of Mount Davidson. Beside it, Castle Towers Creek flows through a wide valley into Cheakamus Lake. Nonetheless, you must climb beyond Singing Pass in order to get a true appreciation for the amazing scope of the valley.

Groves of subalpine fir dot the slopes. Their distinctive deep purple cones stand straight up, fat as your thumb. Deer or mountain goats shelter in these groves: you'll see the smooth beds they have fashioned for themselves and smell their strong, musky scent. They nibble on the interior branches of the conifers, leaving the outside limbs full for protection.

Return trip: You have more time to look around on your way back down. Birds feed in the heather and in the branches of the sturdy western hemlock. They don't seem to be wary of onlookers. Groups of fat ptarmigan launch themselves off rocky outcrops, showing a great expanse of wing with impressive feathering. They moult three times a year, changing camouflage to match the seasons. Beware the gray jays, or whisky-jacks, which will steal your lunch if it's left unguarded.

Across the meadow below the pond at Singing Pass, you will see Bill Bailiff's old winding trail. It links with the BC Parks trail farther down beside the large wooden arrow. The two trails are never far apart; the old one grows faint near the arrow junction, but the old notched logs crossing some of the wet areas remain. There is some magnificent original growth along the old trail. One blowdown near Melody Creek must be the biggest tree to have grown on this mountain in the past thousand years. The wide BC Parks trail is so easy to follow that you might wish to remain at Singing Pass during the "magic hour" before sunset, then walk or ski back down in the afterglow.

18

WHISTLER BIKE ROUTES

. . . . .

> ACTIVITIES: Downhill freeriding and cross-country mountain biking

> HIGHLIGHTS: Uphill for views, downhill for thrills

IN THE mid-1980s, Whistler-based adventure photographer Leanna Rathkelly was the first to describe Whistler as "a mountain bike Mecca." Spurred on by volunteer groups such as the Whistler Off-Road Cycling Association and the Sea to Sky Trail Society, mountain bike trail building proceeds at a pace reminiscent of earlier times when the drive was to cut more and more ski trails.

Although largely invisible to motorists, bike routes proliferate in the forests above Whistler neighborhoods, where mountain bikers confront the sport's physical challenges while pumping their way to places of great beauty. Some trails are steeper than you might want to attempt even on foot, but others follow former logging roads that are much gentler. The overall objective is the same: to explore quiet, enchanting getaways under your own power, in some of the most glorious wilderness on the coast. And although some of these trails, such as those in the Whistler Interpretive Forest and to Cheakamus Lake (see chapters 10 and 11, respectively), have been described elsewhere in this book, here is a sampling of some of the best getaway routes within Whistler's vast trail network.

> **LOST LAKE TRAILS**
Access: *East side of Blackcomb Way, from lot 6; the well-marked Tin Pants Trail leads uphill north from the Centennial Trail just east of the cross-country skier's ticket booth (closed in summer).*
Ability Level: *Novice to intermediate*

Whistler Mountain Bike Park

Much like Nordic skiing, cross-country cycling offers a complete workout—if you want to reach the top of a trail, you'd better be prepared to get there under your own steam. The Lost Lake trails are a good fitness test. In the 1980s, when mountain bikes were just a blip on the recreational radar screen, a network of cross-country ski trails was cleared around the shoreline and on the hillsides above the diminutive lake. Gradually, the trails have become as popular with cyclists as with skiers, whether they're riding the graveled section of the 20-km (12.4-mi) Valley Trail that runs through the park or tackling more challenging terrain, such as the intermediate-rated Vimy Ridge and Upper Panorama Trails.

One of the most appealing things about the Lost Lake trails, particularly for riders just learning to maneuvre a mountain bike, is that trailhead signs depict the level of difficulty of each trail, much as ski trails are designated as novice, intermediate, or expert. Unlike the narrow single-track trails that characterize Whistler's mountain bike park, where even the easiest-rated trails can prove more challenging than first-timers might expect, the Lost Lake trails are also generally wider than most of the cross-country bike routes that have been constructed throughout the valley. Not that you won't also find rocks-and-roots single track around Lost Lake as well. Keep an eye out for these unmarked gems as they lead away from the main trail system.

One of the most welcoming new cross-country trails in Whistler these days is *Tin Pants*, a mixed-use route that winds back and forth above the west side of Lost Lake. Finishing touches are still being applied to the 9.7-km (6-mi) trail, including a wooden bridge that links the intermediate-rated Molly Hogan Trail at the north end of Lost Lake with Tin Pants where it crosses the Old Mill Road Trail.

For starters, Tin Pants (which takes its quirky name from the bug-proof apparel worn by loggers) is more than just a cycling trail. Although it's rarely explored on foot, its smooth, hard-packed construction will appeal as much to those pushing children in strollers as to runners looking for a good place to stretch their legs. Stylish touches, such as bridges built from lodgepole pines, abound, giving Tin Pants the look of a twig-furniture showroom in places. This is particularly true at several prominent viewpoints where Tin Pants intersects with the expert-rated Centennial Trail. One of its best vantage points overlooks Rainbow Mountain as it rises on the west side of valley to its 2314-m (7592-ft) summit.

After your ride through the woods above the lake, it's refreshing to make your way around the shoreline on the *Lost Lake Loop* to seek out sections of other trails. A particularly enjoyable stretch of easy-rated *Lower Panorama* leads away from the north end of the lake past an observation deck overlooking the Lost Lake wetlands restoration project.

> **MAGIC PARK**

Access: *Blackcomb Ski Base, Blackcomb Way*
Ability Level: *Novice*

Magic happens. And nowhere more so than on the trails in the Magic Park at the foot of Blackcomb and in the adjacent Whistler Mountain Bike Park. Try a few runs to see for yourself. The longer you ride, the more convinced you'll become that something truly enchanting is being triggered inside your head.

Riding with a Whistler Blackcomb guide is the wand that catalyzes this spellbinding effect. At the start, they'll counsel you to lift your head, look where you want to go, and your bike will automatically follow. (It's one thing to believe this advice when you're simply coasting along. It's a whole other article of faith when you're speeding downhill atop a 20-kg (44-lb) mountain bike whose geometry looks more like a motorcycle—minus the engine—than your average street cruiser.) Works every time. Gaze ahead around the corners as single-track trails snake through the woods and the bike follows as naturally as if it were pre-programmed to do so. Practice this artful technique. Revel in it. Magic is indeed in the air and nowhere more so than on a series of bike trails specifically designed with beginners in mind in Blackcomb's Magic Park. This is where novice skiers and snowboarders overcome their jitters in winter. This is where freeride-wannabes get started in summer. Don a helmet fitted with full-face protection, plus pads for your arms, legs, and hands, mount a dual-suspension bike, and wheel over to rendezvous with a guide at the bottom of the Magic chairlift. Time for a briefing on some basics, starting with how to load a bike onto the lift. Given the bike's hefty size, this may prove to be a challenging workout in itself. About the only thing one can categorize as small about a freeride bike is its seat, as insignificant as a flea on an elephant. That's because freeriders don't spend much time sitting down. This style of cycling is done almost exclusively in a standing position.

Once at the top of the Magic Park lift, choose from two trails, reassuringly named *Cruise Control* and *Easy Rider.* Head to a level skills area to practice some balancing techniques that will soon come in handy when switchbacking around banked turns, or berms. After a confidence-building run or two in the Magic Park, head over to play on the big-league trails a short distance away on the lower slopes of Whistler Mountain where you'll find yourself surrounded by burly biker buddies stacked up like football defensive linemen, ready to tackle trails with names like Angry Pirate, No Joke, Dirt Merchant, and the ominous Heart of Darkness. Unless you're intent on getting trail mugged, steer away from the pack at the top of the lift and head for Easy Does It, a relatively gentle trail where you can put your newly acquired skills to work. .

Muscle memory is an admirable trait, an acquired response that keeps one's reflexes sharp. Imprint a move on your muscles a hundred times and it then becomes as natural as, say, rolling out of bed. With about that many bermed turns spread out across its 7-km (4.3-mi), *Easy Does It* is the perfect trail to train muscles to automatically handle the challenge of cornering at high speed. And remember to keep your eyes focused as far ahead as possible rather than yielding to the powerful temptation to look down at the trail. At first, this act will take every nerve you can muster to apply. Then when you see that it works time and again, the magic of what your eyes are doing is almost overwhelming. Somehow your peripheral vision senses where the best line to take over the rocks and roots lies while you scope out what's fast approaching up ahead. The magic of the human body is spellbinding. Careful: You'll want spend the rest of your life immersed in what is truly a magic park.

> ## WHISTLER MOUNTAIN BIKE PARK

Access: From Skier's Plaza in Whistler Village, the Fitzsimmons chairlift and the Whistler Express gondola take riders and their bikes to the Olympic Station and the Roundhouse Lodge. From Olympic Station, the Garbanzo chairlift accesses more challenging trails.
Ability Level: Intermediate to expert

To freeride or cross-country? That is the question facing cyclists who journey to Whistler these days. Since 1998, when the Whistler Mountain Bike Park debuted, the trend to armor up like a gladiator, catch a ride uphill on a chairlift, and freeride down trails on a full suspension– and disc brake–equipped mountain bike has proven irresistible to an increasing number of cyclists who once favored cross-country trails. Not that you can't do both, but there's an undeniable thrill to freeriding in a bike park that rivals skiing or snowboarding these same slopes in winter when you speed downhill, then catch your breath as you're whisked back to the top on a chairlift.

From the top of the Roundhouse to the bottom of Whistler Mountain is a vertical drop of 1175 m (3855 ft), covering over 50 km (30 mi) of technical trail.

Running into a tree—or any stationary object, for that matter—makes cyclists appreciate the need to protect heads, backs, arms, and knees. Downhill mountain bikers first began wearing padding in the early 1990s. With the introduction of suspension systems and lightweight bike frames, the speeds that riders can achieve have risen sharply. Armor saves you. Go down without it and you might be laid out for weeks. With it, you'll usually get right off the ground with only a scratch. You've got to put your ego—the hero thing—aside. After all, everyone is suiting up, from kids to grown-ups looking to enjoy a healthy second childhood.

Since 1998, the number of riders using the trails has doubled each year. More than 100,000 riders show up at what is arguably the most unique bike park on the planet. Included in that number are names such as Cedric Gracia and Richey Schley, two of the best-known downhill and slopestyle riders.

Be prepared for a challenge. This is not a cross-country joyride. If you're looking for that, try the trails around Whistler's Lost Lake (also described in this chapter). Don't expect to take in much of the views while riding here either, at least not while you're in motion. One of the biggest surprises is how many families are out riding the course together. The age range is anywhere from eight to sixty. In fact, the mountain bike park is one of the big reasons that almost as many people visit Whistler in summer as they do in the winter. The line of bike riders waiting to get on the chairlift or gondola on weekends is just as long as the line of skiers and snowboarders in winter. There's just one difference. All the trails in the bike park, even the

> **WORCA**

W HEN IT comes to community support for mountain bike trail building, Whistler leads the pack. The Whistler Off-Road Cycling Association, or WORCA, boasts over a thousand members, making it the largest cycling club in Canada. And with over 100,000 rider visits each summer, the Whistler Mountain Bike Park has become the template for other resorts eager to broaden their appeal.

beginner runs, are single-track, and they snake through the forest at an angle much steeper and narrower than most of the ski runs.

Even on the easy trails you can find yourself going faster than you might want. It helps to remember that going too slow is just as bad as going too fast. It may take a couple of runs to find the right balance, which is why I suggest spending some time with one of the park's guides in order to pick up a few pointers. Most of the guides are snowboard or ski instructors here in winter, and they're pros when it comes to helping you find your comfort level. If you're interested in a full immersion, sign up for one of the multi-day bike camps offered May through September. Contact Whistler Blackcomb (www. whistlerblackcom.com) for details.

That's where your armor comes in handy, especially padded gloves. Try a run such as *Rippin' Rutabaga.* It may be slightly above your skill level, but it will show you where your comfort level is. An average ride lasts 30 minutes. You'll quickly find there's more riding in the park than you can probably handle in one visit. Note: Don't cheap out. If you don't own protective clothing or if your bike is an older model with little or no suspension, do yourself a favor and rent some specialized gear for the day. Remember, these bikes retail for as much as $5,000, so it's worth it. With the help of armor, fat tires, and a full-suspension system, you ought to do just fine.

There's not a more intimidating section of the Whistler Mountain Bike Park than the *Boneyard*—a name guaranteed to prompt cyclists of all ages and abilities to have second thoughts before attempting it. Inspiration for aspiring junior mountain bike riders comes from watching the pros of the world of dirt negotiate their way over and around and off the massive berms, drops, ramps, and jumps that define the Boneyard.

> **SEA TO SKY TRAIL** &

Access: Whistler Olympic Village, Function Junction
Ability Level: Novice to intermediate

The Sea to Sky Trail project has been in the works since the early 1990s. Originally envisaged as a greenway linking Squamish with D'Arcy (see chapter 26), it has subsequently morphed into a much more ambitious route between Horseshoe Bay and Lillooet (see chapter 31). One of the best sections begins at Function Junction neighborhood beside the 2010 Winter Olympic Village and leads south to Brandywine Falls Park (see chapter 8). This is one of the best-built trails in the corridor. I think it's going to be around for a long, long time. In particular, the 11-km (6.8-mi) stretch between Whistler and Brandywine Falls is in immaculate shape. Contoured with the terrain, the 1.5-m (4.9-ft) crushed-gravel route is a flagship trail and makes for a lovely day trip as it winds back and forth through the woods, past pothole lakes and amazing basalt rock formations. It's the opposite-end bracket of the Whistler Mountain Bike Park, which likes to think of itself as the biggest, gnarliest, baddest park in the world. In years to come, this free amenity will round out the corridor's regional reputation for superbly built trails.

Just because snowflakes begin to fly doesn't mean the trail is shut down for the season either. Snowshoes and cross-country skis are both good ways to negotiate sections of the trail along old logging and BC Hydro routes that the Sea to Sky Trail Society has brushed out. You'll be keeping company with the Cheakamus River in many places. Allow an hour to reach Sugarcube Hill and beyond to the Cal-Cheak Forest Service Road (see chapter 8). From there, the trail passes through the forested recreation site to a suspension bridge across Callaghan Creek. This may be as far as you wish to come. Tack on another hour to reach Brandywine Falls from here via the Whistler Bungee Bridge. Trail markers help make sense of directions at every major turning point. Information on the Sea to Sky Trail is posted at seatoskytrail.ca.

> ## RAINBOW-SPROATT FLANK TRAIL
(ALPINE MEADOWS TO RAINBOW CREEK)

Access: Turn west off Highway 99 at Alpine Meadows, north of Whistler Village, then follow Alpine Way to its highest point. A dirt road leads uphill from here and connects with the trail.
Ability Level: Intermediate

Alpine Meadows and Emerald Estates are the two most northerly neighborhoods in Whistler. With a little effort you can reach panoramic viewpoints—and monster single-track trails—from the old roads above each. Looking out over the valley is as good a geography lesson as you can experience—next to paragliding or flying. A camera can capture much of the expanse, but at certain spots your eyes will hardly be big enough to take it all in. What you see is Whistler evolving before you. (See chapter 13 for a map of this area.)

Within minutes of starting up a dirt road that begins above Alpine Meadows at the top of Alpine Way, you'll reach *Rick's Roost*, a lookout named for the late local photographer Rick Flebbe. Views of the valley stretching from Green Lake to Alta Lake open up suddenly on your right. There's a bench at the top of the Roost just to the side of the road. Measuring your position here against the slopes of Blackcomb and Whistler mountains across the way helps you gauge your elevation above the valley. Whether you are a first-time visitor or a Whistler pioneer, the vista never loses its freshness. It seems that you can see everything that's happening in the valley at once.

Above the Roost, the road climbs steadily into the watershed. The first two side roads on the left lead towards the Mel's Dilemma Trail network, crossing a small creek that feeds down the south side of Alpine Meadows and into the River of Golden Dreams. Several concrete dams regulate the flow of the creek, channeling some of it into water towers for the neighborhood's use. There is also a satellite-dish communication center nearby. The roads are kept in good shape so service vehicles can drive in.

Not far above the Roost, the dirt road is partly cleared up to the first major switchback, where it deteriorates quickly to an alder-lined path. It heads uphill on a moderate incline with level spots in places, curving one way and then the other. Stick with this path and you will soon reach a clearing where Lost Lake comes into view on the opposite side of the valley. From below, this lake is hidden in the forest; you have to reach a higher elevation than the Roost to see it.

Where the trail divides, the Rainbow–Sproatt Flank Trail begins. One branch heads north towards 19-Mile Creek while the other makes a sharp left turn south. If you keep on going straight ahead towards 19-Mile Creek, you may find that the path soon becomes so overgrown with alder that you must stoop to get through it. The alders are bowed over by the weight of snow in winter, then gradually rise during summer, clearing the path for easier exploration. The path itself takes on the appearance of an old creekbed. It does eventually lead to the banks of 19-Mile Creek, but you may need a machete to clear the way. It isn't all bad though, as there are some clearings with good views along the way, especially from the hillside above the path. (Large piles of bear scat indicate that humans aren't the only ones to use this path—make noise as you ride so you don't take a bear by surprise.)

To the south, the Flank Trail leads upwards onto a level ridge. The farther along this ridge you travel, the better the views are. A moderate climb through open brush leads to the old-growth forest above; along the way you pass more fully developed second growth than previously encountered. After you have been on the trail above Alpine Meadows for about 90 minutes, you'll reach another major trail divide. You may be satisfied to have found the views from this ridge and be ready to retrace your tracks. Or you can carry on, making a 7-km (4.3-mi) loop over to 21-Mile Creek and back along Alta Lake Road to Alpine Meadows. The branch leading uphill has been intentionally blocked by several old tree limbs. If you wish to continue farther, take the open trail to the left.

Tapes help mark the route where the trail is overgrown. Also watch for signs that other bikes have been through here. Mountain bike chain rings often cut into fallen logs, leaving open red marks that are helpful in defining the route. These slashes are as visible as the more traditional orange metal markers nailed to tree trunks.

The open trail passes through old-growth forest for 10 to 15 minutes, the soft ground bouncing under your tires. After the logged area you climbed through on your way up here, you'll find this a pleasant place to be. A small stream descends through the clearing from the side of Rainbow Mountain. Cross this stream on a series of logs. As you ride south along a ridge, you overlook the last section of 21-Mile Creek as it flows towards Alta Lake. Your only clue to the creek's course higher up the mountain is the line of old growth flanking its banks.

A second small stream appears on the open slope, and beside it some very large stumps more than 2 m (6 ft) in diameter. With all the low-lying blueberry and huckleberry bushes around, there will be good fall color here after the first frost. The ground in late spring and summer is quite mucky around the stream for a short distance, then the trail rises to another small clearing. Looking across the valley, you see that you are at approximately the same elevation as you would be at midstation on Blackcomb and Whistler mountains. Pause a moment to enjoy the view. The scope of this panorama is unexpected: Black Tusk, Mount Sproatt, Alta Lake, Fitzsimmons Glacier, Singing Pass, and Whistler Village all vie for attention. In addition, the peaks and ridges around Wedge and Weart mountains now stand revealed.

Watch your traction; it gets muddy again for the next 5 to 10 minutes. The trail doubles as a creekbed as it descends, meeting up with an old road. From here you can see a low watershed building on the south side of 21-Mile Creek, with Mount Sproatt rising above. As the trail nears the creek, it becomes narrower and enters a section characterized by numerous switchbacks. The trail drops steadily from here to Alta Lake Road, where it reaches a clearing with a dozen tall snags still standing among the living old-growth forest. Moss covers much of the rock face. Now 21-Mile Creek is quite close and there are exhilarating views of Rainbow Mountain to the west. Enjoy this; the views begin to disappear below this clearing as you descend towards the valley floor. You may spot hikers and riders on the opposite side of 21-Mile Creek on the Flank Trail as it leads a short distance up the Rainbow Lake hiking trail (see chapter 16), or along the classic *Whip Me Snip Me* biking trail. One of the best viewpoints on the entire journey occurs here. Green Lake is visible in the distance while in the foreground is a stand of old growth. You may want to shoulder your bike here and grip sturdy old growth to help break your slide should you get going too fast.

A web of off-road mountain bike trails begins on the east side of Alta Lake Road, including intermediate-rated *A River Runs Through It* and easygoing *Bart's Dark Trail*, were among the first cut in the valley through the Emerald Forest trail network to meet the *Valley Trail* (see chapter 13). The forest below the road is a warren of old logging roads and newer bike trails. Farther north, watch for the well-marked, paved entrance to the Valley Trail. Directly across the road from this entrance, leading uphill, is the start of *Mel's Dilemma.* Follow it north for 10 minutes as it heads over to the small creek descending from the Alpine Meadows watershed. A crossing will bring you out onto Forest Ridge Drive. Turn left onto Fissile Lane. This leads back onto Alpine Way; you are now within minutes of the trailhead at Rick's Roost, having come full circle.

The Rainbow–Sproatt Flank Trail between 21-Mile Creek and 19-Mile Creek is part of a lengthier route developed by the Whistler Off-Road Cycling Association. It forms a subalpine route between the Callaghan Valley (see chapter 9) and Cougar Mountain (see chapter 19) along Whistler Valley's west side.

> **THE INSIDE TRACK**

> *Maps:* A detailed map of the Lost Lake trail system is posted beside the Valley Trail as it leads from day parking lot 3 beside Blackcomb Way in Whistler Village, towards Lost Lake. Free maps of the Lost Lake Trail system are available from Cross Country Connection (604-905-0071; www.crosscountryconnection.ca), where you can also rent bikes as well as get repairs and advice. A detailed bike trail map for both Whistler and Pemberton is published by TerraPro and is available for $12.95 from most bike shops and bookstores in Whistler. A good trail guide to consult is *Whistler Mountain Biking* (Quickdraw Publications).

> 19

COUGAR MOUNTAIN AND
ANCIENT CEDARS GROVE

. . . . .

> **LOCATION:** 152 km (94 mi) north of Vancouver, 85 km (53 mi) north of Squamish, 27 km (16.7 mi) north of Whistler Village, 30 km (18.6 mi) south of Pemberton

> **ACTIVITIES:** Cross-country skiing, fishing, hiking, mountain biking, paddling, picnicking, snowshoeing, walking, ziplining

> **HIGHLIGHTS:** Small lakes, plentiful berries, a cathedral cedar grove

> **ACCESS:** Take 16-Mile Creek Forest Service Road (called Cougar Mountain Road on some maps), a well-marked, two-lane road that rises uphill on the left (west) side of Highway 99, 1 km (0.6 mi) north of the Emerald Estates. (See map, page 175.) After a short distance you will pass a brown Forest Service sign marking the beginning of the road along 16-Mile Creek. Just past the sign is a widening on the right (north) side of the road where snowmobilers, snowshoers, and cross-country skiers congregate in winter. Snow is not cleared past this point. If you wish to travel the entire 20-km (12.4-mi) round-trip journey by bicycle or on foot in summer, leave your vehicle here, or drive halfway to Cougar Mountain and park at the entrance to the Showh Lakes Recreation Reserve. Take plenty of fluids when you set out on a warm day.

GIVEN THAT the Whistler Valley is walled by mountains—big mountains—one of the sweetest peaks hardly registers on the resort's skyline. To make up for that, it wears the grandiose name of Cougar—the secretive West Coast mountain lion.

Ancient Cedars Loop Trail

When it comes to huggable ancient rain forests, Cougar Mountain displays the finest old-growth western red cedar and Douglas fir found anywhere in the Sea to Sky corridor. This is my idea of visiting a cathedral in the outdoors. And only a short jaunt north of the village.

The best part is—it's free! All that's required is swinging your arms and legs. Take your time. Breathe deeply. Oxygen doesn't come much richer than this. When you feel like a pause, there's even a little waterfall that always buoys my spirit.

> ### 16-MILE CREEK FOREST SERVICE ROAD

Access: 16-Mile Creek Forest Service Road begins at Highway 99 just north of Green Lake and leads 4 km (2.5 mi) northwest to the Showh Lakes Recreation Reserve. From this point the road becomes rougher and is rated as four-wheel-drive only as it leads about 5 km (3 mi) northwest to the Soo River South Forest Service Road.

16-Mile Creek flows into the Green River just north of the Cougar Mountain turnoff from Highway 99. Its headwaters are two small lakes—one of which is Screaming Cat Lake—south of the Showh Lakes (see next page). Soon after you begin traveling up the

> ### BEST ANCIENT FOREST

CORE SAMPLES from western red cedar trees on Cougar Mountain indicate that many are well over 600 years old— with some approaching the millennium mark. And although the Douglas fir on the periphery of the cedar grove are much smaller, they are about the same age, proof that size isn't always an indication of age.

Characteristics of old-growth forests like the one on Cougar Mountain include living trees that are large for their size, dead standing trees (or snags), blowdowns on the forest floor and in streams, and a multi-layered branch canopy. Other ancient forests around Whistler can be found along the Cheakamus Lake Trail (chapter 11), the Rainbow Lake Trail (chapter 16), in Rebagliati Park (chapter 13), and at the bottom of the Seventh Heaven Express chairlift on Blackcomb.

road, watch for the entrance to the expert-rated Section 102 mountain bike trail on the left. Several buildings appear on the north side of the road, the operations base of an adventure company, Cougar Mountain at Whistler (604-932-4086; www.cougarmountain.ca). Proceed past and ignore the logging road branching off to the left. (It leads along the logged south side of 16-Mile Creek.)

For the first 2 km (1.2 mi), the road follows this small, gently inclined valley with 16-Mile Creek on its right side. Some pleasant western red cedar trees overhang small fishing holes along the way. Although the trees are a good size, they will seem like babies after the ones atop Cougar Mountain.

A bridge spans 16-Mile Creek, after which the road begins to climb a ridge above the creek on the valley's north side. From the bridge to the Showh Lakes Recreation Reserve is 1 km (0.6 mi).

BEST RAINBOW TROUT

The Showh Lakes and Cougar Lake are stocked with rainbow trout in a catch-and-release fishery, April to November. Required: artificial flies with single barbless hooks

> ## SHOWH LAKES RECREATION RESERVE
Access: *4 km (2.5 mi) west of Highway 99 on 16-Mile Creek Road*

A series of choices present themselves at the entrance to the Showh Lakes Recreation Reserve, all well marked. A detailed map posted at the information kiosk beside the parking area helps make sense of the options. The 1.6-km (1-mi) Lower Cougar Trail (no bikes) leads uphill on the right and links with the Ancient Cedars Loop Trail, a 5-km (3.1-mi) round trip. Allow two hours to make the complete journey.

Also from here, a rough road leads 1 km (0.6 mi) uphill to the Showh Lakes and another parking lot. There is no easy access from here to the smaller of the two lakes. Continue uphill to the right on foot or by bike for 2 km (1.2 mi) to the Ancient Cedars trailhead. Halfway along, the larger lake appears below you. Watch for the trail to its shoreline on your left, which leads down through stumps and blueberry bushes heavy with fruit in late summer. A choice picnic spot is atop a giant log half-submerged in the shallow water. Fishing and swimming are also possible.

> ## ANCIENT CEDARS LOOP TRAIL

Access: The 4-km (2.5-mi) Ancient Cedars Loop Trail begins 1.6 km (1 mi) from the Showh Lakes Recreation Reserve's entrance or 1 km (0.6 mi) from the larger of the Showh Lakes.

When it comes to a choice between the two approaches to the Ancient Cedars Loop Trail, I prefer the rocky, root-filled Lower Cougar Trail to the steep road. The trail is surprisingly soft in spots from the years of needles and fallen lichen that have accumulated on the forest floor. Moss also carpets much of the forest floor. White snowberries and the red fruits of devil's club stand out vividly among the evergreens by late August. (Beware the rhubarb-like leaves and spiny stems of the devil's club, which can leave you with painful, inflamed scratches.) An atmosphere of absolute tranquility surrounds the trail. A short distance before meeting the Ancient Cedars trail, the splashing sound of a small creek cascading down a waterfall fills the air.

A small wooden bridge spans the creek beside a waterfall at the outset of the Ancient Cedars Loop Trail. If you're not sure about crossing it, follow the trail to the right, which leads to the heart of the forest. Nothing ever prepares me for the sight of enormous centuries-old tree trunks thrusting above the open forest floor. Thanks to the constant nurturing of snow and rain, these cockeyed columns of biomass have grown beyond all proportion. Under their dense canopy of resin-rich cedar boughs, I'm always humbled.

You can tell when you've reached the ancient cedars: trunk diameters suddenly swell to 3 m (9 ft). On a hot day, the shade cast by these giants—the oldest of which has been dated at 900 years old—lowers the temperature in this part of the forest another degree. Several enormous cedars sprout sideways from a common base. Nearby, two giant blowdowns lie at 180 degrees to each other. Fungi climb the trunk of one cedar like a spiral staircase, their orange flesh a rare splash of brightness.

Cougar Mountain's Ancient Cedars Loop Trail never disappoints. I always leave tipping my hat to those who preserved the crown of Whistler's biggest little mountain.

20

WEDGEMOUNT LAKE

Garibaldi Provincial Park

. . . . .

> LOCATION: Northeast of Green Lake in Garibaldi Park, 152 km
> (92 mi) north of Vancouver, 94 km (58 mi) north of Squamish,
> 15 km (9 mi) north of Whistler Village, 20 km (12.4 mi) south of
> Pemberton

> ACTIVITIES: Camping, hiking, viewpoints

> HIGHLIGHTS: Unrivaled jewel-box setting

> ACCESS: Begin by following the blue signs marked "Wedgemount
> Lake (Garibaldi Provincial Park)" that appear beside Highway 99, 4
> km (2.5 mi) north of Whistler's Emerald Estates neighborhood and
> just beyond the Whistler town sign. Turn east off Highway 99 and
> cross the Green River Bridge. Once across, turn left and head uphill
> 2 km (1.2 mi) on a road of packed dirt. Signs at each divide point the
> way to the lake. Alders line the road as it rises through reforested
> slopes, ending at a parking lot with room for a dozen vehicles.
> Visit www.env.gov.bc.ca/bcparks/ for more details and trail updates.

> ABILITY LEVEL: Intermediate

O F THE five trails that lead into Garibaldi Park from the
Squamish-Whistler corridor, the one to Wedgemount Lake is
the most strenuous and least traveled. It's also one of the
oldest. Legendary Whistler pioneer Harry Horstman blazed the
original trail up the narrow canyon between Wedge and Weart
mountains through which Wedgemount Creek drops into the Green
River. He also spent many summers prospecting around Wedgemount Lake, a turquoise gem set between Wedge Mountain (at

Mount Weart with The Owls from Wedgemount Lake

2891 m/9485 ft the highest peak in the park) and its slightly smaller neighbor to the north, Weart (2835 m/9301 ft). (Wedge Mountain was named for its distinctive shape; Mount Weart memorializes the first chairman of the Garibaldi Park Board.) If you arrive with the sun shining in the middle of summer, you'll find the setting for this lake unrivaled: a wide swath of glacier rising at the lake's eastern end, a panorama of peaks, wildflowers in bloom, a million stars at night, clear air, and an immense silence.

Part of the release I guarantee you'll experience on arrival at Wedgemount Lake comes when you give yourself up to the fatigue engendered by simply getting here. There are very few steps along the way that don't go one above the other. If you are just hiking up for the day with a light pack, it will take you between 2½ and 3½ hours one way. If you are carrying enough equipment to spend the night, add another one or two hours to cover the 7 km (4.3 mi) from the parking lot to the lake. The total elevation gain is about 1200 m (3940 ft).

A single-track trail climbs from the parking lot through an overgrown clear-cut towards Wedgemount Creek and crosses it on a cement bridge, testimony to the little creek's strength. One of the larger trees on the trail stands directly above the bridge; go round it towards another bridge crossing a smaller stream. Except for glimpses of Wedgemount Creek from the trail higher up the mountain, this is the last water you'll find until you reach the foot of an avalanche slope about two hours away.

Now it's just a question of climbing. At first, the old growth's canopy of branches is so thick that few plants can compete for light, leaving the forest floor open and green with a thick covering of moss. Mushrooms sprout everywhere in late summer beside blueberry bushes. Soon the girth of the conifers lessens and smaller trunks provide handholds for lifting and pushing yourself forward. Wild azaleas rush to put out blossoms in the short growing season. The trail is a constant series of switchbacks that take you away from the creek then back as it drops straight down through a canyon worn bare by the water's action. You'll have to leave the main trail for a better look at the creek in places, but this requires only a few steps to a viewing point.

After crossing a short stretch of scree at the foot of an old slide that must have occurred several centuries ago, the trail enters its final, steepest stage. This is the most difficult stretch, not only because of the elevation gained with every step, but because in late spring and early summer the path doubles as a creekbed. Stop here for a look around. Weart's Armchair Glacier is to the north. One of the two bookends cradling the glacier, called The Owls, is recognizable by the distinct glacial gouges on its flank.

A short, wiry prospector with a bushy beard, Harry Horstman became friends with lodge owners Myrtle and Alex Philip soon after they arrived at Alta Lake. One autumn in the early 1920s, Myrtle and Alex took two guests on a hike to Wedgemount to visit Harry. His remark on meeting them at the lake was that the new sport of hiking must be catching on, as they were the second group he'd seen since the beginning of the summer!

In contrast to the other four principal park trails into Garibaldi—Diamond Head, Garibaldi Lake–Black Tusk, Cheakamus Lake, and Singing Pass—there are very few markers along the Wedgemount route, and there is no indication you are nearing the top until you have almost arrived. Watch for a large stone cairn, a sign that the end is near. A short distance above here are twenty walk-in campsites plus a small cabin, with room for six around its two tables and a narrow loft. Much like its counterpart at Russet Lake (see chapter 17), its primary appeal will be to those such as the author of the sidebar entry who appreciate any port in a storm. The cabin's outhouse is most distinctive, a bullet-shaped, metal-clad model that looks poised for liftoff back to the valley in case of dire emergency.

In front of you is the broad surface of Wedgemount Lake. The lake lies roughly east-west; the cabin where the trail arrives is on the north slope. Later in summer, the lake turns a deeper shade of turquoise. The surface of Wedgemount Glacier, which feeds into the lake, is quite dirty near the water's edge. In contrast, the snow and ice on Armchair Glacier is very clean, its border well defined against

> BEST HIKING DIARY

THE TATTERED guest book in the little BC Mountaineering Club cabin that stands beside Wedgemount Lake holds the comments of as many guests in a season as the area's first European settler, Harry Horstman, saw there in his lifetime. Some are positively hair-raising. Here's a typical one:

Climbed through deep snow for six hours, minus 20 and blowing; ended up on the wrong side of the lake; thought we'd have to bivy in a snowbank for the night but with 15 minutes of daylight left we spotted the top of the privy sticking up above a drift; feels great to be here even though the cabin was half-full of snow that had drifted in through cracks in the door; the floor is like a skating rink because the roof has been leaking again, but with a little effort we made it cozy and slept for 12 hours straight; never had such a great time in my life.

the coloring of the striated rock. After the stiff climb required to reach this location, I like to simply relax in one of the many windbreaks on the slopes above this inviting side of the lake and watch the shadows slowly lengthen as the sunlight and breeze create shifting patterns on the lake. With the help of binoculars I can usually spot bootprints in the snow high on the ridge of Wedge Mountain.

You'll have to clamber down a rocky slope to reach the lake. The ice of Wedgemount Glacier reaches almost to the shore of the lake's east end. Now that you've made it, you have all the time you need to enjoy yourself—unless, of course, the weather suddenly turns cold, robbing you of precious body heat. Perspiration will have soaked through much of your clothing by the time you reach the lake. Beware the debilitating effects of hypothermia. You'll need all of your remaining strength for the descent, which is even trickier in the first stages than the climb up. And even in dry weather the trail can be slippery.

Views across Whistler Valley from Powder Mountain and around to Rainbow Mountain, with Mounts Rethel and Parkhurst close by, make the descent a joy. The fury of Wedgemount Creek as it rockets out of the lake's western end and over a waterfall can be heard as you hike through groves of subalpine fir and Engelmann spruce. By the time you reach the parking lot, you'll be happy to dry off and head down to Whistler for some refreshment. Be sure to toast Harry Horstman's memory when you do.

PEMBERTON

21

WHISTLER TO PEMBERTON

Highway 99

. . . . .

> LOCATION: Highway 99 from Whistler to Pemberton

> ACTIVITIES: Camping, cycling, dog sledding, fishing, picnicking, swimming, viewpoints, walking, whitewater kayaking

> HIGHLIGHTS: Forest trails to quiet picnic spots along the Soo and Green rivers; a broad-shouldered cycling route

> ACCESS: Highway 99 as it runs for 20 km (12.4 mi) between Whistler's most northerly neighborhood, Emerald Estates, and One-Mile Lake at the southern end of Pemberton.

WHEN HIGHWAY 99 was finally pushed through from Squamish to Whistler in 1964, the citizens of Pemberton expected that it would soon link up with their town. After relying on the railroad for most of the century, the farmers in the secluded valley north of Whistler had lobbied for years for better access to the coast. Like most improvements between Pemberton and the outside world, however, the extension of Highway 99 north to Pemberton did not come as easily or as quickly as the town would have liked, though a gravel version did finally arrive in the mid-1970s. Since then, paving in the early 1980s has made this smooth-surfaced and well-banked 30-minute section of the highway, and its frequent passing lanes, an enjoyable drive.

There are many interesting features to the landscape along the way from Whistler to Pemberton. Some can be glimpsed from the road, while others require short excursions on foot or by bike. The Green River, for example, links the two towns as it flows north from Green Lake in Whistler into the Lillooet River near the Pemberton

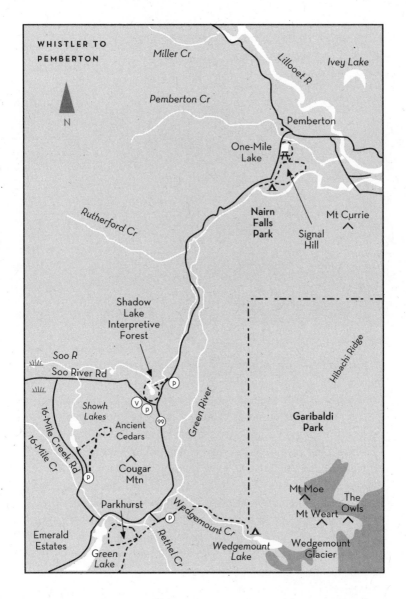

Miller Cr

Lillooet R

Ivey Lake

Pemberton Cr

N

Pemberton

One-Mile
Lake

Rutherford Cr

Nairn
Falls
Park

Mt Currie

Signal
Hill

Shadow
Lake
Interpretive
Forest

Hibachi Ridge

Soo R

Soo River Rd

P

Green River

Garibaldi
Park

V
P

16-Mile Creek Rd

Showh
Lakes

99

Ancient
Cedars

16-Mile Cr

Cougar
Mtn

Mt Moe

The
Owls

Mt Weart

P

Parkhurst

Wedgemount Cr

Emerald
Estates

Green
Lake

Rethel Cr

P

Wedgemount
Lake

Wedgemount
Glacier

airport. Two important tributaries, the Soo River and Rutherford
Creek, feed the Green along the way, and there is a stunningly
powerful waterfall, Nairn Falls, where the Green River squeezes
through the neck of the valley just before the outskirts of Pemberton.

Green Lake

For the best look at these roadside delights, make this journey by bicycle. The highway builders created wide shoulders with cyclists in mind. The only exception is the section of road close to Nairn Falls at the northern end of Whistler Valley, where riders must be extremely careful of traffic for a short distance.

The 40-km (25-mi) round trip takes about four hours, depending on your bike, your stamina, and whether you detour off-road. On the way north there is one mighty steep hill and several long, thrilling descents, making it the easier of the two legs. If you plan to ride the complete circuit, be sure to save enough energy for the extended hill climbs on the way south. In warm weather you will have plenty of company along the way; many Whistler workers who live in Pemberton commute by bike.

Weekends are a good time to attempt this ride, when there are fewer commercial vehicles on the road. The wash from logging trucks on the southbound side of the road in particular can be a concern, as they are fully loaded in this lane; you will rarely, if ever, see logs being trucked north.

As the Valley Trail leads north between Alpine Meadows and Emerald Estates, it parallels Highway 99, winding along the west shore of Green Lake. Where the trail crosses 19-Mile Creek, a paved side road leads to the Whistler secondary school. (A walking trail meanders alongside the creek towards the creek mouth on Green Lake, past some behemoth black cottonwood trees.) The trail and Highway 99 then swing away from Green Lake for a short distance beyond this point, in order to skirt the marshy delta where the creek enters the lake. They pass Whistler Fire Hall No. 2, the new Rainbow housing development, and the Whistler Municipal Heliport. Beyond here, the Valley Trail swings back beside Green Lake. There is a pullout here with two colorful interpretive signs, painted by Isobel MacLaurin, identifying wildlife often seen along the lakeshore as well as a profile of the peaks rising on the east side of the broad lake. This is an excellent spot for photographs. As much as you might want to get close to the lake, the banks drop off steeply. Be patient until you reach the entrance to Emerald Estates, a short distance north.

At Emerald Estates there are three points of public access to the lake, all good places to take a break from the highway. At the south end of Summer Lane is a small, rough approach, not visible from the highway. From here a narrow trail leads beside the lake to the north end of the lane, where there is a formal boat launch complete with dock and picnic area. My favorite of the three is Green Lake Park. Just before the boat launch, watch for Lakeshore Drive; follow it around a short distance to a pullout. A short, open trail leads to a small beach with picnic tables (two with barbecues) and washrooms. Good views open up to the south of Whistler Mountain. Canoes and kayaks stored here give mute testimony to this being the best place to launch on Green Lake. Unseen in the woods on the opposite shore is the ghost town of Parkhurst.

Spacious enough for floatplanes at its south end, Green Lake narrows at its north, where it empties into the Green River. From this point as you head north, particularly by bike, you get a very real sense of how the valley tilts gradually towards Pemberton, encouraging the flow of the Green River north in that direction.

> GREEN RIVER CROSSING

North of Emerald Estates all traffic now follows Highway 99 as it leads beside Green Lake for a short distance and passes the turn-off to Cougar Mountain (on the highway's west side; see chapter 19). Down through the trees you catch glimpses of the Green River, which from this point on will be a frequent companion, accessible at a variety of locations. The highway crosses over 16-Mile Creek, which runs under the road through a culvert just before it joins the river. (The turnoff to the Wedgemount Lake trailhead on the east side of the Green River is several bends in the highway past here; see chapter 20.) At this point you are 17 km (10.5 mi) north of Whistler Village.

As the highway climbs north from here, it passes the large wooden sign for southbound traffic that heralds the Resort Municipality of Whistler. If you're exploring by bike, settle into your ride and carry on up a gentle incline. The grade of the land carries the river to the east side of the valley while Highway 99 stays to the west. The river falls away from view now and won't rejoin the highway for 10 km (6.2 mi).

The forest on each side of the highway has been logged all along this stretch. And although new growth has begun, it provides little shelter from rainstorms or the broiling sun. The road climbs moderately then begins a long, gradual descent to the Green River railway crossing. If you follow the tracks west, you will soon come to a railway bridge over the Soo River with a good view of the canyon that isn't visible from the highway—well worth the quick detour. There is plenty of clearance on each side of the tracks, so there is no need to be overly apprehensive about approaching trains.

Just before the crossing, watch for the Soo River Forest Service Road leading off to the west to eventually meet the 16-Mile Creek Road, forming a rough loop around Cougar Mountain (see chapter 19).

> SHADOW LAKE INTERPRETIVE FOREST

Access: West off Highway 99 on the Soo River Forest Service Road

A short distance along this well-maintained road, watch for a pullout where a sheltered wooden lookout perches above diminutive

Shadow Lake, which lies nestled below beside the Soo River. A series of loop trails runs through the forest and to the viewpoint, making this a well-warranted detour off Highway 99. Segments of these trails go back a century or more. Trappers and traders, both European and First Nations, passed through here on their way to and from Pemberton and the coast. Little remains of the logging operation that flourished at Shadow Lake in the early 1900s.

Unlike the hard-packed trails beside the Cheakamus River in the Whistler Interpretive Forest (see chapter 10), these ones are softened by a thick covering of leaves and evergreen needles. They don't run for nearly the distance of those in the Brohm Lake or Whistler interpretive forests, but the route around Shadow Lake offers other rewards. For one thing, the views of surrounding peaks, including Wedge Mountain and the sunbaked bluffs above the Soo River, are superior. Lush displays of wildflowers, such as Pacific bleeding heart and trailing yellow violet, carpet the forest floor in a wetland zone between the lake and the river. Follow the section of trail that leads through a stand of old-growth fir and cedar onto a sandbank where tall black cottonwood trees tower above the Soo. This is a sunny spot to enjoy a picnic.

In winter, it's worth driving to the "3 km" mark farther west to the Soo Valley Wildlife Reserve, home to Whistler Dog Sledding Adventures. Although full tours must be booked in advance through Cougar Mountain Adventures (www.cougarmountain.ca), visitors are welcome to drop by to watch the dogs in action and perhaps cross-country ski the trails.

On first encountering sled dogs, the biggest surprise—aside from their rather diminutive size and thin coats—is how instantly friendly they are. Unlike the stereotypical image of brawny sled dogs, Alaskan racing huskies are more similar to sleek Australian blue healers than to St. Bernards. In fact, they are a cross between huskies and greyhounds. Dog sledding is full of surprises. Before you even set out on the trail, one of the most rewarding experiences is helping a well-mannered team of six dogs into their harnesses. As eager as they are to run, these mutts display a remarkable degree of patience as you leash them together. And when it comes time to turn them loose, you can either snuggle into the coziness of the sled bag or stand astride the runners and, with help from your guide, drive the sled yourself.

One of the great life lessons from an hour or two of dog sledding is that there is a freedom out on the trail that you just won't find at home. And it's a far more environmentally friendly activity than snowmobiling. Not surprisingly, more Whistler visitors now go to the dogs, so to speak, than to snowmobiles.

> ## SOO RIVER TO RUTHERFORD CREEK

Back on Highway 99, just past the Green River railway crossing, a gravel road leads off to the west past a weigh station to two quarries. It is actively used by large trucks during the week, but on weekends you can ride through the first quarry that you come to on a road that runs down and across the Green River. There isn't much of interest on the river here, but as the road is not steep you may wish to ride down for a look, anyway.

As you continue north, the highway descends through a series of bends in the road, with the Soo River canyon below to the west. This is one of the most enjoyable sections to bike. You will be sailing along by the time the highway levels out. If you plan to cycle round trip, try not to dwell on the thought that on the return journey it will be all uphill.

The Soo River now runs beside the highway for a short way before it joins the Green River, with a pullout beside the highway on the bank of the Soo just before the bridge. This is a popular fishing spot; there are also several rough campsites in the forest beside the river. A short distance farther north, on each side of the Soo River Bridge, are signs of the old highway. The bridge is 6 km (3.7 mi) north of the Green River railway crossing. Just after you cross the bridge, watch for a small road leading down to the river on the east side of the highway. This is another good place to fish.

It's about 2 km (1.2 mi) between the Soo River and Rutherford Creek bridges. Along the way, a series of small side roads leads off to the east. Most of these are BC Hydro service roads. A local Boy Scout troop has planted sections of the hydro right-of-way with Christmas trees. As well, there is a motocross trials area here for dirt bikes.

If you're on a bike, this may be a good place to turn around and head 15 km (9 mi) back to Whistler, for the most challenging part of this section of Highway 99 begins just north of here.

> **NAIRN FALLS TO PEMBERTON**

The highway north of Rutherford Creek is level for 2 km (1.2 mi), with the Green River once more on its eastern side. There are some good picnic spots beside the river; if you're cycling north, this may be a good place to rest before you tackle the steepest climb on the trip. Highway 99 runs underneath a BC Rail overpass, then climbs steadily through a series of tight switchbacks for almost 3 km (2 mi). This is a very difficult passage, especially because the highway shoulder is extremely narrow in places. The Green River cuts through an unseen canyon below the road just before it plunges over Nairn Falls. Once you've reached the crest of the hill, it's a gentle glide to the entrance of Nairn Falls Provincial Park (see chapter 22).

From Nairn Falls, Highway 99 continues its downhill run for another 1.6 km (1 mi) to One-Mile Lake. The water in this small lake is warm. A boardwalk around the shoreline allows wheelchair and buggy access. A trail links the lake with nearby Nairn Falls Park.

> BEST GHOST TOWN

THE GHOST town of Parkhurst lies hidden above Green Lake's northeastern shore—an easy paddle from Green Lake Park or a side trip when cycling the intermediate-rated Green Lake Loop trail. Parkhurst prospered in the 1930s and '40s, shipping more wood than any other mill town in the Whistler Valley. And exploring what remains of the settlement is one of the most interesting ways to discover traces of Whistler's past. The remains of the mill workers' ramshackle residences are located on a ridge above the lake and the railway tracks. Several abandoned cars and trucks of assorted vintages are permanently parked, some buried to their axles. Old stove pieces litter the ground. Privies and bunkhouses have been flattened after years of neglect and the weight of winter snow. Yet the wood in some of the buildings is surprisingly fresh where it has recently been exposed.

Having made your way through the narrow canyon at the north end of the Whistler Valley, it's a release to see the Pemberton Valley open up before you. There's a special feeling to this landscape, with its cleared fields and wide views of the surrounding mountains. And from here a choice of directions for further exploration present themselves where Highway 99 intersects with the Pemberton Valley Road. If you're feeling a bit saddle-sore, there are a number of watering holes and coffee bars a short distance west of the Petro-Canada gas station on Portage Road.

Quench your thirst before you make the return trip or head off around the valley for more adventures. If you've had enough cycling for one day, you can always ride the bus back. For schedule information, visit www.busonline.ca/regions/whi/schedules/schedule. cfm?line=99&

Once you've had a chance to bike the road between Whistler and Pemberton, it won't seem as long or as steep ever again. You'll also have acquired a more intimate knowledge of this stretch of the Sea to Sky corridor and its many off-road sights; you'll want to search for them again on future trips.

> **THE INSIDE TRACK**

> *Dog Sledding:* To book a tour with Whistler Dog Sledding Adventures, contact Cougar Mountain Adventures (www.cougarmountain. ca), Blackcomb Snowmobile (blackcombsnowmobile.com), or Callaghan Backcountry Ski Lodge (callaghancountry.com). Although full tours must be pre-booked, visitors are welcome to drop by Whistler Dog Sledding Adventures' base in Soo Valley to watch the dogs in action and perhaps cross-country ski the trails. To reach the Soo Valley, journey 20-minutes north of Whistler by car on Highway 99 to the well-marked Soo River Forest Service Road which leads 3 km (1.9 mi) west to the dog sled staging area.

22

NAIRN FALLS
PROVINCIAL PARK

. . . . .

> **LOCATION:** 92 km (57 mi) north of Squamish, 32 km (19.8 mi) north of Whistler, 3 km (1.9 mi) south of Pemberton

> **ACTIVITIES:** Birdwatching, camping, cycling, fishing, hiking, picnicking, swimming, viewpoints, walking

> **HIGHLIGHTS:** Blockbuster waterfall, cool green canyon, tranquil campground, neck-craning mountain views

> **ACCESS:** From the well-marked exit on the east side of Highway 99

As the Green River nears Pemberton, it increases considerably in volume, picking up water from the Soo River and Rutherford Creek and a host of smaller streams. Suddenly its broad shape is transformed into a thundering column of white water that drops 60 m (200 ft) at Nairn Falls. Almost as quickly as the drama began, the river then resumes its former character and courses on towards Lillooet Lake.

The neck of the Whistler Valley, where this transformation occurs, is also the route through which the railway, Highway 99 and a string of BC Hydro towers squeeze themselves. I always find this a powerful place to visit. A mist rises to the treetops, the ground shakes, the bald rock face on which you stand seems linked directly to the earth's core, and the forested slopes of Mount Currie rise steeply from the canyon floor. From down here you can't see the peaks of its broad comb, but several come into view as you walk the trail to the falls within the boundaries of this welcoming provincial park. (See page 175 for a map of this area; visit www.env.gov.bc.ca/bcparks for current conditions.)

One-Mile Lake

> NAIRN FALLS

Long regarded as a place of spiritual significance by the local Lil'wat (pronounced "leet'wat") people, the current approach to the falls follows sections of a much older route to Mount Currie and attracts day-trippers to the park year-round. The trail is only 1.8 km (1.1 mi) long, a comfortable 20- to 30-minute walk that begins at the visitor parking lot just inside the park gates. At first you pass along a ridge, high above the green waters of the river. (Do not attempt this when conditions are icy.) Parents with young children should walk cautiously on this narrow path. The embankment drops away sharply as the trail cuts through original forest and climbs the hillside above the river. You'll feel the ground trembling and hear the roar of the water before the falls come into view. Don't worry about the safety of young children here, as viewpoints are fenced for added security. An interpretive sign explains the falls' interesting geological evolution.

Advance precautions will only increase your appreciation for what's to come. Although Nairn Falls is almost as high as Brandywine Falls (see chapter 8), the feeling here is quite different. Whereas the waters of Brandywine plummet straight down to a

Nairn Falls

Meager Creek Hot Springs

Birkenhead Lake

Pacific dogwood, floral emblem of British Columbia

Stein Valley Nlaka'pamux Heritage Park

Wedgemount Lake

Anderson Lake, D'Arcy

Joffre Lake

Seton Ridge

South Chilcotin Mountains

Sky Pilots, Spruce
Lake Protected Area

Stein Valley Nlaka'pamux Heritage Park

Fairyslipper orchids

Barkley Valley Trail

Fountain Valley Road

Cinnamon-coloured black bear

catch-pool and then run off into Daisy Lake, here the Green River boils over the falls, swirls around boulders, then rushes past before dropping again with a roar to join the Lillooet River. When the river's action is heightened by an above-average runoff, pieces of driftwood shoot from the top of the falls as if from a cannon.

> NAIRN FALLS CAMPGROUND &

Aside from the drama of the falls, the park also provides a good spot for picnicking and overnight camping. A park map, several tables, and benches with a view of the Green River are located beside the visitor parking lot at the start of the falls trail. Nearby sit eighty-eight well-spaced campsites, seven of them designed as doubles for visitors who are traveling in a group. (To locate the doubles, check the park map.) The campground is open from late May to October; at other times of the year no-fee camping is possible if you are prepared to walk in from the gated entrance.

BEST MOOSE SPOTTING

The meadow on the south side of Signal Hill, near One-Mile Lake, is prime moose-grazing territory in spring.

When you first enter the park you have a choice of directions. If you bear right past the day-use area you will be on Green River Road, where all of the sites on the right-hand side have views of the river. The sound of the current creates a cocoon of privacy around each one. Surrounded by tall Douglas firs, these popular spots fill quickly. Each site comes with a log table and a fire pit fitted with a cooking grill. Dry firewood is available for purchase from the park facility operator. A tall blue water pump stands across from site 31 at the intersection of Maple and Green River roads. From May to September there is a charge for overnight visitors ($15 at present). You may reserve a campsite in advance through Discover Camping (toll-free 1-800-689-9025 or 604-689-9025 in Metro Vancouver; www.discovercamping.ca).

A short trail runs down to Coudre Point, where the river widens. This is a good place for fishing, for exploring the river on foot in daytime, and for stargazing at night. The trail begins near the intersection of Green River Road and Dogwood Lane. Look for it between sites 14 and 46.

A much longer trail begins next to site 92 at the intersection of

Green River Road and Fir Lane. Known as the *Moose Trail*, it runs 3 km (1.9 mi) north from the park to One-Mile Lake.

> ## ONE-MILE LAKE &

Access: 1.6 km (1 mi) north of Nairn Falls. Road access is from Highway 99, which runs along the western side of the lake.

The municipality of Pemberton maintains a small day-use park beside One-Mile Lake. There are picnic tables beside a large stone fireplace and an outhouse set back in the woods. A small beach with a floating dock invites visitors to take a plunge in the warm waters. In a region where the glacier-fed creeks are too cold for comfort, One-Mile Lake is an exception. From the dock you look north over the broad Pemberton Valley to the tops of the Cayoosh Range. Young children will certainly enjoy a stop here, as there are more activities for them than at nearby Nairn Falls.

A gentle trail circles most of the lake, with a boardwalk across the marshy north end where a small stream drains north into nearby Pemberton Creek. Another dock is located halfway along the lake's eastern side. Beside it is a small rock bench, a good place to rest with a pair of binoculars; there's plenty of waterfowl activity on the lake during spring and fall migration. By midsummer, much of the lake is covered with lily pads. And when you approach Pemberton, just past the lake, look up to the ridge on the west—the white blur you see is a waterfall on One-Mile Creek.

> ## BEST OUTDOOR SPA

EVER WONDER why standing beside a waterfall is so soothing? Studies show that the negative ions generated by waterfalls have a positive effect on the human body—the more negative ions there are in the atmosphere, the better we feel. Bonus: Analyses of air samples have shown that "wild" air (the air we breathe in the wilderness) contains thousands of times the number of negative ions recorded on city streets.

23

PEMBERTON AND AREA

· · · · ·

> LOCATION: 153 km (95 mi) north of Vancouver, 95 km (59 mi) north of Squamish, 35 km (22 mi) north of Whistler, 106 km (66 mi) south of Lillooet

> ACTIVITIES: Cycling, historic site, horseback riding, mountain biking, picnicking, viewpoints, walking

> HIGHLIGHTS: Tranquil rural scenery with a pioneer past

DESPITE THE recent developments along Highway 99 at Pemberton's southern entrance, to my mind this is still a quintessential small Canadian town. Turn left at the Petro-Canada on Portage Road and drive slowly as Pemberton unfolds before you. Mountain bikers gather at the Pony Espresso, often while their battered bikes are being mended down the road at the Pemberton Bike Company, tucked in behind the Outpost Restaurant. Pemberton's main street begins just north of the train tracks where Portage merges with Birch Street for two blocks. Welcome to the heart of town. Finding your way around is not difficult. If you decide to leave your vehicle and explore on foot or by bike, a good place to park is in the large lot beside the BC Rail tracks.

> **PEMBERTON VALLEY ROAD**

Pemberton and environs are ideal for day-tripping cyclists. Most of the roads are paved and level, and though the shoulders on these country roads are not broad, traffic doesn't pass by with the same intensity as on Highway 99. You can relax as you pedal around, checking out the old homesteads and exploring the back roads. There are also several stables in the area from which you can tour the valley on horseback.

To get more of a feel for "Spud Valley," I suggest heading north-west along Pemberton Valley Road, which links downtown with Pemberton Meadows. This road runs up the valley for 46 km (28.5 mi). To find it, follow Prospect Street for a short distance north from the heart of town to the intersection with Camus Street. Look for a small clearing with a picnic table beside the Pemberton Pioneer Museum. This is a good spot to stop and reorganize, check a map, and enjoy the view of massive Mount Currie. Just around the corner, Prospect Street turns into Pemberton Valley Road.

Pemberton Valley Road winds its way gently past cleared acreage. The names on many of the mailboxes you pass—Ronayne, Hartzell, Ryan, Miller, Garling—are those of settlers who arrived generations ago. Many of these family names grace mountains and waterways throughout the valley. One example is Miller Creek, 5 km (3 mi) north of Pemberton. A bridge crosses the creek here and another crosses the Ryan River where it joins the broad Lillooet River, 2.5 km (1.5 mi) north of Miller Creek.

You have now entered the heart of the valley. North of Ryan River, for the next 18 km (11 mi) you pass through the Pemberton Meadows. Mount Ronayne rises above on your right; imposing Mount Samson is straight ahead to the northwest. The meadows stretch north to where the valley narrows and farm cultivation ends.

Pemberton Valley visitors in search of potatoes will find Yukon Gold, Magenta Red, Kennebec, and Norchip (a variety recently developed for french fries that has also found a wider audience) on sale at Jordan and Trish Sturdy's North Arm Farm (1888 Sea to Sky Highway; 604-894-5379; www.northarmfarms.com). Mind the geese that guard the farm's entrance, located on the south side of the highway between Pemberton and Mount Currie. Potato lovers should also note that both white and red varieties, as well as a cornucopia of fresh produce, are advertised for sale at some farms, such as Goat Mountain Farm in Pemberton Meadows for as little as $20. The Yukon Gold potatoes are so flavorful they taste like they've been grown in butter.

Spring is an the ideal time to explore both the upper Pemberton Valley and the shores of the Lillooet River, when wide, gray sandbars lie exposed. Water in the river reflects the pale olive and yellow hues of the tall alder and cottonwood trees that are just beginning to come into leaf. In the river's oxbows, tree trunks washed down during flood season lie jackstrawed together. Paw prints in the soft sand betray the presence of wildlife that otherwise remain entirely unseen. Black-tailed deer, which occasionally stray out to feed in fields where winter crops were sowed, are the exceptions.

It's easy to make your way out onto the sandbars, particularly in the upper stretches of the valley where the Pemberton Valley Road and Lillooet River run side by side. You can park beside the river and walk out on the wide sandy expanses, or walk or cycle along one of the dike trails leading to the river. Both approaches are possible from Pemberton Valley Road's intersection with Lillooet River Road, about 26 km (16.1 mi) northwest of Pemberton. As you approach this junction, watch for two wooden gates shaped like hitching rails opposite Shaw Creek Farms. Leave your vehicle here and follow the dike trail that meanders through the forest beyond the gates to the river.

> ## PEMBERTON FESTIVALS

THE BEST way to get the feel—and taste—of a small town is to enjoy one of the local festivals. Pemberton hosts many such fairs in its community centers on Cottonwood Street and Pemberton Meadows Road. Home-baked pies and rhubarb coffee cakes, which taste as if they've come fresh from the oven of a wood-burning stove, vie for attention with the region's local artisans, who display an impressive range of work.

On Canada Day (July 1), marching bands gather in the center of town, vintage automobiles and horse-drawn carriages roll side by side, bicycles and ponies bedecked with ribbons carry excited youngsters, and sports teams stand resplendent in fresh uniforms. The new Cottonwood community center is located on the north side of Portage Road at the entrance to town. To find the Meadows community center, follow Portage Road in downtown Pemberton to its intersection with Prospect Street. Follow Prospect to Pemberton Meadows Road.

Lillooet River and Mount Currie

Where Lillooet River Road turns east and heads towards the river and beyond into the Lillooet headwaters (see chapter 25), Pemberton Valley Road continues north of this junction and becomes much less traveled as its paved surface gives way to gravel for another 20 km (12.4 mi). Once the snow has cleared and the fields dried out by late May, dust rises not only from the road but also from nearby fields, as farmers ready their land for planting.

This section of the valley is so dominated by mountains that it lies in shadow from December to March. Small wonder that it is rarely visited except by residents and wildlife. I like to head this way in April to experience the giddy sense of release when the sun reacquaints itself with those who live at the foot of Mount Morrison, one of the numerous peaks flanking the massive Pemberton Icefield. Like a tabletop when viewed from floor level, the glacial pan lies unseen to the south. Still, its frozen presence noticeably influences the air temperature when spring breezes waft through the valley below.

The easiest access to the Lillooet River occurs where a sign announces the end of the public road. This is also where you'll be rewarded with the best views of far-off craggy peaks, such as Mount Meager, that rise above the Lillooet River headwaters. Although the massive snowfields on the horizon hint at the presence of a large peak as you travel north through the valley, only here is the mountain's true expanse fully revealed. Its misshapen summits are a reminder of the volcanic activity that rocked this region two millennia ago, when Mount Meager blew its stack.

Before the spring snowmelt begins in earnest, the Lillooet River is uncharacteristically clear. More often its waters are clouded with silt brought down by tributaries draining the Pemberton Icefield and from the river's source in the Lillooet Glacier.

There's a remote, mysterious grandeur to this landscape, suggestive of a mountain kingdom in Tolkien's Middle Earth. An unbroken stand of alder and cottonwood curtains the valley's isolated northwestern enclave. The sense of seclusion is further heightened by an owl's forlorn hoot carrying from the far shore. Pemberton may be experiencing a growth spurt that has spilled over from the overheated Whistler housing market, but you'd never know it here, on the shadowy side of the valley.

> **THE INSIDE TRACK**

> *Cycling:* The Bike Co (1392 Portage Road; 604-894-6625; www.bikecowhistler.com) for all things bike related

> *Fishing:* Spud Valley Sporting Goods (1380 Birch Street; 604-894-6630; www.spudvalley.com) for all things outdoors related, including fishing licenses

> *Trail Rides:* The Adventure Ranch (604-894-5200; www.adventureranch.net); Adventures on Horseback (604-894-6269; www.adventuresonhorseback.ca); Pemberton Stables (604-894-66150; www.pembertonstables.ca); Punch Creek Trail Rides (604-894-6086)

24

PEMBERTON BIKE ROUTES

. . . . .

> **LOCATION:** 153 km (95 mi) north of Vancouver; 95 km (59 mi) north of Squamish, 37 km (23 mi) north of Whistler, 107 km (66 mi) southwest of Lillooet

> **HIGHLIGHTS:** Hot trails, cool lakes, an epic route that honors a legendary Sea to Sky mountain bike pioneer

> **PEMBERTON VILLAGE TRAILS**

Access: Portage Road leads west from Highway 99 into the heart of Pemberton. Turn right on Collins Road to reach the BC Rail Bridge in two blocks.

Ability Level: Novice to intermediate

The logical place for out-of-towners to begin an off-road ramble around Pemberton and the nearby First Nations community of Mount Currie is on the intricate network of double- and single-track trails on the east side of the Lillooet River, opposite the village center. A BC Rail bridge two blocks from the center of town on Collins Road spans the Lillooet. The bridge features a pedestrian walkway that can also be used by cyclists.

After pausing on the railway bridge to admire Mount Currie's brawny profile, which dominates the local skyline to the south, pilot your bike along one of the sweetest trails in the region—*Riverside Park Trail.* The trail makes a quick descent from the train tracks and leads east beside the Lillooet, where the forested slopes on the east side of the river stand in marked contrast to the open western shore. In spring, skunk cabbage and mahonia (Oregon grape) are as thick and golden on the forest floor as the dandelions are in the pastures. Designed to keep a bike's speed in check without the need for much braking, the well-traveled trail snakes through the woods with just enough rises and falls, twists and turns.

Head south along an old road that circles a nearby pond, which on a fine day holds a perfect reflection of Mount Currie's avalanche chutes. You'll soon link up with *MacKenzie Cruise*, the first of three main trails that lead north from the BC Rail tracks. *Indy 500* and *Blood, Sweat & Fear* offer more raw and technical riding than MacKenzie Cruise, which coils through tall stands of western red cedar and monumental black cottonwood. Although the Lillooet can be heard gurgling along nearby, it is mostly cloaked from view by low-hanging boughs as you zigzag back to the rail bridge. Riverside Park Trail will leave you puffing and panting for more. This is the kind of fun for which mountain bikes were designed.

> LILLOOET RIVER DIKE TRAILS

Access: From various points along Pemberton Valley Road, which leads northwest
Ability Level: Novice

Until a series of dikes was built along the Lillooet River in the 1950s, floods were a fact of life in Pemberton. Today, sections of these dikes double as recreation trails for horse riders, walkers, and cyclists. Where gates restrict access when the dikes cross farmers' fields, pathways divert explorers onto riverside trails that circumvent the pastures. (To judge from the size of the sturdy Charolais cattle in one field, these detours are well warranted.) These riverside trails are composed of the soft, silty sediment that washes down off the massive Pemberton Icefield, looming unseen above the town to the northwest.

One particularly good section of the dike system that lends itself to exploration by bike occurs near Pemberton Valley Road's intersection with Lillooet River Road, about 26 km (16 mi) northwest of Pemberton. As you approach this junction, watch for two wooden gates shaped like hitching rails opposite Shaw Creek Farms. Leave your vehicle here and follow the dike trail that leads through the forest beyond the gates to the river.

> MOSQUITO LAKE TRAILS

Access: The easiest access to these trails is from Highway 99 between Pemberton and Mount Currie, just east of the Lillooet River Bridge. The River Trail begins beside the bridge. To reach the majority of the trails, turn north off Highway 99 at the first road east of the bridge, beside an impressively landscaped log home. Follow Ivey Lake Road as it crosses the BC Rail tracks and climbs the knoll. As you ascend, there are often other mountain bikers to quiz about routes. An alternative approach to Mosquito Lake is via the gravel access road that branches west from Portage Road just north of Mount Currie, a 2-km (1.2-mi) ride to Mosquito Lake Regional Park (See map, page 209.). A paved route is Reid Road, which leads west from Portage Road near Owl Creek and eventually meets Ivey Lake Road at the top of the knoll. At this intersection, turn left (north) on Linda Road and watch for a trail kiosk on your right. Turn here on a secondary road that climbs for 1 km (0.6 mi) to a parking lot beside diminutive Mosquito Lake. Vehicle traffic is blocked beyond here. This makes an old logging road that rounds one shore and a lakeside trail that rounds the other the sole preserve of cyclists and hikers—as well as the occasional bear.

Ability Level: Intermediate to expert

Mountain biking in Pemberton is centered on Mosquito Lake. Together with Ivey Lake, it lies tucked behind a knoll on the north side of the valley between Pemberton and the town of Mount Currie. To the south, the namesake mountain dominates the landscape. And from the knoll, views of its expansive north face are sublime. Equally absorbing are the clouds of mosquitoes for which the valley is notorious, particularly from late May to August.

A dozen or more trails crisscross each other adjacent to Mosquito Lake, principal among them the *Lake Trail,* the ominously named *Meat Grinder* and one of the most pleasant combos in the region, *Wolfe's House Trail* and *Jim Jam,* which intertwine on the north side of the knoll. Views are limited on the densely forested slopes, but that's a good thing as you won't want to be distracted, except by berry bushes as you may have to push your bike over some of the more challenging sections.

These trails either go up or down and provide a technical challenge not unlike navigating moguls in winter on skis or a snowboard. The trails aren't built for cruising. Disk brakes and full-suspension systems provide immeasurable benefits when tackling some of the trails' more creative challenges. A maze of narrow log rides and trestle stunts with 5-m (16-ft) drops augment the single-track. Trail

Mosquito Lake Park

building is still proceeding at a steady pace, and you will often find members of the Pemberton Off-Road Cycling Association and Pemberton Valley Trail Association at work on more creations.

A pause at one of the three docks anchored at Mosquito Lake's shoreline is a must. By June, the water is warm enough to tempt riders to hop in. A black bear may also make an appearance on one of the downed logs that juts out from the forest while a vividly colored western tanager alights on a nearby branch, its wing feathers the same shade of florescent yellow-green as the lichen on the forest floor. The longer and more quietly you sit, the more likely this tableau—including a passing family of loons—will unfold before you, and a reward for all that you missed while concentrating on micromanaging your ride.

> **SIGNAL HILL TRAILS**
Access: On the east side of Highway 99 at One-Mile Lake
Ability Level: Intermediate to expert

The granite knob of Signal Hill thrusts up from the base of Mount Currie, on the southern outskirts of Pemberton. Mountain bike trails loop around Signal Hill and along the way connect with nearby Nairn Falls Park (see chapter 23), where two trails—Moose and Tower of Power—converge. The easier of the two is *Moose Trail,* which runs for 3 km (1.9 mi) between the park's campsite 92 and One-Mile Lake, then twists through the forest on the west side of Signal Hill. (The trail takes its name from the moose that occasionally graze in a meadow on the south side of Signal Hill in spring.) There are some particularly large trees near the lake where you can practice the art of cutting your handlebars quickly back and forth as you snake past their trunks.

Once you've gotten your confidence up on Moose Trail, try its expert-rated companion, *Tower of Power,* which leads to the right from the intersection of Green River Road and Fir Lane in the park, then connects with *K2* as it crosses Signal Hill's summit and *Lumpy's Epic,* which loops around both the west and east sides of Signal Hill. This trail is named for Geoff "Lumpy" Leidel. In the 1980s, Leidel was one of the original core group of Vancouver's North Shore riders, and among the first Canadians to ride professionally in the fledgling World Cup mountain bike races. A resident of Whistler, then Pemberton, he died in an avalanche while backcountry skiing in 1998. The single-track Lumpy's Epic is one of the most challenging mountain bike trails in Pemberton and does justice to his memory. Simply hiking, let alone riding, this trail is inspirational.

> **THE INSIDE TRACK**
> *Cycling:* For local cycling tips, maps, and service, visit The Bike Co (1392 Portage Road; 604-894-6625; www.bikecowhistler.com). The staff will helpfully sketch in trails so new that they haven't yet shown up on any maps. They'll also offer advice on travel times and the level of skill needed on various routes, before pointing the way to the nearest trailhead. The shop is an integral part of the village's cycling community as well as sponsor of the annual Tour de Soo cross-country mountain bike race between Whistler and Pemberton. A good map to consult is the *Pemberton Valley Recreational Trail Map.*

> # 25

LILLOOET HEADWATERS

. . . . .

> LOCATION: 179 km (111 mi) north of Vancouver, 121 km (75 mi)
north of Squamish, 26 km (16 mi) northwest of Pemberton, 62 km
(38.5 mi) north of Whistler

> ACTIVITIES: Bathing, camping, cross-country skiing, driving,
hiking, mountain biking, snow trekking, viewpoints

> HIGHLIGHTS: Wildlife and wilderness hot springs in the shadow
of Canada's most recently active volcano

> ACCESS: Follow the paved Pemberton Valley Road north for
26 km (16.1 mi) to its intersection with the Lillooet River Forest Service Road. Turn right and cross the Lillooet River Forestry Bridge.
The graveled Lillooet River Forest Road runs north for 50 km
(31 mi) and ends just past Salal Creek at the southern boundary of
Upper Lillooet Headwaters Park. Watch for the sign on Pemberton
Valley Road that indicates where to turn for both the Lillooet River
and Hurley River Forest Service Roads. There are several signs at
this intersection, including one of which reads "Lillooet 96 km
(60 mi)" and another indicating Meager Creek Hot Springs. The
bridge to both roads is 1.5 km (0.9 mi) north from here. Note:
The Hurley River Road is a summer route north to the upper
Fraser Canyon.

EVERY TIME I visit the Lillooet headwaters I'm reminded of the days before the region's dike system straightened out the Pemberton Valley section of the Lillooet River. For in the headwaters north of Pemberton Meadows, the river braids itself across the narrow valley floor and, at full flow, leaves very little ground uncovered on either side. As the seasons change and levels in the river drop, wide sandbars are revealed, making it possible to walk well out towards the middle of the river in many places.

Until 1975 only one road, which ran along the valley's south side to the foot of Spidery Peak, provided access to the headwaters. Then, when BC Hydro decided to explore the geothermal potential of the Fall Creek volcanic center, which includes the region around Mount Meager, the Lillooet River and Meager Creek roads were constructed. Maintaining these roads has proved to be no small feat as rivers, creeks, and rockslides repeatedly wash out vulnerable sections. Still, the road reopens after every deluge and commercial activity resumes.

From a recreational standpoint, the Lillooet headwaters offer visitors the chance to see magnificent icefields, visit the site of the most recently active volcano in southwestern B.C., soak in a wilderness hot spring, and view wildlife such as moose, wolf, bear, and deer. Summer is a popular time to travel through the headwaters by car or bike; in winter months, cross-country skiers, snow trekkers, and an army of snowmobilers have the region to themselves.

> ### LILLOOET RIVER ROAD
Access: 26 km (16.1 mi) north off Pemberton Valley Road

The Lillooet River Road is hard-packed dirt and gravel—a surprisingly easy surface to cycle, with signs that count off the distance traveled from the bridge in kilometers. A short distance past the bridge beside the Lillooet River, you pass a small group of buildings belonging to the Coast Mountain Outdoor School. The modern facility, Fougberg House, is named in honor of Margaret and Slim Fougberg, a pioneer couple who homesteaded in the Pemberton region. Set back across the road from the school is Heritage Village, where in summer, Girl Guides and other groups use the sturdy log cabins as a base for their jamborees. The centerpiece is an old school with oversized windows to provide as much natural light as possible for learning on overcast days. On the walls inside are several large maps dating from the Dominion of Canada's early days.

The road is wide enough to accommodate large trucks, and you should be prepared to meet one coming south around one of the many bends. The quiet time for logging traffic on the Lillooet River Road is generally 6 PM to 6 AM on weekdays and Friday evening to Monday morning. (Careful, however, for some crews work

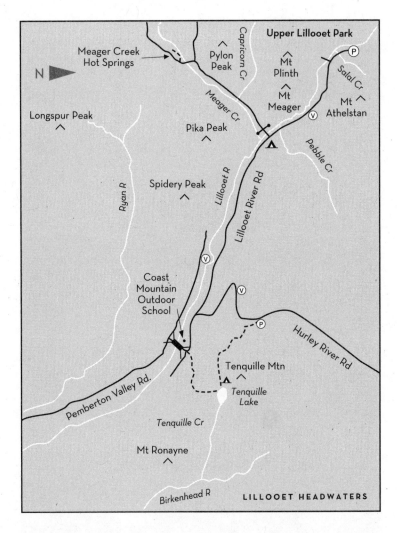

N

Meager Creek Hot Springs

Pylon Peak

Capricorn Cr

Mt Plinth

Mt Meager

P

Salal Cr

Mt Athelstan

Longspur Peak

Pika Peak

Pebble Cr

Ryan R

Spidery Peak

Lillooet R

Lillooet River Rd

Coast Mountain Outdoor School

Hurley River Rd

P

Tenquille Mtn

Tenquille Lake

Pemberton Valley Rd.

Tenquille Cr

Mt Ronayne

Birkenhead R

LILLOOET HEADWATERS

weekends, too, and around the clock.) Also keep an eye out for deer, which wander out of the forest to walk the road.

In the early days of this century, trappers and surveyors both explored the upper Lillooet River. One sign of their presence occurs where the road crosses Railroad Creek. This name seems strangely out of place, since the BC Rail tracks are back in Pemberton. But before that rail route was finally decided, surveyors considered

Upper Lillooet Park

running the line up the Pemberton Valley to this point, then up through Railroad Pass to Lillooet. Once you've driven this way you'll understand why they chose instead to route it through the gentler grade of the Pemberton (Birken) Pass.

> ## HURLEY RIVER (BRALORNE/GOLD BRIDGE) ROAD

Access: 7.5 km (4.6 mi) north of the Lillooet River Bridge on Lillooet River Road

The Hurley River Forest Service Road is an alternative summer route to the recreation options west of Lillooet—centered in the former mining villages of Bralorne and Gold Bridge. Like many similar roads in the region, it was built to carry logging equipment, but the views in the first 10 km (6.2 mi) are worth the side trip off Lillooet River Road. Near the top of Railroad Pass you will also find the trailhead to Tenquille Lake.

The Hurley Road forks to the right of the Lillooet River Road and immediately climbs uphill, marked off in kilometers. The best views of the valley below occur between "km 6" and "km 7." You look west towards the mountains that hold the Pemberton Icefield, and the fields of the most northerly farms in the Pemberton Valley are clearly visible below. If you position yourself here near sunset on a summer's day, when water levels in the Lillooet River are low, you'll see the sandbars shade to gold as the last rays of sun stream down. The river can be seen winding north to the Meager Creek valley before tucking into the folds of its headwaters.

Since the establishment of the Spruce Lake Protected Area in 2004, with its superb hiking and mountain biking terrain, Hurley Road is seeing an increased amount of traffic. I still find this road too rough for my liking and recommend the alternate route via Lillooet instead (see chapter 31).

> ## UPPER LILLOOET RIVER

North past the Hurley Road junction, the Upper Lillooet River Road allows travelers only an occasional glimpse of the river itself. For obvious reasons, builders tried to keep the road high and away from the river to avoid washouts. To see the river, the best places to turn off are around the section of the road between the "km 20/21" and "km 23/24" markers. Watch for side roads that lead towards the river, which is always gray-green and cold, fed by snow and glacier melt. As the summer progresses, sandbars are revealed and side channels dry up, and it's possible to walk out onto the river. This affords panoramic views of the mountains on each side of the valley, from Mount Currie at the southern end to Mount Meager to the north.

An important intersection on the Lillooet River Road occurs at "km 36," site of the Upper Lillooet campground—twenty-nine drive-in sites on the banks of the Lillooet River. (An overnight camping fee of about $10 is charged May to October.) A well-signed road at this junction leads towards Meager Creek Hot Springs.

> **MEAGER CREEK HOT SPRINGS**
Access: 43 km (26.7 mi) north of the Lillooet River Bridge via the Lillooet River and Meager Creek Forest Service roads

When I'm looking for a little sanctuary, a wilderness hot spring does it every time. And there's nothing like bathing in the most geologically active corner of Canada to up the adventure ante. Such is the case at Meager Creek where rainy weather often adds even more *frisson* to these hot springs north of Pemberton. In October 2003, monsoon rains triggered massive flooding in the Pemberton Valley. Fed by swollen tributaries such as Meager Creek, the Lillooet jumped its banks. From the air, the scene looked more like the Gulf Islands than prime agricultural land.

The force of rapidly flowing water overwhelmed a 70-m-long (300-ft-long) wooden bridge that spanned Meager Creek, cutting off road access to the hot springs located a short distance upstream on the west side of the creek. Thanks to an injection of $900,000 from the Provincial Emergency Program, which covers damages to high-value recreation sites such as the hot springs, a new steel-and-concrete structure was eventually installed. On August 1, 2008, Meager Creek Hot Springs officially reopened to the acclaim of local residents and Tourism Pemberton officials alike.

The bridge washout was only the most recent in a long history of cataclysmic events there that stretch back to 400 BC, the date of Mount Meager's most recent volcanic eruption. That earth-shattering event spewed ash as far as the Alberta-Saskatchewan border. An inventory of similar events includes an avalanche on Mount Meager's companion, Pylon Peak, which completely covered a glacier over which Pylon Creek continues to bubble. Nearby stands the jagged remnant of another volcano, Devastator Peak. In 1975, a substantial rockslide on Devastator buried a party of geologists and partly blocked the flow of Meager Creek. The creek's waters backed up, creating a small lake that took several years to drain. Geologists predict that a resumption of volcanic activity is likely within the next several centuries. With these events in mind, a set of sobering roadside markers are placed along the Meager Creek Forestry Road. They direct travelers to refuge areas in case of emergency—any port in a storm.

The sweeping grandeur of the peaks is enough to momentarily take a visitor's mind off the prospect of suddenly finding oneself in the midst of chaos unleashed. The upside of all this geothermal activity is the presence of B.C.'s hottest and most voluminous hot springs, which percolate on an open terrace above Meager Creek's silt-gray waters. "Creek" doesn't do justice to Meager. Even at its annual low flow level, this is not a stream to be trifled with. Still, as you soak beside it in a near-scalding thermal pool with the wild sounds of cascading whitewater in your ears, there's no more relaxing place to be.

Although the hot springs are situated on provincial land, the site and nearby Lillooet River campground are managed by the local Lil'wat Nation's Creekside Resources. For millennia, the Lil'wat have used the springs for everything from poaching fish in the hot water to revering the springs for their natural healing qualities. These days, they look after the place to demonstrate ownership.

Over the decades since a road to Meager Creek was first built by BC Hydro in pursuit of geothermal power production, the springs have been a magnet for both families and party animals. To preserve the peace and insure that both yahoos and dogs are kept away from the springs, a Creekside Resource's caretaker monitors activity, including weather conditions, at the site. Opening hours are 8 AM to 6 PM. A day-use fee of $5 is collected at the springs from those aged 12 and older plus $10 per site at the pleasant campground on the Lillooet River Forestry Road. The hot springs officially close for the season on October 31. From then until snowfall shuts the Lillooet River Road, access to the springs is on foot or by bike from the gated entrance to the Meager Creek Road, 7 km (4.3 mi) west of the campground. For updates, call Creekside Resources in Mount Currie (604-894-6145).

> ## UPPER LILLOOET PROVINCIAL PARK
Access: 50 km (31 mi) north of the Lillooet River Bridge

If you continue on Lillooet River Road past the Meager Creek turnoff, the road follows the river upstream, much of the way uphill, for 14 km (8.7 mi) to where Salal Creek flows into the Lillooet River, becoming progressively rougher and less well marked along the way. Good clearance is a must for all vehicles, especially when crossing rocky creekbeds. Across the river to the west, the craggy volcanic spires of Mount Meager and Plinth Peak reveal themselves, including one sinister-looking crenellated black tower nicknamed the "Finger." With binoculars, you can pick out a sturdy granite gendarme (a large rock outcropping) that juts up on Plinth's north flank.

One kilometer (0.6 mi) before the bridge over Salal Creek the road divides: bear right here to reach Upper Lillooet Park. The road to the left descends to a bridge across the Lillooet River, which leads to the site of a pumice mine on the slopes of Mount Meager. It's worth the short detour to this bridge to appreciate the deep, narrow canyon through which the river plummets. Unseen downstream from the bridge is the rim of Keyhole Falls over which the river tumbles. The gorge is formed from basalt columns.

Immediately after crossing the bridge over Salal Creek, take the first road on the left. This leads 0.5 km (0.3 mi) to a parking area, from where it is an easy 20-minute walk along an old mining road to the east side of the Lillooet River. Sections of an iron bridge framework rear up on the far side of the river. From here a rough trail descends the riverbank and leads north into the upper Lillooet River Valley.

Waterfalls cascade down the slopes of Mount Meager and drain into the Lillooet River's far side. A vast geological formation called Pumice Bluffs is visible on the opposite side of the river. Also apparent on the slopes of Mount Meager and on both sides of the river valley are majestic groups of basalt columns, remnants of the lava flows that cut through the forest at the time of Meager's most recent volcanic activity about 2,450 years ago.

The force of the volcanic explosion blew debris and pumice onto nearby slopes, and you can easily find chunks of pumice beside the road leading to Salal Creek or bobbing in the Lillooet—pumice is an extremely porous rock, light enough to float.

From this vantage point you look north across the open rift valley, where meadows full of bog orchids perfume the air in summer. Tall cottonwoods line the riverbanks, and in early autumn their leaves blaze with a golden hue that lights up the valley. The riverside trail leads north, and, aside from some tricky sections where it climbs the eroded riverbank, takes a comparatively straightforward route. Allow 90 minutes to reach a wide sandbar on the river where, when water levels are sufficiently low, you'll find a good place to camp.

This is a magnificent place to admire the valley's last remaining stands of Douglas fir, white pine, and the occasional huge red cedar, in contrast to the series of clear-cuts that characterize most of the Lillooet Valley. You have now entered a region designated by a coalition of Lower Mainland conservation groups as the Randy Stoltmann Wilderness Area (see sidebar). This 19,996-ha (49,409-acre)

> ## A WILDERNESS HERO

. . . .

R ANDY STOLTMANN was an eloquent B.C. writer as well as an avid mountaineer and dedicated conservationist who died in an avalanche while on a ski traverse in May 1994. Before his premature death, Stoltmann had prepared a detailed study for the Federation of Mountain Clubs of B.C. on preserving a large tract of wilderness north of Squamish. Stoltmann named it the Stanley Smith Wilderness Area for a Vancouver explorer who traversed much of this region a century ago. (Stanley Smith and his companion were accomplished outdoorsmen who carved canoes out of cedar logs and lived off the land for months at a time, all the while searching for two lost British surveyors (who were never found).

portion of the reserve was set aside as the Upper Lillooet Park in 1997. (Northwest of Squamish, an additional 30,330 ha/74,944 acres of this remote wilderness has been preserved as Clendinning Park. See chapter 3.)

Once you reach a sandbar or two, look around. In this wilderness corridor there are bound to be some animal tracks. Pressed side by side in the soft silt of the sandbar may be those of a wolf and a bear. Nearby, the cloven hooves of a hefty moose have likely left an impression where the beast waded across an arm of the upper Lillooet River. There is a reason this is such a major wildlife gathering point. Much of the bottom and slopes of the 200-km-long (124-mi-long) Lillooet River Valley have been logged, and the remaining wildlife has gradually moved up the valley. All that remains of the old growth is found here, in this last 5 km (3.1 mi) as the river winds its way to the face of the Lillooet Glacier above the slate-green waters of Silt Lake.

> **THE INSIDE TRACK**

> *Cat Skiing:* Backcountry Snow Cats (Pemberton; 604-932-2166 or 1-888-246-1111; www.snowcats.ca) set in the broad-ridged South Chilcotin Range around the corner from Whistler, where you won't find any infamous "coast concrete" snow conditions. Arctic outflow winds mound up powder in deep, dry drifts. Backcountry's ten-room lodge sits at the top of the Hurley Pass; half the enjoyment of getting there is the 45-minute snowmobile ride from the fledgling company's base in Pemberton Meadows.

26

MOUNT CURRIE TO D'ARCY

. . . . .

> LOCATION: 159 km (98.6 mi) north of Vancouver, 101 km (63 mi) northeast of Squamish, 41 km (25 mi) northeast of Whistler, 6 km (4 mi) east of Pemberton, 100 km (62 mi) south of Lillooet

> ACTIVITIES: Boating, camping, driving, fishing, mountain biking, picnicking, rafting, viewpoints, whitewater kayaking

> HIGHLIGHTS: Rivers red with salmon, a road rich in history

> ACCESS: From Highway 99 in Mount Currie, at the junction of Highway 99 and the Duffey Lake Road, Portage Road leads 40 km (25 mi) north to D'Arcy.

O F ALL the communities in the Whistler region, Mount Currie has one of the richest histories. Long before the arrival of prospectors on the Gold Rush Trail in the 1850s, the Lil'wat First Nation thrived at the north end of Lillooet Lake in the village of Slalock, near the present townsite of Mount Currie. According to recent archeological findings in the Fraser Valley, the Lil'wat could well have paddled their canoes in this region 10,000 years ago. I find the best place to appreciate both the Lil'wat and Squamish bands' ties to the land is the Squamish-Lil'wat Cultural Centre in Whistler (www.slcc.ca).

The Lil'wat were a people who perfected the art of survival by maintaining the status quo. Early Europeans reported that in contrast to the hostile reception they received from the aboriginals of the Thompson Plateau to the east, the Lil'wat gave them a far more gracious welcome. Kinship with the Interior Salish (the Lil'wat are that group's most westerly members) did not shield the Lil'wat from attack by raiding parties, which would cross over from the Fraser Canyon on the Stein Valley Trail. In fact, one of the reasons Europeans were welcomed in Slalock was the protection they afforded residents from these hostilities. The Lil'wat also found work as guides, paddlers, and packers for European travelers. Their navigational skills, developed over generations of handling cargo canoes as long as 15 m (50 ft) through the Lillooet River's treacherous rapids, were very much in demand on the Gold Rush Trail.

After the Cariboo Gold Rush played itself out, one of the prospectors returned to make his home in the area. John Currie married into a Lil'wat family, built a cabin in what is now Pemberton, and opened the area's first store and post office. His children were among the first postal employees.

Today there are few signs left of the old Lil'wat settlement of Slalock along the Duffey Lake Road, which leads east from Mount Currie. But you can visit the Sam Jim house at the Pemberton Museum (see chapter 23) to get a sense of the snug interiors of early cabins.

> **PORTAGE ROAD**

Access: *From Highway 99 in Mount Currie*

The 40-km (25-mi) road that links Mount Currie with D'Arcy was once an important section of the old Gold Rush Trail. When travelers had made their way up the river and lake system to Mount Currie, they still had to clear the Pemberton Pass before reaching the shores of Anderson Lake. Passengers rich enough to afford travel by stagecoach had to hang on for dear life as a teamster whipped his horses up the rocky road. Today, this paved road is a pleasant, albeit winding, journey by car or bike. And surprisingly, the total driving time from Mount Currie to D'Arcy is an easy 30 minutes—not long when you consider how much history lines the way.

Pemberton Pass, at the south end of Gates Lake, is 280 m (920 ft) higher than the road's beginning in Mount Currie. Because the road climbs through the pass, some cyclists prefer to transport their bikes to D'Arcy and cycle south from there. This quiet, rolling stretch of road has a unique personality, perhaps because of the nature of the narrow Birkenhead River valley through which much of it passes. (The road to D'Arcy covers the same ground originally surveyed by Britain's Royal Engineers in 1860.) The Birkenhead River valley is so narrow that there isn't room for more than one

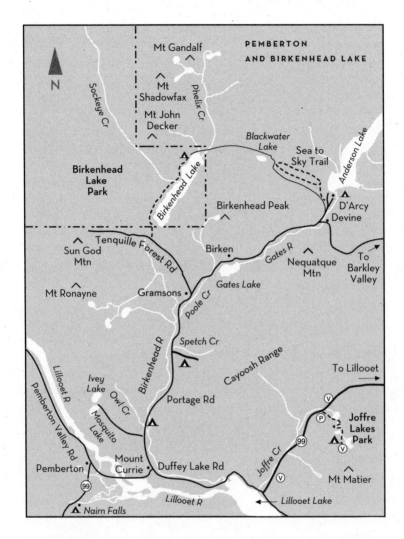

trail, and the existing road and the railroad bed have been laid over the old road.

Few opportunities for farming exist except in the Gates Lake district, and even here, cultivation is hindered by the long, cold winters. As the frozen ground thaws, it heaves up stones that must be cleared each year before plowing and seeding can commence. Since Hudson's Bay Company trader Alexander Anderson (after whom the big lake at D'Arcy is named) first entered the area 150 years ago, few European settlers have settled permanently in this valley. Most of the current residents arrived only recently, with the influx of logging activity.

> **OWL CREEK FOREST SERVICE RECREATION SITE**
Access: 7 km (4 mi) north of Mount Currie
    As you drive north of Mount Currie towards D'Arcy, Portage Road climbs briefly after it crosses the railway tracks, then begins to level. At approximately 7 km (4 mi), watch for a bridge over Owl Creek, followed immediately by a clearing on the right where a hydro substation is located. It is marked by a Forest Service sign that indicates the Owl Creek recreation site. Cross the railway tracks, then turn either left or right when the road divides. Located at the confluence of Owl Creek and the Birkenhead River are fourteen charming, pleasantly spaced campsites with picnic tables, fire pits,

> **5 TOP SPOTS FOR WILDLIFE VIEWING**
. . . .

1 Nothing epitomizes life on the B.C. coast more than the sight of spawning salmon—and the Birkenhead is one of the best examples of rivers that run red with the sockeye species in late summer and early fall (see chapters 26, 27, 29, and 30). Bonus: Salmon runs on the Squamish River, principally between November and January, also attract thousands of eagles (see chapter 3).

2 The Squamish estuary is a birder's paradise, especially in winter when trumpeter swans and golden eagles are in residence (see chapter 1).

3 On the slopes around the Whistler Olympic/Paralympic Park in the Callaghan Valley, you're sure to spy black bears (see chapter 9).

4 Mountain goats share space with hoary marmots on the peaks above the Barkley Valley (see chapter 28).

5 Upper Lillooet Provincial Park—for wildlife viewing par excellence (see chapter 25).

and outhouses. To the right are sheltered campsites at the mouth of Owl Creek; to the left more open campsites are located on the banks above the Birkenhead River. The voices of both river and creek help mask other sounds, creating a sense of privacy at each site. An overnight camping fee of about $10 is charged May to October.

A fish hatchery operated in this clearing beside the river from 1907 to 1937; it has since been relocated downstream, closer to Mount Currie. All that remains is the old orchard that once surrounded it. It's a miracle that these trees still blossom at all: they're at least seventy years old and have endured the coldest winters of the past century. Picnic tables spread with white petals await travelers in May, though the sites are just as appealing at other times, and particularly when the sun shines and the river sings. In September, the Birkenhead churns with spawning chinook and coho salmon. (If you wish to visit the hatchery, run by the Pemberton Sportsmen's Wildlife Association, turn right just before crossing the railway tracks in Mount Currie as you head north. Cross the Birkenhead River and bear left.)

The Owl Creek sites are popular with both anglers and whitewater kayakers. If you're looking for some exercise, explore beside the railway tracks where they lead south over Owl Creek on the sturdy ties of the bridge. One of the best views of Mount Currie is found just past here, particularly near sunset as the last rays climb the mountainside to its rugged white crags then fade away into the afterglow.

> ### OWL CREEK TO D'ARCY

North of Owl Creek, Portage Road runs past rock faces that were reshaped with black powder by early road builders. Because this part of the Gold Rush Trail is so smooth, it's hard to connect it with the more difficult southern sections on In-SHUCK-ch Road. Today anglers quietly work their lines where prospectors with horses, mules, and camels once grunted their way up the grade. (The use of camels was not very successful, as their smell was so offensive to other animals.) All along the Birkenhead River you will see the cars of anglers who have pulled off to try their luck with the river's salmon, trout, and char. Drive slowly and watch for rough pullouts. These occur frequently north of the narrow bridge crossing the Birkenhead.

The river is now on your left side until just south of Gramsons, where it veers to the northwest. Poole Creek takes over as a companion to the road and railway. The road crosses the Poole Creek Bridge, then passes several clearings on the left where Ab Gramson homesteaded in the 1920s. A British veteran of the First World War, Gramson emblazoned his colorful cabin, self-styled as "Number 10 Downing Street," with names of battle sites from that war.

A number of other creeks feed into the Birkenhead River from both sides of the valley. At Spetch Creek, on the road's right side, halfway between Owl Creek and Gramsons, there is another recreation site. (The Forest Service sign at roadside is much smaller than the one at Owl Creek—if you miss it you will have to double back.) The dirt road seems steep as it climbs immediately into the forest, but is not hard to handle if you drive slowly. It circles past ten well-spaced campsites with picnic tables heavily sheltered by deciduous trees in summer. The bubbly sound of the creek is enough to brighten any visit, as is the fact that camping here is free.

At Gramsons, an unmarked gravel road runs left off the pavement, crosses the railway tracks next to the cabin, then heads northwest. Almost immediately a sign warns of active logging in the area. The rough road climbs to the south end of Birkenhead Lake and far beyond to the ridge on Tenquille Mountain. This is part of an arc that links with the Tenquille Lake Trail and the Hurley River Forest Service Road (see chapters 24 and 25) that brought backcountry adventurers into the north end of the Pemberton Valley. There is very limited public access to Birkenhead Lake on this route, and you cannot reach the Birkenhead Lake Park campsites by following it. (See chapter 27 for more information.)

Portage Road climbs past here to the highest point on the Gold Rush Trail, the Pemberton (sometimes called Birken) Pass. Poole Creek rushes down from its headwaters on the side of Birkenhead Peak. The road then bends northeast, skirting the lower slopes, and Gates Lake appears, with the small settlement of Birken midway up its shoreline. Dominated by the white peak of Nequatque Mountain and the Cayoosh Range rising to the north, this lake always strikes me as the quintessential vision of the quiet life in Canada, one shared by citizens and visitors alike. Who hasn't dreamed of owning

Birkenhead River

a cabin on such a postcard-perfect lake, with a small dock on which
to sit on long, hot days?

At this altitude and latitude such days are precious indeed. The
growing season here is short, and records kept over the past century
show that frosts can strike in any month of the year. Yet the winters are said to be a touch milder and sunnier in Birken and D'Arcy
than in the Pemberton Valley. Those who have experienced the outflow of Arctic air that slashes through the Pemberton Pass in winter
months might be excused for thinking that such comparisons are
academic.

Just north of Gates Lake, before the pavement reaches the Mars
Crossing on the BC Rail line, a dirt road turns right and heads back
beside the lake. Day-use access is much easier from this side.

The Gates River flows beside the road on its way north to Anderson Lake. Cleared fields are more common here, as are farmhouses,
old and new. The turnoff to Birkenhead Lake Provincial Park is near
the small settlement of Devine. D'Arcy is 5 km (3 mi) north of it.

The N'quat'qua Indian Reserve, home to the Anderson Lake Band, occupies most of the land at Anderson Lake's southern end. This means that the village of D'Arcy is partly on reserve land. As you enter the town, Highline Road leads off to the left, then crosses the railway tracks and heads north along Anderson Lake to Seton Portage, a distance of about 25 km (15.5 mi). Although recommended for 4x4s only, parts of this back road have been upgraded by BC Hydro, and it warrants exploration at least as far as McGillivray Falls, about 8 km (5 mi) beyond D'Arcy.

At the end of the pavement lie the southern shores of Anderson Lake. Heritage Park overlooks the lake here, with a public boat launch, dock, beach, picnic tables, and ample parking. Free-range cattle are also a feature at D'Arcy—watch for them on the road. (Keep an eye out for the occasional buffalo as well. It's that kind of town.) The N'quat'qua Band operates the spacious Red Barn Campground (604-452-3380). There's usually room for all comers here on the banks of the Gates River where it enters the lake, at a charge of about $15 per night.

Deep, dark Anderson Lake is 22 km (14 mi) long, with high, snow-covered ridges lining each side: the Bendor Range on the west and the Cayoosh Range to the east. A paddlewheeler named *The Lady of the Lake* (whose sternwheel is exhibited in the Pemberton Museum; see page 188) once transported passengers and freight to Seton Portage at the lake's northern end. From there it was a short distance overland on road or narrow-gauge railway—complete with wooden rails and cars hauled by mules—to Seton Lake, at the top of which sits Lillooet, Mile o on the trail to the Cariboo goldfields centered on Williams Lake. Despite its rather forbidding appearance, Anderson Lake has attracted a string of settlers and cabin owners along its western shoreline, particularly at McGillivray Falls and Seton Portage.

27

BIRKENHEAD LAKE PARK

. . . . .

> LOCATION: 211 km (131 mi) north of Vancouver; 153 km (95 mi) north of Squamish; 95 km (59 mi) north of Whistler; 58 km (36 mi) north of Pemberton

> ACTIVITIES: Boating, camping, cross-country skiing, fishing, hiking, mountain biking, picnicking, snowshoeing, swimming, wildlife observation, windsurfing

> HIGHLIGHTS: Big lake set among big mountains, easygoing bike trail

> ACCESS: To reach Birkenhead Lake, follow Portage Road north from Highway 99 at Mount Currie for a distance of 35 km (22 mi). The well-marked Blackwater Forest Service Road opposite the small settlement of Devine leads 17 km (10.6 mi) west to Birkenhead Lake.

BIRKENHEAD LAKE lies tucked in the folds of the Coast Mountains' Cadwallader Range, near D'Arcy. And there's no other place like it in the region. Sheltered from the strong winds that rake nearby Anderson Lake, its north-south 6-km (3.7-mi) length is just the right size for exploring on foot, by bike, by boat, or on snowshoes or skis. Even if you're just visiting for the day, you're bound to fall in love with the idea of returning to spend the night at the forested provincial campground here.

In 1963, at the same time that Whistler Mountain was being developed, Birkenhead Park opened. For the first few years it was the preserve of locals. Once Highway 99 linked Pemberton with the rest of the Lower Mainland in 1975, however, visitors from farther afield began to discover its beauty. In 1996, the size of the park tripled to 9755 ha (24,105 acres) with the addition of the pristine Sockeye Creek watershed. (Visit www.env.gov.bc.ca/bcparks/ for current conditions.)

On the way to Birkenhead Lake, watch for signs of wildlife. In fall, spawning salmon turn the waters of the Birkenhead River bright red. Deer spring from the roadside back into the forest. At roughly the halfway point from Portage Road you pass Blackwater Lake, screened from view by the forest, where a Forest Service recreation site provides access for fishing. Just beyond here are a few barns and open fields, signs of the homesteading that has gone on in the area since the mid-nineteenth century. Hangover Hill Ranch is one of the larger spreads.

Upon entering the park, either turn in to the campground or drive to the day-use parking lot next to the boat launch. (In summer, canoe rentals are available on site.) Picnic tables dot the grassy bank above the lake here. An even better location to stretch out is the nearby beach, visible from the boat launch and just a few minutes' walk from the parking lot. A broad lawn fronts the beach, where the drop-off into the lake isn't as abrupt as at the boat launch.

Birkenhead is typical of many glacier-scoured mountain lakes in the region, with steep-sided hillsides plunging into deep water and only limited shallows. Windsurfers and those traveling with young children will appreciate the safety of the campground's beach, where the water warms to a slightly higher temperature than elsewhere around the lake's rocky perimeter. (Come fall, when fish are spawning in nearby Phelix Creek, the beach is a good place to view eagles and black bears. While one must always exercise extreme caution around bears, during spawning season they are almost entirely focused on feeding. One of the best—and safest—vantage points is from offshore in a boat.)

An enjoyable way to explore Birkenhead Lake on foot or by bike is to follow the old logging road that runs for 8 km (5 mi) along the lake's western side. Watch for the well-marked entrance to the *Birkenhead Lake Trail* just north of the boat launch. A gate bars access to motorized vehicles, but bicycles are allowed. This road has been maintained as an emergency fire road and more recently as a section of the Sea to Sky cycling and hiking trail.

A narrow wooden bridge spans Sockeye Creek. Water flows full bore beneath the bridge during spring freshet season and fall rains. An open valley to the west reveals the distant headwaters feeding

Birkenhead Lake

Sockeye Creek. This is one of the few open areas around the lake. Looking up the creek from out on the water, you can see a tall, unnamed white peak in the distance to the west of the creek. Mount John Decker is in the foreground on the north side of the lake.

Viewpoints from the road are few. Watch for a clearing just off the road 10 minutes past the Sockeye Creek bridge, where a stand of tightly spaced lodgepole pine appears. The open forest floor makes it easy to walk to the ridge, from which you can see down to the lake and across to Birkenhead Peak (elevation 2523 m/8278 ft).

Along the way, the road climbs gently through shaded second growth. This makes for a pleasant walk, particularly early in the day. Although views are limited, a lovely sense of calm prevails. There are remnants of some impressive old-growth forest in places, particularly Douglas fir.

Forty minutes' walk beyond Sockeye Creek is a large washout. You will have to do some scrambling to make your way around this major slide area. The southern end of the lake is 20 minutes beyond here, where a number of private cabins at Birkenhead Estates are located. Birkenhead Road and the Tenas Valley logging road lead towards this end of the lake from a turnoff at "Number 10 Downing Street," the colorful cabin beside the BC Rail tracks south of Birken.

One of the pleasures reserved for those who boat on Birkenhead Lake is the view of the mountain range to the south that gradually reveals itself. Tenquille Ridge rises as a broad white wall of snow and ice stretching off to the west. Nearby is Sun God Mountain. The snow on all the peaks is quite white in spring and early summer, before the melt reveals the darker ice beneath; the white looks especially dazzling reflected in the lake. Looking north from the lake you see a long, tall ridge that separates Birkenhead from Anderson Lake. Allow two hours to canoe the length of the lake. The best landing spots are on the northern half; rocky cliffs dominate other parts.

Fall is a particularly good time of the year to nose around the Birkenhead Lake woods, when the forest floor is covered with a remarkable variety of mushrooms.

For hikers interested in exploring the east side of the lake, *Goat Lookout Trail* leads from the campground to a viewpoint above. The 1-km (0.6-mi) trail allows hikers in spring and fall to watch for mountain goats on the ridges above the valley's north side. Soon after you begin walking Goat Lookout Trail, watch for another, lengthier trail, equally rough, that branches south and follows the east side of the lake for about 4 km (2.5 mi). This trail is unofficially referred to as *Bear Trail*—probably for good reason.

From May to October, a fee of about $15 is charged at Birkenhead's ninety-four campsites, seven of which are doubles. Owing to the elevation, nights can be cool even in summer. Campsites can be reserved March 1 to September 15 by calling 1-800-689-9025 or visiting www.discovercamping.ca. Although the park is often full on the long weekends of Victoria Day, Canada Day, B.C. Day, and Labor Day, at other times there is usually plenty of room. The Thanksgiving weekend in October, when early frosts bring out the color in the surrounding forests, is an especially pretty time to be in the area. Signs on Portage Road beside the turnoff tell campers in advance if the park is full so that they can make alternative plans, such as to head for the private campground in nearby D'Arcy (see chapter 26) or find a wilderness campsite.

The forest around the lakeshore provides shelter and privacy for each campsite. Some are almost right on the beach; others are tucked in beside Phelix Creek. In summer, the road that runs through the campsites gets quite dusty and is heavily traveled by traffic to the boat launch; if space allows, choose a low-numbered site as close to Phelix Creek as possible. There are a dozen small overflow campsites for those who arrive after the park is full, but they are quite tightly spaced and provide little more than a place to park beside the road.

At the point where Sockeye Creek tumbles off the mountain slopes and creates a gravel bar is some of the best rod-fishing of kokanee and rainbow trout on the lake.

In winter, the road in to Birkenhead Lake is plowed as far as the bridge over Phelix Creek, 2 km (1.2 mi) from the entrance to the park. Cross-country skiers, snowmobilers, snowshoers, and ice fishermen enjoy these cold, clear days.

> ## TRAIL-BLAZING

B.C.'S SEA to Sky Trail was started in the early 1990s by renowned trail builder Ross Kirkwood. Although far from complete, the trail will ultimately link Horseshoe Bay with Lillooet and encompass more than 300 km (186 mi) of off-road trails, deactivated logging roads, and BC Hydro service roads. Designed for recreation, the trail does not follow a straight line but meanders, to give riders and hikers a better feel for the countryside. The Sea to Sky Trail Society's mandate is to construct a touring route accessible to both novice and intermediate riders (seatoskytrail.ca). At present, besides the routes in the Birkenhead Lake region, the best sections run from Brandywine Falls to Whistler (see chapter 18).

Access: Five entry points off Portage Road and the Blackwater Forest Service Road to Birkenhead Lake
Ability Level: Novice to intermediate

Mountain bikers interested in getting a taste of the Sea to Sky Trail north of Mount Currie should head for the region around D'Arcy, where much of the initial thrust of trail building was concentrated. You'll find a variety of options here for exploration around Birkenhead Lake, including a 50-km (31-mi) loop that will put even the most road-hardened posteriors to the test. Decide for yourself how much of the territory you can comfortably cover during a day's visit. Perhaps it will be the 8 km (5 mi) of single-track Birkenhead Lake Trail that runs along Birkenhead Lake's western side. Double that when you make a round trip of it, and you have an easy two-hour ride with plenty of breaks for admiring the lake and fall colors in the surrounding forest. This section is particularly well suited to those who are just getting the feel for what off-road cycling is all about.

If you've got enough wind in your lungs, you can tack on another 17 km (10.5 mi) while riding between Birkenhead and Blackwater lakes and onward to D'Arcy. Much of what you accomplish will ultimately be determined by where you leave your support vehicle. To assist you in making your decision, roadside markers are handily placed at a number of locations along this section of the Sea to Sky Trail. Watch for these distinctive brown posts positioned beside Portage Road and on the Blackwater Forest Service Road that leads to Birkenhead Lake. Distances and ability levels are clearly marked on them. Park at any of five locations where these trail markers are situated and begin your explorations from there.

28

BARKLEY VALLEY

. . . . .

> **LOCATION:** 210 km (130 mi) north of Vancouver, 152 km (94 mi)
> northeast of Squamish, 82 km (51 mi) northeast of Whistler,
> 57 km (35 mi) northeast of Pemberton

> **ACTIVITIES:** Camping, hiking, mountain biking, nature observa-
> tion, viewpoints

> **HIGHLIGHTS:** Goat-haunted peaks that echo the 1960s

> **ACCESS:** Follow the Haylmore Main Forest Service Road that
> leads 16 km (9.9 mi) east from Devine on Portage Road. The Bar-
> kley Valley Road begins almost anonymously on the north side of
> the road, just before the "km 16" marker. Hidden just uphill from
> view is an information signboard with an enlarged topographic map
> detailing the immediate area. The Elliot Creek campsite is located
> 5 km (3.1 mi) northeast of here. Elevation gain is 325 m (1066 ft).
> The alpine region around Twin Lakes lies a further 3 km (1.9 mi)
> beyond the campsite. To reach it requires a thigh-burning 455-m
> (1493-ft) climb. For more information, consult Canadian Geo-
> graphical Survey maps 92 J/8 (Duffey Lake) and 92 J/9 (Shalalth).
> Interestingly, though the old Barkley Valley mining road appears on
> topographic maps of this region from the 1960s, it does not appear
> on more recent editions.

> **ABILITY LEVEL:** Novice to intermediate

THE LATE 1960s were a turbulent time, and no year more so
than 1968. That summer, several prominent Americans,
including Martin Luther King Jr. and Robert F. Kennedy Jr.,
were gunned down. At the Democratic convention in Chicago that
August, then-mayor Richard J. Daley unleashed his police force on

peaceful anti–Vietnam War demonstrators in a naked display of brutality.

Baby boomers who witnessed these indelible events found themselves in the embrace of an "assassination generation" psychosis. Small wonder that clusters of disillusioned youth banded together and headed for the hills. While North American society seemed hell-bent on flameout, pockets of isolated tranquility offered the promise of sanctuary and reconnection with the natural world.

In 1968, one such group, originally based in the Fraser Valley, made its way north to the secluded Barkley Valley southeast of D'Arcy. The U-shaped valley rests among the Coast Mountain's Cayoosh Range. Historically called Lawlaton, a N'quat'qua word that connotes a paradise where food and game are plentiful, the valley took its post-contact name from miner Tom Barkley, who prospected here in the early 1960s. Perhaps the religiously inspired Fraser Valley group found comfort in the fact that this was a place of spiritual significance within the traditional N'quat'qua territory.

Lord knows, they couldn't have taken much solace from the sight of Tom Barkley's dilapidated cabin. It had fallen victim to an avalanche, a common winter occurrence in the steep-sided valley. Still, the group hunted, fished, kept cattle, and logged with horses to build their homes and barns, and they must have enjoyed some happy summer days getting back to the land. However, today their stoved-in log cabins testify to the fact that winter did them in. According to longtime D'Arcy resident Frank Rollert, who occasionally hauled in stove oil for the group, the winter storms of 1969–70 were so extreme that the group found itself in trouble and had to be escorted to safety by the RCMP.

The times have changed, but it's still not safe to venture into the Barkley Valley between December and April. If you're interested in sampling paradise, it would be wise to seek out the obscure trail that leads into the valley during snow-free months. You'll be pleasantly surprised by what you find. The B.C. Forest Service and a local group, the Cayoosh Recreation Society, have chosen to protect and enhance the valley. Under their stewardship, a series of interpretive signs have been put in place along the well-worn route, informing visitors of the history of the valley and its unique natural features.

Upwards of 350 mountain goats, for example, inhabit the upper reaches of the Cayoosh Range, which hems in the little valley. Although you'd be hard-pressed to spot the sure-footed goats, even from the stillness of one of the rock-walled blinds erected near the peaks, you might be lucky and find a fistful of their thick white hair, discarded during the molting season, trapped on a low-lying juniper bush. Even if you don't see a goat, their unmistakable musky aroma marks this as their territory. (As you ramble through the alpine, keep a wary eye open for grizzly bears. They are usually just as keen to avoid human contact as the goats, but the bears dislike being surprised, so keep a line of chatter going as you move about.)

Avalanches have cleared long paths down the slopes of the Cayoosh Mountains. By midsummer these subalpine tracks are thick with thistle stalks, paintbrush, aster, and droopy-leafed lilies.

At the outset, the trail passes beneath sturdy, lichen-draped Douglas fir. As the trail enters the Barkley Valley, the lush rain forest gives way to more open sections of spindly subalpine fir. A local logging company clearcut a strip through here in hopes of halting the spread. You can choose to make the campsite beside Elliot Creek your base (the Cayoosh Recreation Club has an A-frame cabin here) or continue following the trail, which divides about 1 km (0.6 mi) up the valley from the campsites. (Watch for an abandoned 1954 Willys truck that sits flattened in the field there.) For the best views of the surrounding peaks and a chance to glimpse wildlife, turn left at the divide. From here, a trail follows Crystal Creek as it leads upwards towards Twin Lakes in the alpine zone.

Although the main trail ends at 2165 m (7103 ft), just below the first of the two alpine lakes that feed Crystal Creek, it's not difficult to follow a series of game trails leading to the open ridges. From these lofty heights you look down into the headwaters of Melvin Creek and Lost Valley Creek, the last two unlogged valleys in the Cayoosh Range. Off to the south, the ice-encrusted spires of the Joffre group of peaks crown the horizon above unseen Duffey Lake.

29

IN-SHUCK-CH
FOREST SERVICE ROAD

Lillooet Lake Road

. . . . .

> LOCATION: 174 km (108 mi) northeast of Vancouver, 166 km
  (103 mi) northeast of Squamish, 58 km (36 mi) northeast of
  Whistler, 21 km (13 mi) east of Pemberton

> ACTIVITIES: Boating, camping, driving, fishing, mountain bik-
  ing, paddling, picnicking, swimming, viewpoints, walking

> HIGHLIGHTS: Lakeside campgrounds, hot springs, historic
  church, heritage trail

> ACCESS: The well-marked In-SHUCK-ch Forest Service Road
  begins 15 km (9.3 mi) north of Mount Currie on Highway 99 at the
  head of Lillooet Lake and runs 81 km (50 mi) south to the head of
  Harrison Lake.

B Y LATE May, the Lillooet River and its tributaries swell to lake-
sized proportions with spring runoff. The contrast between
their turbulence and the peace of mind induced by listening
to them is truly astonishing. All this frenetic energy has a soothing,
hypnotic effect. Find a spot by the shoreline of Lillooet Lake or the
Lillooet River where you can sit entranced while kingfishers flash by
and finches flit among the underbrush. Sunlight dapples the boughs
of cedar trees above while mason bees adorn salmonberry blossoms
beside you. All of nature is responding to spring's call to get on with
life. And to get on with it passionately.

The first road skirting Lillooet Lake was built in 1858 as the
quickest route to the Cariboo goldfields in central B.C. The In-
SHUCK-ch Forest Service Road (also called the Lillooet Lake Road)

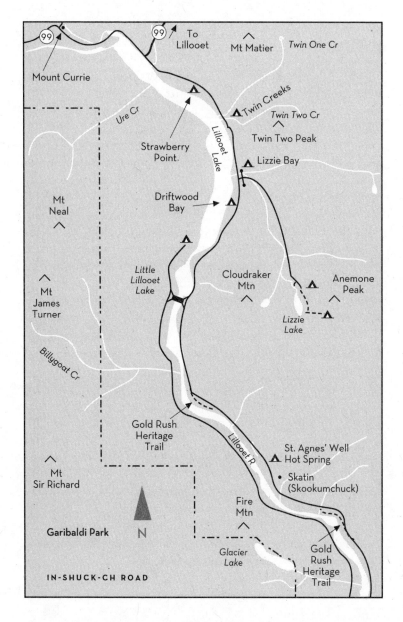

that now runs along the lake's eastern side is a recent arrival, built to accompany the string of hydro towers that were put into service in the 1960s. In places the high-voltage lines droop near enough to the road to merit warning signs. In keeping with its name, In-SHUCK-ch Road is also an important link for the Samahquam, Skatin, and Douglas First Nations reserves dotted alongside it between Mount Currie at the northern end of Lillooet Lake and Port Douglas at the northern end of Harrison Lake. (Together, as the In-SHUCK-ch Nation, the three groups are negotiating a treaty with the federal and provincial governments.)

Travelers today face few of the challenges experienced by the gold rush stampeders who passed this way; however, as there are no services along this road, be certain that you are carrying enough fuel to last the journey. One thing that hasn't changed is the beauty of Lillooet Lake. Depending on the time of day and weather conditions, the color of the water varies from a pale jade green to jet-black.

Soon after its outset, In-SHUCK-ch Road crosses over Joffre Creek, which tumbles down the last part of its run from the icefields high above. At roadside in summer you'll find a host of wildflowers: white daisies, pink wild roses, saffron lilies, blue lupines, and a profusion of other species and shades.

The road gently climbs and falls beside the lake. It is wide enough for cars going in opposite directions to pass, but take care at several

> ## THE LILLOOET DELTA

LILLOOET LAKE is fed by three major rivers: the Green, the Birkenhead, and the upper Lillooet, which enter the lake within a short distance of each other. The accumulation of silt where these three major sources converge accounts for this being the fastest-growing delta in North America. It is estimated that in the past century more than 1.6 km (1 mi) of waterfront at the northern end of Lillooet Lake has been filled in. This is clearly evident around the Mount Currie rodeo grounds on Highway 99, where the land is largely composed of sand. The buildup has been accelerated since the late 1940s by the installation of flood-control dikes in Pemberton Meadows. The silt that once fertilized those fields during flood times is now channeled downstream into the lake.

blind corners—especially as there may be cyclists on the road. Count on averaging 50 km/h (30 mph) as you drive this gravel road.

> LILLOOET LAKE CAMPSITES

Access: A series of four Forest Service campgrounds dot a 10-km (6.2-mi) stretch of Lillooet Lake's northeastern shore. At present, a charge of $10 per night is collected between May and October at each by Creekside Resources, a First Nations campground management and maintenance company based in Mount Currie (604-894-6145).

Strawberry Point at "6 km" is the first campground you'll pass as you make your way along the lake, and one of the best beaches on the lake is located here. Although the water in this big lake rarely gets warm enough for long swims, a beach where you can toast up is inviting enough. Unlike at other campgrounds in the area, you must park and walk in to Strawberry Point's eight sites. There is usually plenty of driftwood washed up on the beach to provide shelter from the wind that often blows on the lake.

You can launch a boat onto Lillooet Lake at Twin One Creek, at the "10 km" point. A rough logging road across from the fifteen-site campground leads up the north side of Twin One Creek, providing views of the northern end of the lake. Between Twin One and Twin Two creeks is the *Lillooet Lake Lodge* (604-905-9246), with five small cabins and seven campsites for rent.

There are even better views from above the *Lizzie Bay* campground at "15 km." The fifteen sites here plus seven more at nearby *Driftwood Bay* (at "16 km") offer forest shelter; some of these sites also have their own small beaches.

A logging road halfway between the Lizzie and Driftwood campgrounds runs up the south side of Lizzie Creek to Lizzie Lake, 12 km (7.4 mi) east. In October 2003, flooding washed out sections of the road, making access only possible on foot. Although the Forest Service is committed to repairing the road, it won't happen soon. Those seeking an alternative approach into Stein Valley Nlaka'pamux Heritage Park should consider alternate routes such as Blowdown Pass (see chapter 30) or Lytton (see chapter 31). Lizzie Lake rises in the folds of Anemone Peak on the park's western boundary.

Lillooet Lake

South of Driftwood Bay, the lake narrows and Lillooet River briefly resumes its run to the Pacific, then widens once again to form Little Lillooet Lake. By early May, anglers are out in force, testing their casting skills from the shores of this short stretch of the Lillooet River. At "31 km" the Tennas Narrows Bridge spans the river and links up with a well-maintained logging road on the west side. If you cross here and head north alongside Lillooet Lake, you will find an open campsite on a point of land favored by anglers near the big lake's southern end. This road leads south 50 km (30 mi) to another bridge at Fire Creek, which links up once again with In-SHUCK-ch Road.

> **GOLD RUSH HERITAGE TRAIL**
Access: 46 km (28.5 mi) south of Highway 99
South of "31 km," the road is also referred to as the Pemberton-Douglas Forest Service Road. This used to be the roughest part of the journey, but, thankfully, the worst sections have been smoothed over. Ever since the road was first put through in the 1850s, one spot

in particular has bedeviled travelers. But with the recent improvements the rock outcropping called "Mile 29" on the Gold Rush Heritage Trail no longer eats mufflers. From this point south, watch for small side roads leading down to the banks of what has become the Lillooet River once more after the interruption of Little Lillooet Lake. In several places (notably near "46 km"), you can pick up traces of the old trail known as the Douglas Road. It is mossy, littered with blowdowns, and surfaced with well-worn stones, but open enough to allow exploration.

BEST FREE SOAK

The St. Agnes' Well hot spring had a reputation among early prospectors as "the only free thing in the province."

> ## ST. AGNES WELL HOT SPRING (TSEK)
Access: 50 km (30 mi) south of Highway 99

Near In-SHUCK-ch Road's "50 km" point is a small but extremely hot spring. Named for one of Colonial governor James Douglas's daughters, it is known as St. Agnes' Well. A hotel and stagecoach relay station once stood here during the gold rush, and the old Douglas Road still passes by, which you can follow for quite a distance north of the hot spring's campground along the riverbank.

Depending on your timing, you may be the only visitor, or a rugby team may have taken up residence for the weekend. Still, the water in the tubs is often so hot that it limits the amount of bathing time most visitors can endure, so even if you do find the site crowded, the wait won't be long. May and October are two of the best months to visit: traffic is light and with school still in session, there's regular road maintenance for the sake of the school bus—and no bugs.

Thanks to the efforts of the former owners—the Trethewey family, who sold the land on which the spring seeps to the federal government in 2007 (who in turn plan to return the property to the In-SHUCK-ch Nation following the completion of treaty negotiations)—four tubs of various sizes and temperatures are positioned near the source of the spring. A system of pipes draws steaming thermal water into these for bathing.

Soak contentedly before walking over to the nearby river. You'll have to tiptoe to avoid treading on the Pacific bleeding heart that lines the trail. The Lillooet is usually running too high, fast, and cold for swimming, but the riverbank is a good place to relax after bathing in the hot spring. On the opposite side of the valley, steep slopes of scree rise sharply, the rocks covered with a gold lichen.

> SKATIN (SKOOKUMCHUCK)
Access: 51 km (31.6 mi) south of Highway 99

Just south of the spring is the small settlement of Skatin, or Skookumchuck. Make the drive here, if only to see the Church of the Holy Cross with its three steeples. There are two entrances to the town, one at each end of a loop road that connects with In-SHUCK-ch Road.

The front doors of the church are loosely wired shut against the elements, but through a crack in the doors you can see the elaborate hand-carved interior. Skatin residents are justifiably proud of the building and the fact that it is still standing after a century—almost all such early wooden structures in B.C. were destroyed by fire, including the original St. Christopher's in Mount Currie, the former companion to this church.

Standing in the midst of a dozen modest frame homes and surrounded by forest and the peaks of the Garibaldi Range, this stunning piece of folk art patterned on an Oblate church in France testifies to the strength of its builders' faith. Horses were used to drag timber to the site when the church was constructed in 1905, and when the horses were exhausted, the villagers would take over the task of hauling the cedar beams.

The interior of the church is even grander than its baroque exterior suggests. Italian leaded-glass windows in rich shades of green, orange, blue, and yellow—along with a rose window above the choir loft—infuse the inside of the church with brightness even on a dull day. Every piece of wood has been hand carved, from the smallest candleholder to the life-sized statues of the Holy Family, each with its own altar. Overhead, a white dove of peace floats.

> SKATIN TO HARRISON LAKE
The road south of Skatin is well maintained, and you can drive the 25 km (15.5 mi) to the head of Harrison Lake in 30 minutes. If

you decide to stop along the way to bushwhack through the undergrowth, you'll find stretches of the Gold Rush Heritage Trail on the bank of the Lillooet River, south of Gowan and Livingston creeks. When you reach Little Harrison Lake, you'll also come to the steep hill leading down to the water, the first challenge tackled by the builders of the trail. Unfortunately, a logging company with good intentions but no historical perspective leveled the last of the old buildings at Port Douglas in 1989. But you can still do some interesting exploring, by boat on the sheltered waters of Little Harrison Lake, especially in the narrow channel leading to the big lake.

A bridge crosses the Lillooet River 6 km (3.7 mi) north of Port Douglas, linking In-SHUCK-ch Road with the logging road that runs along the west side of the river. Head north on it and you will reach Tennas Narrows Bridge at the "31 km" point of In-SHUCK-ch Road. Watch carefully for extra-wide logging trucks, which are often preceded by small pilot trucks. If you turn left along the west side of the Lillooet River you will soon reach Harrison Lake. Unless you have a sturdy 4×4 and five hours, do not attempt the drive to Harrison Hot Springs at the lake's southern end. The road is all but washed out in several places.

Take your time retracing this route. Lillooet Lake always presents a show for the eyes. Depending on the time of day and the amount of cloud cover in the sky, its surface displays a wide range of hues. In the early hours, water near the shoreline is a mottled tortoiseshell; at midday, a murky malachite; towards dusk, jet-black. And after a trip along its banks your mood may well be as iridescent as the sunlight that plays on its waves.

30

DUFFEY LAKE ROAD

. . . . .

> LOCATION: 160 km (99 mi) north of Vancouver, 102 km (63 mi) north of Squamish, 44 km (27 mi) north of Whistler, 7 km (4 mi) east of Pemberton

> ACTIVITIES: Boating, camping, cross-country skiing, cycling, driving, fishing, hiking, horseback riding, picnicking, snowshoeing, swimming, viewpoints

> HIGHLIGHTS: Jewel-box lakes nestled in stunning alpine scenery

> ACCESS: At its southern terminus, the Duffey Lake Road begins next to St. Christopher's Catholic Church in the heart of Mount Currie, then crosses a series of Lil'wat First Nation reserves for the first 16 km (10 mi) of its 96-km (60-mi) journey to Lillooet.

THE DUFFEY Lake Road section of Highway 99 links Mount Currie and Lillooet, a distance of 96 km (60 mi). This winding road skirts the head of Lillooet Lake, climbs a high pass, then traces Duffey Lake's eastern shore before entering sagebrush country on the Thompson Plateau, where an ancient aboriginal trail preceded the road by thousands of years. At the time of the building of the Gold Rush Trail, Sapper Duffey (a private in Britain's Royal Engineers, who sometimes spelled his name without an "e") was the first European to be guided along it. He reported that the 11 percent grade from Lillooet Lake to Cayoosh Pass was too intimidating for further consideration. Many travelers who drive this stretch today, particularly on the descent, would agree with his assessment.

The Duffey Lake Road was first built as a logging road, then opened to the public in 1975. The residents of Pemberton and Mount Currie welcomed it as a land route linking them with the Fraser Canyon, for the old Gold Rush Trail favored by prospectors

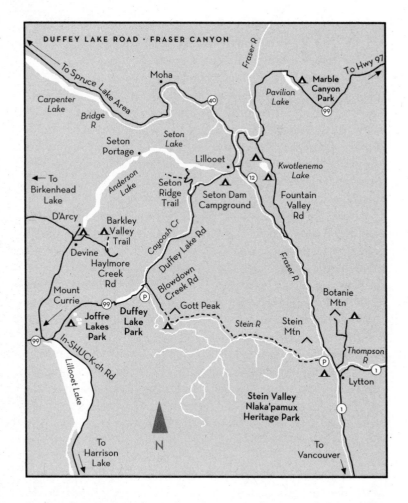

in the 1850s required a journey across Anderson and Seton lakes to reach Lillooet at the north end of the canyon. Such travel was impractical in winter months, when the water routes froze over, leaving the railway as the residents' sole link to the outside world. Covered by mud and snow though it might be for much of the year, the Duffey Lake Road allowed vehicles access to Pemberton before a route was punched south to Whistler and Squamish.

Beginning in Mount Currie, the road follows the Birkenhead River. It is shaded by tall cottonwood trees, and the massive mountain after which the town is named rises above in the southern sky. This is farm country and the major crop is hay, grown to feed the horses that run free in the adjacent fields. When driving, keep an eye out for pedestrians and cyclists, who rely on your courtesy to compensate for the absence of shoulders in places along the two-lane road. If you're traveling by bike, you'll also enjoy yourself, as this section of the Duffey Lake Road is mostly level. The only bother is the occasional barking dog, and the fact that in summer this is a predictably hot place to ride. Fortunately there are several spots beside the river to rest en route to Lillooet Lake, an easy 30- to 45-minute pedal from Mount Currie.

Beyond the rodeo grounds, the road passes through the eastern end of the Mount Currie Reserve, where a bridge spans the Birkenhead close to its merger with the Lillooet River. For a short distance you'll have Lillooet Lake for company. Silt and driftwood carried down by the river are responsible for the infilling at the lake's head. A dirt road leads down from the highway to the boat launch beside the bridge here, suited to both cartop- and trailer-launched watercraft.

From here, the Birkenhead River is a joy to explore by canoe or kayak. Keep an eye out for ancient red-ocher pictographs on the cliff face below one of the hydro towers straddling the mountainside. Even if you don't spot the stone paintings, you'll be delighted by the quiet river, with its clear green water and herons, kingfishers, and ducks. Beginning in August, successive runs of sockeye salmon enter the Birkenhead from the lake, having made their way this far from the Pacific via the Fraser River and Harrison Lake to spawn. When they do, the river runs red. This is an awesome sight, an autumn treat that rivals the changing colors in the forest along the riverbank. And although the salmon aren't feeding, you can sometimes catch a rainbow trout following in their wake.

About 1.6 km (1 mi) beyond the Birkenhead River Bridge, the road divides. Stay left. The In-SHUCK-ch Forest Service Road (see chapter 29) heads south, following the shoreline of the lake, while the Duffey Lake Road climbs steeply past a sign reading "Lillooet 84 km" (52 mi). The highway soon crosses Joffre Creek, whose whitewater tumbles from high above. A series of switchbacks leads to a pullout on the left (west) side, where a viewpoint offers an illus-trated geography lesson on the valley below, including Lillooet Lake, the rivers that feed it, and the open prairie around Mount Currie. Xit'olacw (sometimes referred to as "New Mount Currie") is visible on the hillside to the west. Shafts of sunlight beam down on the long ridges below the peak of Mount Currie, and Joffre Creek can be heard chattering in the canyon below.

Past here, the Duffey Lake Road climbs gently as it heads towards Cayoosh Pass. A number of small creeks flow down off the banks beside the road, adding to the volume in Joffre Creek. Hidden from sight on the left, a massive field of glaciers called the Place Group covers the Cayoosh Range; on the right is the Joffre Glacier Group. These two icefields abut each other to the northwest of the Duffey Lake Road. Joffre Peak rises on the south side where the Matier and Anniversary glaciers, among others, predominate. From this side of the pass, the peaks of the Cayoosh Range seem less imposing than those of the Bastion Range on the west side of Lillooet Lake, but once you're through the pass their full height is revealed. At 2233 m (7325 ft), Duffey Peak is the tallest in the Cayoosh Range though it is all but invisible from Highway 99.

> **JOFFRE LAKES PROVINCIAL PARK**

Access: East of Highway 99, about 30 km (18.6 mi) north of Pember-ton as the highway climbs towards Cayoosh Pass and Lillooet
Ability Level: Intermediate

Three small lakes—Joffre Creek's headwaters—lie cradled at the top of Cayoosh Pass. The largest of the trio is easily reached in a few minutes' walk from the parking lot. The upper two lakes are a stren-uous 12-km (7.4-mi) hike away (a trek not recommended for chil-dren under the age of ten, or anyone who doesn't exercise regularly). Close-up views of the surrounding glaciers are your reward for mak-ing the effort. The icefields around Squamish and Whistler may appear more accessible to local climbers, but the ones above the Jof-fre Lakes are actually easier to reach. The Vancouver Alpine Club opened a trail to them many years ago. There is a map of the trail system as well as an outhouse and four picnic tables here, a good place to do some warm-up stretches and finalize your approach.

Reaching the shoreline of the largest of the three Joffre Lakes is a breeze—a short pathway leads here from the parking lot. There isn't a prettier jewel box in the Sea to Sky corridor. Ringed by an evergreen forest that is, in turn, surmounted by the wrinkled whiteness of the Matier Glacier, Lower Joffre Lake sports a shallow collar of lemon-lime that intensifies to a brilliant turquoise at its center. Although boating is rarely done here, all that's required to paddle Lower Joffre is an easy portage from the nearby parking lot. The lake is stocked with rainbow trout, fingerlings almost big enough to warrant keeping. Almost. The water is so cold that it limits the nutrient content of the lake and, consequently, the size of the fish. Still, angling is a great excuse to float lazily around the lake while drinking in the scenery.

BEST WILD

WEST WORKOUT

The Mount Currie rodeo grounds, where the bleachers and corrals stand empty most of the year, come alive on the Victoria Day and Labor Day weekends.

The lowest lake is just a prelude, however. Hidden in the folds of the slopes above are two companion lakes. Glacial melt fills each to the brim, and whitewater spills from one to the next. A moderately challenging trail links them, and hikers will appreciate the gentle note on which the journey begins and ends. Smooth and welcoming at its outset, with none of the toe-stubbing rocks and trip-wire roots that characterize upper stretches, the trail provides a gradual warm-up at the start and a soft landing at the conclusion of its knee-knackering descent.

As the trail climbs through the forest, it switches back to allow views of the surrounding peaks mirrored in the Lower Joffre's smooth surface. A large red patch of iron-rich volcanic rock shows up vividly on the face of the range to the west. Above the lake, the trail reaches a short, open stretch of debris left behind by the retreating tongue of the glacier, then enters the forest once again. The musical sounds of water and wind fill this part of the woods.

A skillfully laid stone staircase heralds the transition between the gentler and rougher sections of the route. Aside from this touch, and the addition of several sturdy bridges that in places span Joffre Creek, little has changed about this trail in decades. You'll still encounter climbing parties with ropes and ice axes. Most visitors, however, carry not much more than a fanny pack. It's better to travel a little heavier, as weather conditions in these mountains are notoriously fickle. And while it *is* possible to hike the trail in sandals, footwear with good ankle support is advised, particularly when crossing scree slopes and mucky sections. Step cautiously. Although there's nothing dainty about the size of most of the boulders you'll be hopping across, some are surprisingly unstable.

After concentrating on moving your feet carefully over rocks and roots, Middle Joffre Lake comes as a surprise, suddenly appearing after a 75-minute puff. The trail crosses a lively stream, then hugs the banks of the lake. The first wide-open views of the glacier occur here.

In early summer, patches of snow may persist in the gullies and shaded north-facing slopes between Middle and Upper Joffre lakes, one of the prettiest—and steepest—stretches of the trail. As you ascend, it's as if the calendar is being turned back. Sitka alder, devil's club, and Indian hellebore are in full leaf between the lower two lakes. At the upper one, most plant life is just starting to make an appearance.

There's nothing shy about the flow in Joffre Creek. Unleashed from its frozen glacial state, whitewater froths pell-mell down the slopes. Only when it empties into the temporary tranquility of the three lakes does the water assume its gemlike demeanor. The creek's cooling voice is a welcome companion. So are the views of snow-capped Cayoosh Peak to the west and the granite summits that jut through the glaciers above the lakes.

If you're traveling with less than a full pack, allow two to three hours to make the journey one way. This is because each lake will stop you in your tracks. They're individually so exquisite that you might even wonder why you should bother heading higher. Think again. If possible, the uppermost lake is the most captivating of all. Its water is of unparalleled clarity, rivaling the finest emerald ever unearthed. When the sunlight plays upon the lake's surface, which in turn is stirred by the breeze coming down off the glaciers, patterns are set in motion that hypnotize the senses. Add to this the sight of orange monarch butterflies flitting among the red heather blossoms and the rich aroma of subalpine fir resin, and you have a creation that surpasses any heirloom brooch. Should you make the effort to spend the night at one of the twenty-four small lakeside campsites here, all the stars in the world will be spread like diamonds across its surface.

At the far end of Upper Joffre Lake are the glaciers you've also come to see. The trail divides as it reaches the lake, winding around the rocky shoreline in both directions. Stay to the left and you will find some good picnic spots near the outflow of Joffre Creek. Stay right for a winding journey to the far end of the lake, 30 minutes farther along. A large rock cairn marks the end of the trail and the beginning of a number of informal routes to various glaciers. From here, in 15 to 30 minutes you could climb scree to your heart's content for an even better look. Keep your eye on the Matier Glacier though, as chunks of blue ice break off, exploding on the rocks below. You can also admire at a distance; it's all done on such a grand scale that everyone up here has a good view. The adjacent icefields are more popular than ever with alpinists, who come equipped with the right gear to do some serious exploring, summer and winter. There is much terrain from which to choose, and parties of weekend climbers are as numerous as families on this trail.

> **DUFFEY LAKE PROVINCIAL PARK**

Access: 18 km (11 mi) northeast of Joffre Lakes on the Duffey Lake Road

Without leaving the Duffey Lake Road you can still experience dramatic views of the glaciers around the Joffre Lakes: the crest of the Cayoosh Pass is just beyond the park entrance. As you pass through it into an open valley, the road levels. Drive slowly, as the views change from moment to moment. Previously concealed mountain peaks suddenly rise above the ridges, with the white snow and rutted blue ice of the glaciers spread between. Foremost among them are the Anniversary and Matier glaciers. Mount Chief Pascall, Joffre Peak, Mount Matier, and Vantage Peak present a panorama seemingly designed to use up a roll of film or a digital camera's memory card.

Cayoosh Creek flows along beside the road through open meadows. Casper Creek Main and Van Horlick Main, two well-maintained logging roads, run off to the south of the Duffey Lake Road on the eastern side of Cayoosh Pass. You can drive in along Van Horlick for about 15 km (9 mi) to a campsite overlooking the Stein Valley Basin. The area is prone to slides, as is evidenced by long chutes cutting down the slopes of the surrounding mountains. There were once many grizzlies here, but they are rarer now. Logging has driven much of the wildlife in the region south into the rugged landscape at the head of Harrison Lake.

Duffey Lake and the provincial park that surrounds it is an easy 18-km (11-mi) drive northeast of the Joffre Lakes, midway along the road that bears its name. The town of Lillooet, the northern terminus of the Duffey Lake Road, is another 50 km (30 mi) past here. At the eastern end of the lake is a drive-in boat launch. To the south, the view of Mount Chief Pascall from lakeside is captivating. You'll want to sit quietly, enjoying it as long as the insects allow. There is often a breeze blowing that will help keep these irritants at bay, but there is a chill edge to the wind, carried like a message from the nearby glaciers. If you really want to get away from the road, boat across to the lake's west side, where there are rough campsites in several locations. The water in Duffey Lake is scarcely warmer than in nearby Lower Joffre Lake, and the fish don't appear to be much bigger. If you're in a small boat, be wary of the strong winds that occasionally blow up whitecaps. Aside from the boat launch at the lake's eastern end there are few places to land on the shoreline.

Duffey Lake is slender and dark, ranging in color from olive green to black, depending on the light. Its north bank rises steeply; the south side, which the road runs along, is more open but barely more accessible.

> **BLOWDOWN PASS**
Access: East off the Duffey Lake Road, about 3.5 km (2.2 mi) north of Duffey Lake
Ability Level: Intermediate

The logging road is in fair condition (albeit hemmed with alder in places) for much of the distance to Blowdown Pass, about 15 km (9 mi) on. Most vehicles will have to stop at a level area after about 10 km (6.2 mi), beyond which the road deteriorates as it climbs. It is a two- to three-hour hike from here to the pass, where you are likely to still find snow in July. A moderate-sized lake lies at the foot of Blowdown Pass, and though the ground around much of it is marshy, there are several good campsites. Engelmann spruce and subalpine fir surround much of the lake, providing a critical windbreak should conditions take a turn for the worse. This can happen with amazing swiftness, so come prepared on even the warmest days. Should you cross the pass you will be descending into the Stein Valley Nlaka'pamux Heritage Park's Cottonwood Creek watershed. From here it's a four-day hike to the Stein River's confluence with the Fraser River and the nearby town of Lytton (see chapter 31).

At an elevation of 2176 m (7140 ft), Blowdown Pass is an expanse of alpine rubble strewn down to the treeline on either side. Rising above is Gott Peak, an easy climb for even better views of wildlife and scenery. Come July the slopes around the pass are carpeted with thousands of yellow glacier lilies. Watch carefully from a distance and you may spot a grizzly bear digging for the tender roots of this plant, a prized delicacy.

> ### CAYOOSH CREEK
Access: along the Duffey Lake Road north of Blowdown Pass
From the Blowdown Pass turnoff north, the Duffey Lake Road follows closely beside the bubbling waters of Cayoosh Creek, crossing bridge after bridge as it switchbacks towards Lillooet. Five user-maintained Forest Service recreation sites dot the riverbank and provide ample opportunity to pull off the road should you need a break from navigating the winding road or wish to spend the night.

As you drive Highway 99 between Duffey and Seton lakes, try your luck for rainbow trout at the Forest Service recreation sites at Downton or Melvin creeks where they enter Cayoosh Creek. Fly-fish with a small spoon, such as the dependable "Deadly Dick," favored by area anglers.

> ### SETON RIDGE
Access: To find the unmarked access road that leads to Seton Ridge, head 71.5 km (44.4 mi) north on the Duffey Lake Road (Highway 99) from Mount Currie. Watch for a yellow bridge that spans Cayoosh

Creek, where a sign warns of trucks turning. If you overshoot this mark, watch for another sign that reads "Lillooet 20" and backtrack to the bridge. Five generously proportioned switchbacks lead to a flat area on the ridge where the trail begins, one of the most exciting drives in the Sea to Sky region.

Ability Level: Novice to intermediate

Seton Lake near Lillooet is one of the prettiest sights in B.C. And in this province, that's saying something. For starters, while the hues in many mountain lakes change with the seasons, Seton's intense turquoise coloration remains almost constant year-round.

Another reason to single out Seton is that, for such a large lake (over 20 km/12.4 mi long), there are only a limited number of vantage points, which further augments its exclusivity. The easiest viewpoint is from the BC Hydro recreation area (see next section). To appreciate the lake from an entirely fresh perspective, hike Seton Ridge, a wedge of crumbling granite that rises between the Duffey Lake Road and Cayoosh Creek on the south and Seton Lake on its north. So steep is the arid slope above Cayoosh Creek that until a logging road opened the area, one could reach the ridge only on foot or by horseback. Decades ago, that's exactly how a local prospector cut the original trail. Thanks to ongoing logging on the more

> THE LEGEND OF DUFFEY LAKE

AN ANCIENT N'quat'qua legend has it that Duffey Lake is home to the spirit people: when moonlight strikes the surface they rise in their canoes. Spirit chief Ne-Wah and his followers inhabit the south side and ride in golden canoes; Chief Cul-Ne-Wah's people are from the dark side of the lake and ride in jet-black dugouts. According to the legend, after much fasting and prayer, warriors visit Chief Ne-Wah in the spirit world to learn to see with inner vision, though not all have the strength to persist and reach the golden spirit world—some succumb to the dark side. If a warrior is successful, Chief Ne-Wah presents the victorious with a crystal shaped like an eye, which will allow him to see through all things.

Duffey Lake

moderately inclined lakeside, a wide and well-maintained gravel road switchbacks 6 km (3.7 mi) to the ridge. From here, a single-track trail leads an equal distance into the alpine. Allow six hours for the round trip on foot.

Seton Ridge rises west in a long, gradual arch to the foot of a string of glaciated peaks that top out at 2880 m (9450 ft) above Downton Creek, one of Cayoosh Creek's major tributaries in the region north of Duffey Lake Park. (Duffey Lake is Cayoosh's headwaters.) If you come in early July, when the route is usually snow-free, the most pleasant discovery about the trail that leads up and along the ridge is the profusion of wildflowers lining the way. Orange-yellow western trumpet honeysuckle blossoms and bright orange tiger lilies stand out in sharp contrast to the dark forest floor, augmented by splashes of blue-green as the surface of Seton Lake, with its constant wave trains of whitecaps, intermittently flashes into sight.

Two hours of steady hiking—parts of it the up-and-down variety—brings you out of the forest into a clearing, from where you sense that the wide open alpine isn't far ahead. A change in the tree composition, from mountain hemlocks to subalpine firs, silently confirms this place as a transition zone. Stubby black cones adorn fir branches and give the thumbs up to carry on. And while the trail proves challenging at times (particularly if you mountain bike), the fact that it was cut to suit packhorses means the route is never flat-out extreme.

In another hour, lush, grassy meadows appear, speckled with paintbrush in a spectrum of red and orange. Blue Arctic lupine and creamy-white western anemone grow so thickly that you'll be hard-pressed to find a resting place where you won't crush any when you sit down. With all the blossoms, don't be surprised to be dive-bombed by hummingbirds. At the same time, it's so quiet that a passing bumblebee sounds like a bomber. Dark-eyed juncos appear from the knee-high bushes, the same ones that, with the first snow-fall, flock to backyard bird feeders at lower elevations.

Binoculars come in handy for scanning the peaks that rise in a broad array before you. This is a mountaineer's dreamscape, which explains why the Cayoosh Range has been a favorite with local climbers and backcountry skiers for decades. Look for the enormous gendarme that thrusts up from one scree slope. These snow-draped peaks contrast vividly with arid Mission Ridge on the northern side of the lake. Beyond that, in the far distance, a row of peaks marks the Dixon Range in Spruce Lake Protected Area (see next chapter).

It hardly matters that the trail peters out above the treeline. The terrain is so wide open that on a clear day you no longer need a path to make your way, just more time than you may have budgeted to explore. Few people visit here. Other than birds, the only signs of life you may see are occasional ropy white lengths of wolf scat.

> **SETON LAKE**

Access: 97 km (60 mi) north of Lillooet Lake, 3 km (1.8 mi) south of Lillooet

As Highway 99 approaches Lillooet, a series of switchbacks announces the impending appearance of BC Hydro's Seton Beach recreation site on the north shore of Seton Lake. (BC Hydro also maintains the nearby Seton Dam campground and Naxwit picnic area.) Pause here to enjoy the view. A self-guided interpretive trail leads beside the upper parking lot to a group of smooth, round depressions in the earth. Called *kekuli*, these ancient excavations were once the foundations of homes constructed with poles and hides by the ancestors of the local St'at'imc people. They provided not only shelter from the strong winds that frequently blow across the lake but also an excellent vantage point from which to view the surrounding countryside. A service road leads below the viewpoint to the chilly lake's eastern end. Here you'll find a broad stretch of sandy beach with picnic tables, a drive-in boat launch, canoe rentals and change rooms.

A leafy row of acacia trees planted in 1942 by Lillooet residents to honor their war dead shades the shoreline, a welcome relief in summer. Typically, a strong onshore wind helps moderate the heat, which in this region routinely tops the daily Canada-wide high-temperature readings in July and August. The rough splendor of the Seton Bluffs dominates the skyline on the shore opposite the beach, where they tower above the lake. (To preview, view www.cayoosh. net/mcneils.)

Trails link the beach with the Seton Dam campground, which lies just downhill on the south side of Highway 99, where Cayoosh Creek rushes past on its last run to merge with the Seton River. (There's no charge to stay at any of the forty-five pleasantly shaded sites, open May to September.) One of the campground's more unusual features is an old Chinese stone oven, a remnant of the gold rush days of the late 1800s. A marker points to its location near the east end of the campsite.

As the Duffey Lake Road covers the final 3 km (1.8 mi) north to Lillooet, it skirts a network of fish hatchery channels and a reservoir where rainbow trout, mountain whitefish, sturgeon, and kokanee school. Angling is best during spring and fall, with pink, chinook, coho, and steelhead salmon all found in the Seton River. Two spawning channels are also located near the south side of the river, allowing spawning salmon to bypass the Seton Dam. A large parking lot at the Naxwit picnic area caters to tour buses, but everyone is welcome to stop and enjoy the recently planted riverside gardens.

> *Fishing:* Knowledgeable sources to consult about angling in
these waters include Valley Fishing Guides (1-877-858-7688;
www.valleyfishing.com) and Whistler Fishing Guides
(604-932-4267; www.whistlerriver.com). Note: Be wary of
the soft, silty sandbars where the Birkenhead River meets the fast-
flowing Lillooet River. If you care to explore Lillooet Lake, an
hour's paddle south from the boat launch will land you on
the beach at Strawberry Point (see chapter 29).

> 31

LILLOOET AND BEYOND

· · · · ·

> **LOCATION**: 260 km (161 mi) north of Vancouver on Highway 99 or 334 km (207 mi) via Highway 1 (Trans-Canada Highway) and Highway 12, 202 km (125 mi) northeast of Squamish, 144 km (89 mi) northeast of Whistler, 107 km (66 mi) northeast of Pemberton

> **ACTIVITIES**: Backpacking, camping, driving, fishing, hiking, ice climbing, mountain biking, nature observation, viewpoints

> **HIGHLIGHTS**: Sagebrush and ponderosa pine country, ancient trails, Native heritage

> **ACCESS**: Three highways and a maze of back roads fan off from Lillooet: the Sea to Sky Highway enters from Whistler to the southwest and Hat Creek to the east, while Highway 12 leads south to Lytton and Highway 40 leads northwest to Gold Bridge.

LILLOOET WILL be forever linked to the days of the 1850s Fraser River gold rush, when it was known as "Mile 0" on the road to the Cariboo. As many as 10,000 stampeders camped here in summer at what was then called Cayoosh Flats. These days, Lillooet is the staging area for backcountry exploration by bike, on horseback, or on foot in Spruce Lake Protected Area (formerly South Chilcotin Mountains Provincial Park). In January, the town hosts an annual ice climbing festival that celebrates the joys of clinging to frozen waterfalls. The mighty Fraser River flows past the town in a wide, muddy smear. In summer, watch for First Nation anglers drying salmon on smoke racks near the river.

Lillooet (population 2,750) is just the right-size town for a leisurely walk that not only leads past mementos of the 1850s gold rush but also more recent landmarks, such as the 1913 suspension bridge spanning the Fraser River at the northern end of town. The bridge

Spruce Lake Protected Area

hasn't seen vehicle traffic since 1981, when the modern Bridge of 23 Camels opened downstream, which means that it is ideally suited to walking. In fact, do a loop from the heart of Lillooet over one bridge and cross back on the other. Both bridges provide splendid views of the roiling river.

I suggest heading to the town's Visitor Info Centre (780 Main Street; 250-256-4308; www.lillooetbc.com) to gain an inside perspective on Lillooet, both past and present, as the former church is also home to the Lillooet Museum. Then cross the street to the Lillooet Bakery, one of the finest in the Sea to Sky region.

Fishing is one of the most popular pastimes around Lillooet. Rainbow trout dominate the forty-odd lakes, rivers, and streams just as salmon and sturgeon rule the Fraser. Carpenter and Gun are big lakes with strategically placed boat ramps located along Highway 40 west of Lillooet. As well, at the dock at the BC Hydro recreation site on Seton Lake beside Highway 99, just west of Lillooet (see chapter 30), you can cast for rainbow trout, steelhead, and Dolly Varden char up to 6 kg (15 lb).

Unlike the other three major towns in the Sea to Sky corridor (formally named the Squamish-Lillooet Regional District), Lillooet is served by two paved roads, Highways 99 and 12, and graveled Highway 40. Depending on your approach and final destination, they present a variety of choices. Here are several of my favorite drives, including a loop route from Lillooet to the Sea to Sky's southern terminus in Squamish via Highway 1 and Highway 1/99A, one of B.C.'s most scenic circle tours.

> ## SPRUCE LAKE PROTECTED AREA

Access: 95 km (59 mi) west of Lillooet via Highway 40 and 150 km (93 mi) northwest of Pemberton via the Hurley River Road. Both roads lead to Gold Bridge. The Slim Creek Forest Service Road begins at the eastern end of Gun Lake, 10 km (6.2 km) west of Gold Bridge, and climbs 12 km (7.4 mi) to the start of the Spruce Lake Trail at Jewel Creek. The park may also be accessed from Tyaughton Lake via Highway 40, east of Gold Bridge. Many of these roads require a four-wheel-drive vehicle. For more information, check the BC Parks website: www.env.gov.bc.ca/bcparks.
Ability Level: Intermediate to expert

One of the most extensive networks of hiking, mountain biking, and horseback riding trails in the Lillooet region is the 160 km (100 mi) of routes in the South Chilcotin Mountains around Spruce Lake. The weather around Lillooet is much drier and hotter than elsewhere in the Sea to Sky region, so be prepared to consume plenty of fluids as you explore.

Jumping-off points to popular areas in the 713-square-km (275-square-mi) park such as Spruce Lake and Tyaughton Creek lie little more than a one-hour drive from Lillooet. Well-worn trails lead past mountain lakes, cross mid-elevation grasslands, and climb timbered slopes surrounded by spectacular mountain peaks to alpine meadows, a testament to the length of time both humans and wildlife have journeyed through here. Above the treeline lies a stunning visual panorama of rainbow-hued Chilcotin Range peaks that bump up against the more familiar glaciated forms of the Coast Mountains. The pastel shades exhibited here rival those of New Mexico's Sangre de Cristo Mountains, made famous in many of Georgia O'Keeffe's paintings.

Access: 35 km (22 mi) northeast of Lillooet on Highway 99. The Sea
to Sky Highway runs east of Lillooet for 75 km (47 mi) to its junction with the Cariboo Highway (Highway 97) at the restored heritage
site of Hat Creek Ranch, a roadhouse stop on the original Cariboo
Wagon Road that offers guided tours. The Trans-Canada Highway
(Highway 1) lies 11 km (7 mi) south of the Highway 97 and 99 junction at Cache Creek.

Limestone cliffs tower above Marble Canyon Park's thirty-six
tightly packed campsites, attractively situated in the Pavilion Range.
The placid waters of Pavilion Lake reflect the sky above. A waterfall
on the opposite side of the lake helps mute all other sounds. There is
a charge of about $14 per site from May to September.

The walls of Marble Canyon are easy to reach. Lower Mainland climbers have opened dozens of routes over the past decade
in this area, which has come to be known as the "Cinderella of B.C.
rock" because of its still relatively undiscovered beauty. Highway 99
makes its way through the main canyon as it passes beside brilliantly
hued Turquoise, Crown, and Pavilion lakes. From here, a maze of
canyons runs off on both sides. Chimney Rock—known as Coyote
Rock by members of the Fountain First Nation—dominates the
crenulated skyline. In winter, Marble Canyon Park has one of the
best and most easily accessed icefalls for climbing in the region.

The limestone canyon in which Marble Canyon Park is located
is a rather rare geological formation in British Columbia. The white,
chalk-faced slopes are not composed of granite like the nearby Coast
Mountains, and the weathered peaks, surmounted by the remarkable Chimney Rock, have the appearance of a crumbling castle wall.
This canyon was once part of a Pacific island chain, another section of which lies in the northwest corner of the province. Thanks to
continental drift, they got separated.

> **FOUNTAIN VALLEY ROAD**

Access: The 25-km (15.5-mi) Fountain Valley Road runs northeast
between Highway 12 (about 20 km/12 mi south of Lillooet) and Highway 99 (about 13 km/8 mi north of Lillooet).

Mention going for a scenic drive on a B.C. back road and I involuntarily reach for the Gravol or don anti-motion-sickness wristbands.

Only then am I ready to even consider tackling the dust and switch-backs that many such routes serve up. Yet making the effort yields mind-blowing vistas you wouldn't otherwise see. At the very least, these roads are an opportunity to explore beyond the humdrum of major highways.

As much as Highway 12 itself between Lillooet and Lytton counts as a back road, especially where it hugs a steeply inclined slope above the Fraser River, now that it's been paved and avalanche debris routinely cleared, those in search of a route more in keeping with B.C.'s pioneer past might want to seek out Fountain Valley Road, which runs through Xaxl'ip First Nation territory.

This is sagebrush and cowboy country, with hayfields and corrals spread beside the road. Barns adorned with antlers add a frontier touch. Consider camping at one of four Forest Service recreation sites sprinkled around Kwotlenemo (Fountain) Lake, where signs warn to be wary of the feral cattle that come down to the lake to drink. That said, this is a pleasant place to pause for the evening as a steady breeze helps keep bugs at bay. In summer, a fee of $10 per night is charged (except on Tuesdays and Wednesdays, which are free).

Fountain Valley Road's most scenic stretch occurs north of the lake on an open benchland above the Fraser Canyon near Highway 99, where fields of organic produce, such as carrots and tomatoes, are grown for shipment to Vancouver. (For a preview of Fountain Valley and its history, visit www.cayoosh.net/fountain.html.)

> ## LYTTON

Access: 270 km (124 mi) northeast of Vancouver and 85 km (53 mi) south of Cache Creek on the Trans-Canada Highway (Highway 1). Highway 12 provides an alternative and equally scenic route between Lillooet and Lytton, a distance of 64 km (40 mi).

Lytton, the self-styled rafting capital of Canada, is a crossroads in more ways than one. For millennia, the large Nlaka'pamux First Nation community of Kumsheen, or "the meeting place," was here in the Fraser Canyon where the mighty Thompson and Fraser rivers merge in muddy amalgam. This is also where the fir and hemlock rain forest of the Coast Mountains yields to the pine-forested highlands of the Interior Plateau. With summer temperatures consistently among the highest in Canada, Lytton is also the place where the craggy landscape, sodden by winter storms that blow in off the Pacific, begins to dry out. And one of the most pleasant ways to enjoy yourself during hot weather is to join a rafting expedition to run the Thompson River's eighteen sets of rapids along the 40-km-long (25-mi) colorful canyon from Spence's Bridge. Hikers also journey to Lytton to reach the eastern entrance to Stein Valley Nlaka'pamux Heritage Park or to explore Botanie Mountain Park.

> ## STEIN VALLEY NLAKA'PAMUX HERITAGE PARK
Access: *Head about 2 km (1.2 mi) north of Lytton on Highway 12, then turn left on Lytton Ferry Road. The two-vehicle, free ferry runs on demand from 6 AM to 10:15 PM, with half-hour breaks at 10:30 AM and 6:30 PM. The park's eastern trailhead lies 6 km (4 mi) north via West Canyon and Stein Valley roads.*
Ability Level: *Novice to expert*

When you hike massive 1070-square-km (413-square-mi) Stein Valley Nlaka'pamux Heritage Park, don't be surprised to hear phantom voices calling out. Perhaps it's simply a trick of the wind—or your mind. But don't count on it. Ocher-tinted pictographs depicting supernatural beings adorn the rock walls in a variety of locations here, suggesting a magical realm, one where generations of Nlaka'pamux, or "people of the canyon," came in quest of *xa'xa*, "the power of nature." In addition, the Stein River casts a spell of its own. Its volume and velocity propel a wall of humid air before it as it races east to meet the Fraser. Channeled between sharply rising granite ridges and cloaked with ponderosa pine, Douglas fir and corduroy-barked black cottonwoods, the Stein elbows its way along a tight course. Birdcalls are caught up in the breeze as it hurries along and rephrased like a whispered secret.

Unlike the rugged four-day western approach from Blowdown Pass (see chapter 30), the route into the Stein from its eastern entrance is a gentle one. The *Lower Canyon Trail* leads west from the parking lot. Several campgrounds are located at regular intervals along the trail between the parking lot and a bridge over the Stein, 8 km (5 mi) upstream. Each site features sturdy food lockers anchored to cement pads (to deter wildlife, particularly bears and pack rats). The trail, mostly soft river sand, passes a series of pictograph tableaux and makes a perfect two-day, 30-km (19-mi) introduction to the park. For more information, consult the BC Parks website: www.env.gov.bc.ca/bcparks. *The Stein Valley Wilderness Guidebook*, by Gordon White, is an invaluable resource.

> BOTANIE MOUNTAIN PARK

Access: Botanie Creek Road begins on the east side of Highway 12, just north of the Thompson River Bridge in Lytton. The road is paved for much of its 16.5-km (10-mi) length to the Forest Service campground, where three user-maintained campsites are located. The best approach to the Botanie Mountain fire road begins about 8.5 km (5.3 mi) from the junction of Highway 12 and Botanie Creek Road. Turn north here and stay left as you approach Lions Club Park. Follow this road for about 1 km (0.6 mi) along the base of Botanie Mountain. Park at a pullout where the eroded fire road begins to sharply climb the hillside. Note: Water is not available at the campground or on Botanie Mountain. Pack plenty of fluids for this hike.
Ability Level: Novice

Evidence of the convergent biogeoclimatic zones around Lytton is nowhere more apparent than just north of town on the steep-sided slopes and flattened ridges of Botanie Mountain. Ponderosa pine predominate as visitors begin their ascent, while stands of old-growth Douglas fir supersede at higher elevations. One characteristic that these thick-barked pine and fir share is an ability to withstand the licking flames of forest fires, as their severely blackened bases indicate.

The aridity that minimizes ground cover at the lower elevations gives way to a moister environment as you climb. Lush bunchgrass covers much of the forest's understory here. Higher up Botanie Mountain, profuse drifts of wildflowers crowned by red paintbrush, lavender aster, creamy mountain ladyslipper, and yellow tiger lily spread across the southern face of the mountain.

In times past, visitors came not just to view the wildflowers but also to gather the tender roots of yellow avalanche lilies as a food source. Upwards of a thousand Nlaka'pamux once journeyed here each spring from across the Thompson Plateau for the harvest. The word "botanie" (a derivation of "bootahnie") means "covered, walled, enclosed all around" in the Nlaka'pamux dialect.

You may find that the going quickly becomes too rough for your car. From this point, hike up the steep fire road that switchbacks like a seismic graph gone haywire. Under the glare of the strengthening midday sun your water bottles will be making frequent appearances.

After two hours of plodding and panting, you reach the top of the ridge (marked as the Devil's Leap on some maps), where the road finally levels out. Gnarled, moss-tressed Douglas fir shade a viewpoint here and provide a welcome place to enjoy lunch. Due west across the Fraser Canyon lies the Stein Valley. The clear-cut mountain slopes and valleys immediately south present a stark reminder as to what might have been had the Stein not been protected as the Stein Valley Nlaka'pamux Heritage Park in 1996. Whitewater flashes like lightning as the Stein River flings itself towards its union with the Fraser. Farther downstream from the Stein, the green waters of the Thompson have muscled the Fraser's muddy current to one side, and the two rivers share the same channel in ragged alliance before melding as one. Directly below, the wind-whipped

> ## BRIDGE TO THE PAST

· · · · · · · · ·

ALEXANDRA BRIDGE Provincial Park lies about 1 km (0.6 mi) south of the Alexandra Lodge on Highway 1—an interesting place to picnic or just take a short walk to check out the original site of the Cariboo Wagon Road bridge. From May to October, interpretive displays posted beside the spacious pullout give visitors an idea of the Fraser Canyon's history. Since the Cariboo gold rush days of the 1860s, a strategically positioned bridge has spanned the river here. A short trail leads from the parking lot to an old iron bridge that was decommissioned in 1965. The bridge leads nowhere and, like a monument desecrated by rebellion, has been stripped of officialdom. From midspan you can just spy the newest structure, the Alexandra Bridge, about 2 km (1.2 mi) south.

west face of Botanie Mountain bakes in the sun, its gullies dotted with pine.

Continue through the forest along the ridge in search of more wildflowers. Although you might assume they bloom in sunbaked subalpine meadows, look instead for sunlit openings where colorful companion groups blossom in the forest. Butterflies flit about and augment the range of hues, including orange-and-black monarchs hanging suspended from the saffron stamens of bright-orange tiger lily petals, spotted red and purple. Here is a dazzling visual payoff for your efforts.

The telltale buzz of a western rattlesnake will make you jump. Just a glimpse of its earth-toned skin is enough to fire the imagination. As you walk the ridge road that leads half an hour farther north to a Forest Service lookout, you may not be able to distinguish between the sound made by rattlers and that of the crickets whirring in the afternoon sun. Whole sections of the forest drone with high-pitched, electric voices as you pass by, feeding both curiosity and fear. As much as you may want to see a rattler, you'll probably be just as content to not cross paths with the shy creatures that overwinter in writhing colonies deep within the rock face of Botanie Mountain's western slope. Your apprehension may be such that a grouse flushed into sudden flight by your passage will make your adrenal glands flutter.

> **THE INSIDE TRACK**

> *Camping:* Over 20 routes and 18 Forest Service recreation sites are detailed in a guide map *(Spruce Lake Trails Area)* available from the Forest Service website (www.gov.bc.ca/for).

> *Fishing and Cycling:* Camelsfoot Sports (633 Main Street; 250-256-7757); Winner's Edge (644 Main Street; 250-256-4848) for licenses, gear, and advice.

> *River Rafting:* Fraser River Raft Expeditions (1-800-363-7238; www.fraserraft.com); Hyak Wilderness Adventures (1-800-663-7238; www.hyak.com); Kumsheen River Raft and Adventure Resort (1-800-663-6667; www.kumsheen.com).

> *Rock Climbing:* The best description of climbing routes is *Central B.C. Rock,* by Lyle Knight, a comprehensive climbing guide that includes the Lillooet region.

> *Trail Rides:* Chilcotin Holidays (250-238-2274; www.chilcotinholidays.com); Red Rock Trail Ride (250-256-4495; www.redrocktrailrides.net); Spruce Lake Wilderness Adventures (250-283-2375; www.sprucelaketours.com).

Index

Activities Index

. . . . .

Other titles from Jack Christie and Greystone Books

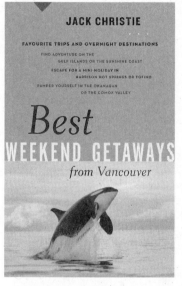

52 Best Day Trips from Vancouver
REVISED & UPDATED
From Delta to Whistler, West Van to Maple Ridge—find the best short excursions from Vancouver.
ISBN 978-1-55365-301-1 · $21.95 CAD

Best Weekend Getaways from Vancouver
Whether you're looking for a rugged outdoor adventure or a relaxing long weekend, this book will point you in the right direction.
ISBN 978-1-55365-256-4 · $22.95 CAD

JACK CHRISTIE (dubbed "Mr. B.C." by the *Toronto Sun*) is one of North America's most trusted travel writers. Outdoors columnist with Vancouver's *Georgia Straight* and host of CBC Radio's *Beyond the Backyard* series, Jack was the recipient of the 2004 Tourism BC Tourism Media Award. Visit www.jackchristie.com for more information.